# AMBUSHED

# AMBUSHED

## A WAR
## REPORTER'S
## LIFE ON
## THE LINE

### IAN STEWART

ALGONQUIN BOOKS OF CHAPEL HILL   2002

Published by
ALGONQUIN BOOKS OF CHAPEL HILL
Post Office Box 2225
Chapel Hill, North Carolina 27515-2225

a division of
Workman Publishing
708 Broadway
New York, New York 10003

Library of Congress Cataloging-in-Publication Data
Stewart, Ian 1966–
   Ambushed : a war reporter's life on the line / Ian Stewart.
      p. cm.
   Published also as: Freetown ambush : a reporter's year in Africa. Toronto,
Ont., Canada; New York, N.Y., U.S.A. : Penguin/Viking, 2002.
   Includes bibliographical references.
   ISBN 1-56512-380-8 (hardcover)
      1. Stewart, Ian, 1966–   2. War correspondents—Canada—Biography.
   3. Sierra Leone—History—Civil War, 1991–   I. Title.
   PN4913.S764 A48 2002
   070.4'333'092—dc21
   [B]
                                             2002071111

10  9  8  7  6  5  4  3  2  1
First Edition

*For Mom and Dad*

In memory of
Myles Tierney (1964–1999)
Miguel Gil Moreno (1967–2000)
and
the many victims of war in Africa

"I went a little farther," he said,
"then still a little farther till I had gone so far that
I don't know how I'll ever get back."

—Joseph Conrad
*Heart of Darkness*

# CONTENTS

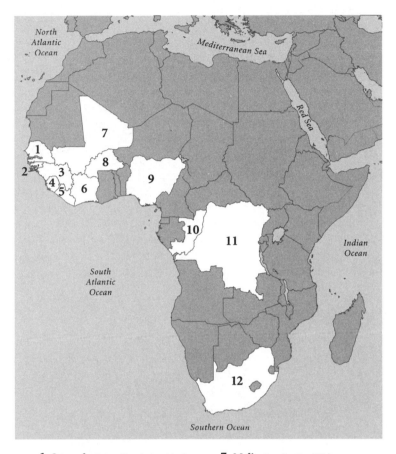

1  **Senegal** – Dakar, Zinguinchor, Mpak

2  **Guinea-Bissau** – Farim, Bafatà, Canchungo, Mansoa, Bissau

3  **Republic of Guinea** – Conakry

4  **Sierra Leone** – Lungi, Port Loko, Makeni, Kenema, Magburka, Freetown

5  **Liberia** – Monrovia

6  **Ivory Coast** – Abidjan, Assini, Grand Bassam, Yamasoukra

7  **Mali** – Bamako, Gao, Kidal, Timbuktu

8  **Burkina Faso** – Ouagadougou

9  **Nigeria** – Lagos, Abuja, Enugu, Onitsha, Port Harcourt

10 **Republic of Congo** – Brazzaville

11 **Democratic Republic of Congo** – Kinshasa

12 **South Africa** – Cape Town

# AUTHOR'S NOTE

TO WRITE A FIRSTHAND ACCOUNT of a brain injury, I had to accept certain limitations. Although written in the first person, a small number of the narrative details in *Ambushed* are borrowed in order to supplement my own missing memories of the events of January 10, 1999, and the first few days thereafter.

Brain injury patients are often unable to recall the moment of their injuries and a period of up to twenty minutes prior to the injury. Maybe the mental images of memory—like film exposed to light—never had time to be processed. Perhaps the memories never registered, or were knocked loose by the damage caused by swelling; the experts have numerous theories but no sure answers.

In my case, I have no recall of the moment I was shot and only a foggy, dreamlike recollection of my evacuation. I have many memories of my first hours of consciousness in the hospital, but they are cluttered and confused with the pure fiction of my nightmares and hallucinations. The narrative of this book is a collaborative effort—a compilation of my recollections along with the memories of those who lived with me through this ordeal.

Through most of 1999 and parts of 2000 I pestered my
parents and sister, my friends and colleagues, along with
my medical staff in London and Toronto for details of the
shooting, brain injuries, my evacuation, and the very early
stages of my recovery. Through dozens of interviews with
David Guttenfelder, Tim Sullivan, and other AP colleagues,
I began reporting on my own story—albeit without the
requisite disinterested vantage point of a good journalist.
For details of my arrival and awakening at the hospital, I
have relied on the accounts of my mother and father, and
the nursing staff of London's National Hospital for
Neurology and Neurosurgery. I have also used numerous
journalistic accounts of the shooting to complete the
picture. Any errors, omissions, or misstatements are my
own. All the events of this book are true, based either on
my recollections or on those of the people who experienced
them with me.

# PROLOGUE

LIKE THE HOLLOW RUMBLE of a hammer pounding sheet metal, artillery shells slammed into the palm-tree-covered slopes of Mount Aureol in central Freetown. War had overrun the picturesque capital of Sierra Leone, and I was there to bear witness. Along with my Associated Press colleagues Myles Tierney and David Guttenfelder, I was covering a heinous conflict about which the world had little knowledge and—to my increasing despair—in which it had little interest.

As the Associated Press's West Africa bureau chief, I coordinated news coverage of twenty-three countries, including war-wracked Sierra Leone. In this forgotten corner of West Africa, I reported on rebel forces from the Revolutionary United Front (RUF) who were kidnapping children to be treated as disposable resources—used as sex slaves or forced into suicidal combat. I wrote about how the rebels had systematically killed or maimed tens of thousands of people, mostly civilians. Yet, no matter how compelling I thought these stories were, newspapers were burying them in the back pages or not running them at

all—and the world remained oblivious. So it was with a
failed sense of mission that I had made my way to
Freetown.

It was Sunday, January 10, 1999, and I had linked up
with a government convoy driving through the city to
collect dead bodies.

FOR ABOUT TWENTY MINUTES our convoy snaked around
Mount Aureol, inching its way toward downtown
Freetown. Rebels armed with AK-47s and grenade launchers had overrun the city four days earlier, and they still
controlled some areas. As we drove through the abandoned
streets, evidence of the RUF's slaughter was everywhere.
From my vantage point in the backseat of our white station
wagon, I saw stiffened, blood-caked corpses littering sidewalks like macabre manikins placed there to haunt the
living. The stink of death—dried blood, stale urine, and
monkey-house fear—hung over all of Freetown. Black
smoke billowed from dozens of arson fires that still smoldered from combat several days earlier.

Although I had covered wars and disasters before,
nothing had prepared me for this. My head swam as we
passed pile after pile of rotting corpses topped with black-
winged vultures that hopped from one body to the next,
pecking and tearing at flesh. I sucked at the humid air to
keep from blacking out, while my sweat-soaked shirt glued
me to the car's vinyl seat.

Myles, a television cameraman, and David, a still
photographer, were wedged on either side of me. The heat

in the cramped backseat was becoming unbearable. In silence we drove through the city toward the downtown districts still controlled by RUF rebels. Even the troops in our convoy were unsure which parts of town were in rebel hands and which were held by the Nigerian-led West African coalition force, known as ECOMOG (Economic Community of West African States Military Observer Group).

At Congo Cross our ECOMOG convoy blundered into a brief, fierce fire fight. For a few minutes, submachine gun fire rattled in my ears and the sharp smell of cordite filled my nostrils. I clutched my notebook and squeezed my eyes shut, questioning my judgment in joining the convoy.

The closer we came to the center of the city, the stronger my feeling of sick dread became. Every building was shuttered, but scores of wide-eyed corpses—civilian men, women, and children, along with soldiers—had been tossed into the narrow street. I scribbled in my notebook that the killing seemed designed for terror, not for any strategic purpose.

Ahead of us, the lead trucks in the convoy rolled past a group of young men armed with AK-47s. The bodyguards in our car wanted to question the men and they ordered our driver to stop. I clenched my teeth to keep from blurting out my only compelling thought: *Keep going, for Chrissakes, just keep going.*

The car slowed and we pulled up to within a few meters of the men. One of them was dressed in American-style jeans, rubber flip-flops, and a jaunty black bowler hat like one of the droogs from Stanley Kubrick's film *A Clockwork Orange*. He gripped the wooden stock of his assault rifle.

One of the ECOMOG bodyguards leaned out the window and shouted something at the gunmen. The man in the bowler stopped and hesitated momentarily. A coy smile spread across his face as he chuckled to himself. I sat perfectly still and held my breath. *Please God, get me the fuck out of here.*

Without warning the muzzle of his rifle erupted with a brilliant flash. The side window exploded into thousands of fragments as a spray of bullets tore into the car. My head jolted backward. For a split second my left side went rigid, then slack. I slid sideways onto David's shoulder. Myles slumped forward over his camera, dead. But I didn't know that, I didn't even know that one of those bullets had punched through my skull and lodged in the back of my brain.

# AMBUSHED

# PART 1

# 1

# BEGINNINGS

I SUPPOSE I WAS DESTINED for a career in journalism. It was in my blood: in the 1960s my great-aunt Dorothy worked briefly as a writer for the now-defunct *Ottawa Journal,* while my aunt Heather wrote the social column for the erstwhile Toronto *Telegram* during the 1970s. Then, of course, there's my uncle, Brian Stewart, who rose to fame as a foreign correspondent for the CBC and later NBC.

As a young man at Queen's University, I was introduced to Canada's media elite: Brian's friends included Peter Mansbridge, also of the CBC, and Mike Duffy, now with CTV, though at the time an influential CBC reporter on Parliament Hill. Brian inadvertently influenced my decision to enter print journalism. Not wanting to live in his shadow, I chose to stay away from television to avoid charges of nepotism. If I were to become a journalist, I wanted to do it on my own.

Eight years before setting off for Africa as a bureau chief and foreign correspondent, I was a mediocre graduate student at Columbia University's renowned journalism school. While at Columbia I lived on Manhattan's Upper

West Side on 122d Street, between Broadway and
Amsterdam Avenue—just three blocks south of Harlem's
Martin Luther King Jr. Drive.

My graduate housing at Columbia was austere, a two-
bedroom apartment that I shared with writing student
Charlie Rogers. Still, it was a vintage brownstone, and it
was a thrill for someone who had grown up in the suburbs
of Toronto and Montreal to be living in Manhattan. For the
first time in my life, I experienced true ethnic diversity, and
I was exhilarated by the bustle and excitement of New York
City. Together, Charlie and I endured Columbia's grueling
course schedule as it wreaked havoc on our social lives;
romances sputtered and failed.

Having finished my master's degree in 1991, I began
applying to Canadian daily and weekly newspapers from
coast to coast, but I found that jobs in print journalism
were scarce. Most major North American dailies were
locked in a hiring freeze, or were cutting back on staff.
Soon, rejection letters papered the walls of my apartment. I
applied to any newspaper I could think of for a job as an
entry-level general assignment reporter. This is the kind of
reporter who covers all news and is not confined to a "beat"
such as cops, courts, or business. Coming up empty, I
lowered my sights and began applying for internships at the
larger metropolitan newspapers that could still afford to run
their apprenticeship programs. Through the cash-rich
1980s, internships had been an accepted route into full-
time journalism. But by the early 1990s, internships had
become a low-paid source of extra labor to supplement

shrinking editorial staffs at newspapers. Employment at the
end of an internship was an unlikely prospect.

After I had been interviewed by some half-dozen larger
newspapers in Ontario and Quebec, my break *finally* came
at the *Toronto Star*. There I got my first taste of life in a
major city newsroom. Like a scene out of the film *The
Front Page*, the seasoned pros in the newsroom called me
"kid," even though I was twenty-five. I was frequently
assigned to overnight duty in the "box." Filled with police,
fire department, and ambulance scanners, the box was a
stuffy eight-by-ten-foot room off the main newsroom.
Veteran reporters used the box for news tips or to follow
breaking stories, but interns typically monitored the radios
and alerted the more senior reporters to possible stories. For
most of the summer of 1991 I sat in the box from 11 P.M.
until 5 A.M. listening to the police handling domestic
disturbances and petty thefts. Occasionally I picked up on
a shooting or other serious crime.

It was mind-numbing work that almost snuffed out my
desire to be a journalist. In fact, I'd have quit and sought out
another vocation had it not been for my other overnight
duty that summer: taking dictation from the *Star*'s foreign
correspondents. Over the phone I met Stephen Handelman,
Olivia Ward, and Peter Goodspeed. They and the *Star*'s
other foreign correspondents often asked me to scan the
wires for news tips on breaking stories in their regions. I
soon became very familiar with Canadian Press, Associated
Press, and Reuters wires. Possibly the purest form of reporting, wire service, or news agency journalism, began over 150

years ago with the AP's first network of telegraph wires linking major American cities. Today, the "wires" are a global network of high-speed telephone lines and satellite uplinks that transmit news from around the world in seconds. News from the wires arrives in newsrooms via computer terminals or dot matrix printers, replacing the slow Teletype machines that dominated the industry into the early 1980s. Although the cost of transmitting news articles has dropped dramatically over the years, wire service journalists have retained their brief, concise writing style. I enjoyed the crisp dispatches, but the real lure of the wires was the exotic datelines that I had long dreamed of visiting. I read about events taking place in Colombo, Kabul, and Phnom Penh. That sense of adventure captured my imagination, fueled with images of my favorite book, Joseph Conrad's *Heart of Darkness*. I saw myself as a young Charles Marlow steaming up the Congo River in search of adventure and intrigue in forbidden places. The wires also had that true sense of urgency that I had always expected in daily journalism. They rekindled my resolve to be a journalist, only now I wanted to be a wire service reporter working overseas.

When my summer internship ended in late August, I again began looking for work. Nine months and some three hundred applications later, I landed a job as a reporter covering the health beat for the *Watertown Daily Times* in upstate New York. For ten months I honed my skills at the *Times* and saved enough money to buy a one-way ticket to China, where my girlfriend at the time was working as an

English teacher. Then I packed my bags in the early summer of 1993 and set off for Beijing to find work as a freelance reporter. While still at Queen's in 1989 I had been horrified when the Chinese government used the military to disperse unarmed student protesters. The Tiananmen Square Massacre became one of the driving forces behind my zeal to get to Asia.

The People's Republic of China, with its xenophobic perception of the foreign media, was not the best place to launch a freelance career. Although I had arranged to sell articles to several newspapers in North America and Europe while doing radio commentaries for several broadcasters, I found it difficult to obtain government press credentials, making even routine reporting almost impossible.

Within two months, I set off for Hong Kong and immediately found work with the *Hong Kong Standard* as a copy editor. Weeks after that I was hired by UPI (United Press International) as a news correspondent covering preparations for Hong Kong's 1997 transition from British to Chinese rule, as well as other regional stories.

For the next eight months I traveled to Taiwan and throughout southern China. I was sent on assignment to the Philippines and Thailand. Getting my first taste of life on the road as a foreign correspondent was everything I had dreamed of. Under the tutelage of Paul Anderson, UPI's regional editor, I learned the ropes of wire service reporting. There was nothing fancy about it, just plain and simple writing about the daily events of Asia. Hong Kong, like much of Asia, was booming economically and people were optimistic about the future. After years of post-colonial turmoil and war, Asia was finally on a path of development and growth, and reflecting this good fortune, most of the people I met were happy and friendly.

Most of my reporting was done from UPI's Hong Kong bureau in Telecom House, overlooking Victoria Harbour. I wrote simple stories about economic growth and newly made millionaires who were cashing in on Hong Kong's burgeoning Hang Seng Stock Index. I lived in a clean, two-bedroom apartment on Lantau Island, a thirty-minute ferry ride from Hong Kong proper, and I made great friends with whom I went out for dinner at fancy restaurants or loud, thumping nightclubs. Soon I joined the Hong Kong Foreign Correspondents Club, or FCC. This colonial institution, founded in 1943, was an oasis of dark wood paneling and black leather chairs that offered refuge from the frenetic streets of Hong Kong's central district. Here I played pool and sipped gin-and-tonics. In khaki pants and brown loafers I played up the image of what I thought was the quintessential foreign correspondent, loving every minute of it.

Within a year of joining UPI, I was sent to India. At the age of twenty-seven, I was the New Delhi bureau chief in charge of South Asia, zipping about the Indian subcontinent with energy and zeal, often making up my own assignments. I met Prime Minister Narasimha Rao, and drank tea with Tibet's exiled leader the Dalai Lama. I traveled south to Sri Lanka, and spent a day in Pinawalla at an orphanage for baby elephants. Amid towering palm trees on rolling tea plantations lived several dozen elephants—the youngest at four months came up to my waist—whose parents had either died or abandoned their young. The orphanage raised the baby elephants to young adulthood, and then they were donated to Hindu temples in Sri Lanka or India, where the animals would live like worshipped and pampered gods.

MY FIRST REAL FLIRTATION with danger came in the spring of 1995 in Afghanistan, the most turbulent part of my turf in the Indian subcontinent. Fighting between factions of the once-unified anti-Soviet mujahideen rebels had ended months earlier and a tenuous truce was holding. It was a simple assignment: I was to travel to Kabul to report on the plight of tens of thousands of displaced residents.

A light dusting of snow blanketed the Afghan capital of Kabul, which already looked like a movie set for *Blade Runner* or *Mad Max*. Eighty percent of the city lay in ruins, leaving the few remaining inhabitants to wander aimlessly in search of food and shelter amid the piles of concrete rubble and twisted metal. The day I arrived, a late-season snow squall had blown in from the Hindu Kush. Children wandered barefoot through the snow, wearing threadbare blankets for warmth.

My Pakistani translator, Behroz Khan, and I checked in to one of the few operational rooms at the Kabul Inter-Continental. Although it had no heat, no running water, and no electricity, the Inter-Con's manager still fleeced us $120 a night.

In the morning, we prepared to set out for a day of inter-

views for a story on how city officials would rebuild Kabul.
In the hotel lobby, a shifty-looking man in black pants
and a black leather coat sidled up to Behroz and began chat-
ting with him. I ignored the exchange and headed for the
door.

"Ian, wait!" Behroz called behind me.

Impatient to begin my interviews, I rolled my eyes.
"What—"

I turned to see Behroz standing at gunpoint, his hands in
the air. A teenager had appeared with an AK-47 trained on
his rib cage.

"We've got a problem," Behroz said calmly. "They think
I'm a spy."

"Screw that!" I snapped. "Let's get out of here."

I began walking. Behroz tentatively followed me. We
both froze when the man in black shouted "Stop!" in
English and Dari.

The man in black then explained that his name was
Eshan Ullah and that he worked for the government. (I
found out later he worked for KHAD, the Afghan secret
police.)

"This is the condition," he said. "We need to wait for my
superiors to check Mr. Behroz's papers. And then you can
go."

"How long will that take?" I asked impatiently. In the
excitement of the moment I had forgotten that three
Pakistani journalists accused of supporting the new Taliban
militia had been summarily executed in Kabul just weeks
earlier. News of the executions had been slow to filter out of

Afghanistan, as the government repeatedly denied any knowledge of the journalists' whereabouts.

"We'll wait here," Eshan Ullah replied impassively.

We did wait, hour after hour.

As word of our arrest spread, colleagues from the BBC and the Associated Press visited the lobby of the Inter-Con where we were held at gunpoint. Photographer Craig Fuji, a friend of mine from New Delhi, pointedly took a series of photos of both Behroz and me. He made it clear to Ehsan Ullah that if anything happened to us, our faces would be on the front pages of newspapers around the world. Peter Greste, the BBC's Kabul correspondent, did the most to help, slipping me notes of encouragement and meeting with senior government officials to try to negotiate a speedy release.

At nightfall Eshan Ullah told us we could return to our room; we would meet his superiors in the morning. Armed teenagers escorted us upstairs and stood guard through the night. At six in the morning Behroz and I wandered down to the lobby, our rifle-toting teens just behind. Eshan Ullah was waiting for us and ordered that we move to the front parking lot. My eyes squinted against the bright sunlight reflected by the snow-covered peaks of the Hindu Kush.

An old Russian Lada squealed up to the front door. I assumed it was Eshan Ullah's shadowy superiors arriving to question Behroz, but three men in army fatigues jumped out of the car and began waving AK-47s in our faces.

"Get in!" Eshan Ullah barked at Behroz.

"You can go now," he said, waving me off like a pesky fly.

I turned to leave, then hesitated, looking closely at Behroz. He was here because of me. I couldn't abandon him now.

"No. I want to stay with him," I said, my heart thumping in my ears. Eshan Ullah shrugged, opened the car door, and shoved me as I bent to step in.

Behroz and I sat in the back with a guard on either side of us. As we neared the city's outskirts, the blindfolds came out: fetid, raw burlap was tied around my eyes and nose. I began to hyperventilate as my world was reduced to the sweaty space of dappled light in front of my nose.

"Behroz?" I asked.

"Yeah."

"You OK?"

"I'm scared," he said.

"Yeah. Me too."

Blind to the world, with AK-47s jammed into our ribs, we drove for about twenty minutes. When the car stopped, Behroz and I were led into a building. Once inside, the blindfolds came off and we found ourselves in a nondescript room right out of a John Le Carré novel: bare walls, two wooden chairs, and a large wooden desk behind which sat a man in a black leather coat. He pointed the bare lightbulb of his desk lamp toward our faces. For twelve hours this man grilled Behroz and me. *What were we doing in Kabul? Did we know why Pakistan was supporting the Taliban?*

When our interrogator was finally satisfied that we posed no threat to President Burhanuddin Rabbani's government, we were released and driven to the foreign ministry, where we chatted politely with some ministry officials over green tea and biscuits. The episode was a bizarre demonstration of Afghanistan's legendary hospitality even in the midst of treachery. As we stood to leave, one ministry official handed me a piece of paper. It was a bill from the Inter-Con for $120.

"Cash only," the official said politely.

When I returned to my base in New Delhi, I was high on adrenaline—thrilled to be alive and raring to go on my next assignment. The experience in Kabul, rather than scaring me away from reporting in dangerous places, spurred me to seek them out. But UPI was slowly going broke, and the bureau in New Delhi was slated to be closed. I began looking for another job that would keep me in South Asia, where the stories were exciting.

UPI's rival, the Associated Press, was looking for a correspondent for their office in Pakistan to help with coverage of West Asia, including Afghanistan. I jumped at the offer despite a hefty cut in my salary. In August 1995, I moved from New Delhi to Islamabad. An orderly city of modern, neatly arranged subdivisions and government buildings, Islamabad was tame by comparison with the chaos of New Delhi. Unable to afford better accommodations, I lived in the one-bedroom servant's quarters on a retired Pakistani general's estate.

I settled into work for the AP and was quickly brought up to speed on the major stories of the region: rising discontent with Prime Minister Benazir Bhutto's government, the Taliban movement in Afghanistan, and the worsening

conflict in Kashmir between India and Pakistan, at a time
when both nations were trying to acquire nuclear weapons.
Conflict and violence were the primary stories in Pakistan
and Afghanistan, and I began to make the transition from
foreign correspondent to war reporter.

On one of my first major assignments, my bureau chief,
Kathy Gannon, sent me to Kashmir. I was to gauge whether
this volatile region was indeed on the brink of its fourth war
since 1947, as many analysts in the West were claiming.
Specifically, I was to check out reports that India was firing
artillery shells across the border. The Pakistan military had
arranged to escort me to the disputed region. There they
assigned me a guide, who led me on foot to a town that had
reportedly been hit by dozens of Indian shells over the past
several weeks.

WE HAD BEEN WALKING for a little more than an hour. At
over 16,000 feet, the thin mountain air was biting cold. My
chest heaved and my heart pounded from the effort of the
hike at that altitude. The sun was slipping behind the snow-
capped peaks of the Karakoram Range, which divides
Indian-controlled Kashmir from Pakistani Kashmir.

My Muslim guide, Ahmed Younis, was about fifty meters
ahead of me on the dark, winding dirt road. Although it
was little more than a narrow mountain pass along an
escarpment, the Neelum Valley Road ran along the
Pakistani side of the contested region, parallel to the United
Nations–demarcated line of control. It thus formed a de
facto border between Pakistan and India. Indeed, in some

spots where the road bent in sharp hairpin turns, Indian territory is as close as twenty meters away from Pakistan. This road was the lifeline linking Pakistan's remote Kashmiri villages to each other and to the capital, Islamabad; however, it reportedly had been cut for weeks by Indian sniper fire.

"They have night vision now," Ahmed warned, as the dusky sky darkened to a star-speckled inky black. "They'll shoot at anything they see moving."

I concentrated on keeping pace with him. In the intense blackness, I lost all sense of space or direction. Although the Indian side of the border was several kilometers away, paranoia played tricks with my senses, making it seem as if it were just a few meters from me. As we approached a hairpin turn that jutted sharply toward India, Ahmed grabbed my khaki vest. He pulled me toward him and whispered in my ear, "We call this part of the road 'the shooting gallery.'"

To reduce the chance of detection, we had to spread out. Ahmed crawled fifty meters ahead of me. The sound of his movements against the gravel path faded as he moved away. I waited and held my breath. When a small rock hit the path near me and bounced past, our preplanned signal, I crawled up to Ahmed's position.

Copying his movements, I rolled from the gravel road into the shallow cover of a watery ditch. Frigid water immediately saturated my pants, photographer's vest, and notebook. I began pulling myself forward, slowly and cautiously. I hadn't gone more than ten meters when the first yellow tracer bullet whistled in and pinged with a sharp ricochet off the rocky escarpment that rose beside the mountain pass. I blinked my eyes to get rid of the blinding yellow streak that was now burned into my retinas.

For an instant, I wanted to stand and run. Then my stomach knotted and I felt like vomiting. Filled with dread, I almost jumped up and shouted, "Don't shoot! I'm Canadian!"

Instead, I lay in the freezing ditch as my legs grew numb. Desperately, I began to rationalize: *Nothing will happen to me. I lived in New Delhi for two years. I know India. They won't hurt me. I'm from Canada. Canadians don't die in Kashmir!*

Following closely behind the first round came a barrage of tracer bullets—some red, some yellow. Sparks flew in every direction off the escarpment in periodic bursts of light. My breathing became shallow and panicky, which was potentially life-threatening in the oxygen-starved mountain air. Although it only lasted minutes, the gunfire seemed to rage on for hours.

After the shooting subsided, Ahmed, who had crawled further ahead pitched another rock my way. I resumed my plodding crawl forward. When I finally caught up with him we both scrambled behind a small clump of bushes. Concealed from the snipers, we both lit cigarettes.

"Now you see what we live with," Ahmed said bitterly. He blew out a long column of smoke that lingered in the air as the vapors from his breath dissipated.

As I crawled on, I considered his words, which somehow

seemed calculated. I worked through the shooting in my mind, and it occurred to me that I couldn't say for sure where that first shot had come from. Did it come from the Pakistani or the Indian side of the border?

It struck me that this assignment might be nothing more than a propaganda exercise by the Pakistanis. I had always understood that governments used and manipulated the media, but this was more ruthless than I had anticipated. *How can they do that?* I thought at the time. *How can they risk my life just to make their point?*

I felt used, manipulated, and angry.

For the remainder of my three days in Kashmir, my blood surged with the excitement of someone who had cheated death. That had been my first time under fire; I had survived it, and I felt invincible. At the age of twenty-nine, I had discovered I had a taste for the rush of adrenaline that comes in life-threatening situations. In the years to come, that taste would become insatiable, until it nearly killed me.

I BEGAN SEARCHING OUT increasingly dangerous assignments, pushing my limits, and testing my mettle under fire. I continued in this way on the Indian subcontinent until June 1996, when I got a call from the AP's then international editor, Tom Kent. He asked if I would be interested in transferring to Vietnam, where I'd be focusing primarily on Vietnam's transition from Marxist-Leninist communism to a free-market economy. Hanoi was a small, one-person bureau, and I'd be writing mostly business and economic stories.

Although I was not thrilled about having to write about business, the transfer would bring me closer to my former status and salary as a bureau chief for UPI. So in September I packed my bags once again and moved to Hanoi.

It was a tough transition at first. I had found it easy to operate in the Indian subcontinent, where English was common, even if not the first language for many. Government officials in both New Delhi and Islamabad, while somewhat disorganized, had been very friendly and welcoming. In Vietnam, though, I was forced to work with a translator, and I could no longer read newspapers for local news tips. The legacy of the Vietnam War and Washington's nineteen-year economic embargo on Hanoi had produced a government paranoid about all Westerners. I had to live with the irritation of wiretaps on my home and office phone lines, and I was frequently followed by Interior Ministry officials.

Slowly, I learned to cope with the restrictive conditions for foreign journalists in Hanoi. I studied Vietnamese and began understanding newspaper headlines and whispered comments. For months, as I covered mundane government politics and economic stories, I was a Politburo-watcher. I wrote about subtle power shifts in the supreme government body of one of the few remaining hard-line communist countries in the world. Despite the AP's efforts to cover the new Vietnam, many American newspapers were still interested only in stories on the search for MIAS (servicemen missing in action), or anniversaries marking some significant event from the Vietnam War.

Most of the journalists assigned to Hanoi did not roam on assignment; they stuck pretty close to home, traveling only within the country. So for a time, I became more grounded and less adventurous than I had been in South Asia. Evenings after work I stopped by my favorite pub to meet colleagues for a couple of beers. I became the host of a renowned Wednesday-evening poker game in my white-walled house at Hanoi's Flower Village on Thuy Khue road. I decorated my house and taught myself to cook.

But my longing for adventure and war reporting never waned. When I got restless I asked to spend time in nearby Bangkok, to help with the task of covering much of Southeast Asia. It was during one of these trips to Thailand that Cambodian co-premier Hun Sen staged a coup to oust his counterpart, Prince Norodom Ranariddh. I immediately offered to help cover the story. It was late June of 1997, and most of the Asian press corps, including several of the AP's reporters from Bangkok, had converged on Hong Kong to cover the end of British colonial rule. When I called my friend and the Bangkok news editor, Patrick McDowell, he immediately told me to come to Bangkok to help edit stories from the area. The day after I arrived in Bangkok, Hun Sen staged his coup.

Although I was clamoring to head to Phnom Penh to cover the coup, the AP's resident Cambodia expert, Grant Peck, was already there. However, after about ten days of struggling through curfews, checkpoints, and heavy fighting in the city, Grant requested a break. We switched places. I was in Phnom Penh—once again in a war zone. But not long after the first days of the coup, the fighting had shifted upcountry, toward the northwestern city of Siem Reap. Surprisingly, charter flights were still operating to the city, a popular tourist destination because of its proximity to the fabled Angkor Wat temple complex. I flew to Siem Reap, where I hoped to link up with local military commanders who would take me to the front-line fighting, not far from the temples of Angkor.

In Siem Reap the AP's regular stringer suggested we try to talk our way onto a military helicopter headed for the front line. However, the local district commander refused us a seat on his helicopter. Determined to reach the action, we hired motorbikes and drivers to make the treacherous nine-hour journey over land-mined dirt roads and washed-out bridges.

I had come prepared for the typical torrential rains of the season, but we hit an unusually dry spell. I was caught off-guard without sun block for the relentless sun of the Asian tropics. By the time I reached the front-line fighting near the village of Khtum, I was exhausted and a boiled-lobster red.

Khtum was controlled by troops loyal to Hun Sen. Once settled in the hamlet, I befriended a boyish soldier in his midteens who took pity on my sunburn. He led me to an abandoned house in the center of the village. On the teak-wood porch there was a barrel of rainwater, which he invited me to use to cool my skin. Introducing himself as Chea Mai, he then produced a small aloe plant in a red earthenware pot. Chea broke off a stem from the plant, dabbed some of the jelly-like sap on his fingers, and motioned that I should rub a bit on my face. The smooth-faced Asian boy smiled curiously at the rough stubble on my chin. He then offered to share his army rations and a swig of rice wine with me.

We sat in the shade of the porch and smoked my Marlboros as Chea showed off his assault rifle with pride.

"Have you ever shot anyone?" Chea asked me through my interpreter. Several older soldiers joined us on the porch and listened to our conversation.

"No," I answered. "I don't like guns."

The other soldiers laughed, and Chea gave an admiring look at the gleaming black barrel of his Kalashnikov. He pulled a long drag of smoke into his lungs and squinted against the bright sun. I handed him my sunglasses and watched him explore them. He held them up to his eyes and stared directly into the sun. He flinched and quickly looked away. The older soldiers chuckled. I couldn't believe these teenaged soldiers would soon be facing combat; they still acted like children.

Blinking and rubbing his eyes with closed fists, Chea tossed the brown plastic Vuarnets back into my lap. "These don't work," he announced with contempt.

We sat cross-legged on the porch of the abandoned house, comparing notes about our lives in our vastly different worlds. We took turns drinking the potent home-brewed rice wine. Like most of the boys conscripted into the Cambodian army, Chea drank for courage in the imminent battle.

"How old are you?" he asked.

"I'm thirty-one," I replied.

"How many children do you have?" he asked.

"None. I'm not married yet," I answered.

He let out a soft, boyish chuckle—almost a giggle. In a country like Cambodia, many would think something was wrong with me to be single and childless at such an advanced age. I switched subjects and began interviewing Chea about his views on the fighting in Cambodia, the ongoing threat of the notorious Khmer Rouge and Hun Sen's coup. There was an innocence about Chea. He had all the trappings of a tough, battle-hardened soldier: his gun, his hunting knife, and the torn army fatigues he wore. But in reality he was just a kid with wide, wondering eyes, in a country that has known little but war since the late 1960s.

My conversation with Chea was cut short when the platoon sergeant called the troops to get ready to press ahead. Chea slung his rifle and a small rucksack over his shoulders and headed over to the other soldiers gathering near the sergeant. Finally Chea's platoon headed down the dusty road toward where the opposition troops had last been spotted. I lingered to let the lead soldiers get a head start. After a few minutes I motioned to my translator that we should follow.

THE FLASH FROM THE EXPLOSION caught my eye a split second before the percussion impact tore through the thick jungle foliage that lined National Highway 68. The power of the shockwave snatched my breath away. My ears rang for minutes afterward, drowning out the sound of the birds

in the banana trees. Then I saw a small swarm of flustered
troops heading toward me along the red dirt highway. They
hauled a makeshift stretcher made from a green hammock
tied between two long stalks of bamboo. As they stumbled
toward me, I saw a young man's face peering out at me from
inside the folds of the stretcher.

It was Chea. His plump, mocha-tinted Khmer face was
turning ashen as blood spilled from the veins, arteries, and
mangled muscles that dangled from his groin, where his leg
had been blown off.

Khmer Rouge rebels had rigged an old mortar shell into
a booby trap. A thin trip wire had been cleverly strung
across the one-lane road. When Chea tripped the wire with
his rubber-sandaled foot, the blast sent a shower of red-hot
shrapnel into his groin and abdomen.

As the three troops hauling the stretcher lurched past
me, Chea looked up with those same wide eyes he had used
to examine my sunglasses, but now they were shadowed
with terror. I watched them through a viewfinder as I
walked beside him, callously taking photographs. I had
been conditioned as a journalist not to become involved
with a story, which really means not to be human.

For several paces I hid behind my camera, but when
Chea reached out to me with his right hand, I lowered it
from my face and took his hand in mine. The blood on his
fingers and palm was warm and slippery; it soon became
thick and tacky as it dried.

Chea squeezed my hand and tried to speak. His pale lips

formed words, but his throat was silent. I watched intently and could sense him letting go. His eyes closed and his grip eased, but the sticky blood kept our hands together until I gently pulled mine free. Chea's arm drooped limp and dangled by the side of the stretcher.

The three troops—now pallbearers—scampered out of sight down the empty dirt road. I was slow to realize that we had come under heavy gunfire from the rebels. Then I heard the crack of a gunshot and I dashed for the ditch by the road. It took me a moment to notice that the soldier behind me had been hit in the thigh by that bullet. His comrades dragged him out of harm's way and tended to his bloody wound in the ditch. Once again, I began taking photos.

I slid further down and listened as bullets whistled by. I heard round after round as they pinged off the hard-packed dirt road, and I understood for once how close I had come to being hit. I could have reached out and touched the ground where that bullet had skipped by; my head was just inches away.

I shifted back in the ditch and looked up to watch in astonishment as a backup platoon of government troops arrived and fought their way forward on the highway. I stared at one unlikely soldier who seemed impervious to the incoming rounds whistling past him. An older veteran soldier, probably in his twenties, he also wore plastic sandals. A blue-checkered Khmer-style scarf hung from his neck, and his dusty black-and-yellow Caterpillar baseball cap was turned backward. He wore no shirt, only a pair of baggy, soiled briefs that did little to conceal his erection. As he marched past, he looked down quickly and smiled at me as I cowered in the ditch. I felt both exhilarated and shamed by his foolhardy bravery. Still looking at me, he began firing his assault rifle from his hip until the banana clip was emptied of bullets. Shiny brass shell casings danced off the dirt road. In one smooth motion he grabbed the spent clip, pulled it from the rifle, tossed it aside, slapped in a full clip and again began firing. As he marched and fired, he screamed at his enemy down the highway. My translator told me he was shouting: "Kill me! Why don't you fucking kill me?"

I lay there in the ditch and watched, amazed, as this lone soldier marched on the enemy.

WEEKS LATER, I WAS BACK in Hanoi, struggling with boredom. The waning summer of 1997 was filled with sweaty afternoons, chaotic traffic, and in a post–Cold War world, very little news that I considered important. The big stories had been done months earlier, as communist Vietnam's bitter, decades-long feud with the United States was drawing to a close. By comparison to fire fights in the jungle, my work seemed unendurably safe and routine. I had become a war junkie—juiced as much on the thrill of combat as by the chase for a good story. It's not uncommon for photographers, but less typical of print journalists.

Although I was only eighteen months into my assignment in Vietnam, I began seriously considering my options for alternative job postings. Months before my firefight experience in Cambodia, I had begun taking notice of

Africa and what was beginning to look like an endless tide of war flowing from that troubled continent. For almost a week straight, I kept hearing the names Kinshasa, Zaïre, Freetown, and Sierra Leone on the BBC and CNN. Zaïre—that African land of kleptocracy—I certainly knew. But Sierra Leone and Freetown were new to me.

I first really took notice of Sierra Leone on a Sunday late in May 1997. I had slept in late to minimize the effects of my late-night, beer-soaked poker game with friends from Reuters and the *Vietnam Business Journal.* When I finally got going around noon, I jumped on my motorbike and headed to the AP bureau on Le Thanh Tong Street to check for messages on the wire from New York or Tokyo. There was nothing for Hanoi, but streams of paper had gathered in a bundled mass at the foot of the message printer. Messages and copy were pouring in from West Africa, and a one-line urgent news bulletin from Freetown was the first hint of trouble in Sierra Leone: "Army officer seizes power in coup."

I logged on to the AP's editorial system and began reading about a little-known army colonel's coup in Sierra Leone. The president, Ahmed Tejan Kabbah, was fleeing his capital to escape certain death at the hands of coup leader Johnny Paul Koroma—a corrupt, middle-ranking officer with ties to Sierra Leone's infamous Revolutionary United Front (RUF).

Toward the end of 1997, the AP's West Africa correspondent resigned to join *Newsday* as its new Johannesburg bureau chief. I applied for the AP job in West Africa and was informed just before Christmas not only that I had been given the job but that my title would change from chief correspondent to bureau chief. Tom Kent, my editor at the time, called to inform me.

"When do you think you can be there?" he asked.

"I'll try to make it by February."

# 2

# INTO AFRICA

IN EARLY FEBRUARY 1998, after a quick visit home to Canada, I was on my way to Africa via New York, London, and Paris. The final leg of the journey would take me to Abidjan, the commercial capital of the Ivory Coast, where I would be based. But even before arriving there, I was pulled into the bloody turmoil of West Africa, which over the next year would eclipse my life and challenge all my assumptions about who I was and what I hoped to achieve.

During a stopover in London, I spent some time in the AP's bureau. Sitting behind a computer terminal, I read about the latest developments in Sierra Leone. A Nigerian-led coalition army known as ECOMOG was staging a massive offensive to depose a junta that had seized power in a bloody coup. The elected president, Ahmed Tejan Kabbah, had been overthrown in the spring of 1997 and replaced by an army junta backed by the notorious rebel Revolutionary United Front. Reading the wire copy filed by my AP colleagues based in Abidjan, I learned that Nigerian fighter jets had begun bombing Sierra Leone's capital, Freetown, as a prelude to a ground assault.

I called Tim Sullivan, the senior AP correspondent in the Abidjan bureau.

"Tim, what are you planning to do for coverage of the ECOMOG attack on Freetown?" I asked.

"I was going to ask you the same thing," Tim responded.

"We've got to send a reporter and a photographer," I told him.

"Who do you want to send?"

I paused a moment, suddenly realizing my unease about sending somebody into harm's way. I couldn't imagine having to call someone's parents or spouse to tell them that their loved one had been hurt or killed while on an assignment I had sent them to. Tim was relatively new to Africa, since he had come straight from the editing desk in New York, so I assumed he was too green for a war zone. There was also Glenn McKenzie, a locally hired reporter who had just joined the AP, but I figured he didn't know the ins and outs of filing while on the road. That left me.

"I guess I'll go," I finally told Tim. "Can you help with the arrangements?"

"Yeah, sure, but don't forget the Pope is going to be in Nigeria in March, and Clinton's heading to Senegal and Ghana in April," he reminded me.

Over the phone we quickly worked out the logistics of covering several major stories in West Africa at the same time. I would head to Sierra Leone and aim to be back in time to cover Pope John Paul II in Nigeria. Meanwhile, Tim would make travel plans for Senegal and Ghana to cover President Bill Clinton's historic trip.

After several more days in London to pick up office supplies and other provisions for the bureau, I set out to collect my visa for the Ivory Coast and fly south from London to Paris and on to Abidjan.

WITH YOUTHFUL WONDER, I pressed my nose up against the window of seat 12-H aboard the Air France flight to the Ivory Coast. From 35,000 feet, the expansive Sahara resembled a rippled blanket of red, brown, and orange. Staring down at the parched but majestic landscape, I realized how little I knew about Africa. I had signed on for this job with romantic notions based on a smattering of *National Geographic* articles and an exaggerated sense of self as the modern-day Livingstone or Stanley setting out to explore the so-called Dark Continent. It was an absurd notion, really, yet my heart raced with the anticipation of a schoolboy on a field trip.

During that Thursday afternoon flight, I spent about seven hours in the sterile tranquility of my plush, business-class surroundings. I was pampered with cocktails, fine entrées, and first-run films. I didn't know then that these would be my last seven hours of luxury—with working air-conditioning and clean, functioning toilets—for months to come. I was unprepared for the imminent assault on my every sense.

As our Airbus descended for its final approach into Abidjan's Houphoüet-Boigny International Airport, sub-Saharan Africa came into clearer view. The desert gave way to patches of vegetation in the Sahel's scattered scrubland.

The Sahel, in turn, evolved into a thick canopy of palm trees, banana mangroves, and rubber tree plantations. Only patches of shadowy darkness interrupted this seemingly impenetrable world of lush green.

The lumbering jet bumped down on the hot runway in the late evening of Thursday, February 12, 1998. The flight attendants popped open the hatch, letting in a flood of humid air, and the windows inside the aircraft's cabin immediately fogged over. Drops of condensation formed on the plane's bulkhead. My heart pounded as I stood at the top of the staircase that had been rolled up to the front passenger door of the jet. A hot, dusty breeze swept across my face. The industrial odor of aviation fuel blended awkwardly with the tantalizing smell of chocolate from the nearby cocoa refining factories. In my head I hummed the horn-blaring theme music to *National Geographic* television specials.

Dark patches of perspiration formed under the armpits of my shirt and down the small of my back as I stood there in the heat. My first inkling of foreboding hit me as I watched gun-toting, khaki-clad paramilitary police scurry back and forth on the tarmac below. Sure, I had been in several war zones, and guns were nothing new, but there was something a little more sinister here. The armed men somehow seemed random and lawless. I felt overwhelmed in these first few moments in Africa and I sensed I had made a monumental mistake. I wanted to stay on the plane and return to Vietnam. Of course I did not—I ignored my dread and kept moving toward the terminal.

Standing in line behind African businessmen, UN diplomats, and budget travelers, I waited for the immigration inspector. An hour crept by before I finally reached the counter, where an officer with a smile of crooked, nicotine-stained teeth beckoned me forward. I handed him my passport and arrival card. Sweat beaded on my forehead and ran down my cheeks. I watched as he intently perused every page of my passport, pausing at the Afghan visas. For an instant I panicked, thinking he might suspect me of smuggling drugs. Scenes from the movie *Midnight Express* flashed through my mind as I eyed a German shepherd being led by leash near the luggage carousel. In time, however, the inspector stamped my arrival and slid my passport halfway back to me. His hand held the document firmly to the counter. I tried, but I couldn't pick it up.

*"Avez-vous un petit cadeau pour moi?"* (Do you have a little present for me?) he asked. It was my first of many brushes with Abidjan's ubiquitous corruption.

Having been warned about the incessant requests for bribes or gifts in Africa, I feigned ignorance of French and replied in English, "How about a nice big smile?"

The inspector chuckled heartily and let go of my passport.

FOR THE NEXT SEVERAL WEEKS I adjusted to life in Africa and began learning the ropes of my new job. As bureau chief for West Africa, I was expected to coordinate the news coverage of twenty-three countries, a great many of which I knew precious little about. In the bureau I worked with

American journalist Tim Sullivan and Glenn McKenzie, a fellow Canadian who until recently had been working in South Africa for Agence France-Presse. Also in the bureau was Amba Dadson, a soft-spoken woman from Ghana. Amba was a lawyer who had taken an interest in journalism when she moved to Abidjan from Ghana's capital of Accra. She had the thankless job of helping all the reporters arrange travel plans and other administrative tasks. In exchange, we helped train her in basic reporting and writing. Together we divvied up the workload.

On my first night shift I got a call from the AP's stringer in Cameroon. A fuel car had derailed near the capital, Youndé, and exploded in flames, engulfing a suburban neighborhood. Many people had been killed and dozens more were being rushed to hospitals with third-degree burns. My heart raced with the thrill of a breaking story. It took more than fifty phone calls from Abidjan that night to get the basic facts of the story. At first we reported six dead. Later that night we updated the figure to twelve. When I closed the bureau at the end of the evening, the death toll stood at twenty-four. In the morning, however, we received a telex from our stringer reporting the death toll was, indeed, six—the number we had started with. As I wrote a correction for the wire, I flew into a rage and spent forty-five minutes trying to get the stringer on the phone. When I reached him, he explained that hospital officials and police officers had counted the same bodies several times. It was the first of many eye-opening experiences I had with practicing journalism in Africa.

Outside working hours, most of my time was occupied by registering as a resident with the Ivorian government and applying for the many visas I would need to cover the region. African bureaucracies move so slowly that most journalists make a habit of keeping valid visas in their passports at all times to avoid the rush in the event of a breaking story. Quickly, the pages of my passport filled with visas for Guinea, Ghana, the Democratic Republic of Congo, the Republic of Congo, the Central African Republic, and many others.

As I moved about Abidjan, my eyes were opened. I had expected poverty and desperation in Africa, but not in the city known as the "Little Paris" of Africa. The streets were strewn with trash and raw sewage. Children in rags begged for handouts or offered to guard my jeep for a few hundred West African francs (less than a dollar). *Patron, patron,* they called out as I parked in front of the city's main Ecobank branch.

On almost every street, I was swarmed by clusters of scurrying little urchins, filthy with street grime. Pushing and shoving, they fought to get to me first. At night, the children were replaced by malnourished and scantily clad prostitutes whose spindly legs were often covered with open sores, and whose arms were lined with needle track marks. Heavy layers of makeup did little to conceal their desperately ill health, and I marveled at the foolhardiness of the Western businessmen who took these women back to their

$300-a-night rooms at the Novotel, the Inter-Continental, or the archaic Hotel Ivoire. Behind all the misery lay ostentatious wealth. Abidjan's suburban streets were lined with enormous mansions hidden away behind high security walls. Parking garages were filled with Mercedes, BMWs, and Land Rovers, most of which seldom left the safe confines of their driveways. When they did, chauffeurs drove them.

In central Abidjan, meanwhile, the frenzied streets were congested with traffic. Dented and rusting Peugots, Renaults, and Nissans skittered from lane to lane, kicking smog and dust into the already choking heat of the day. The sun in Abidjan blazed unrelentingly through the day, while 60 to 75 percent relative humidity left a sticky film over everything. Daily chores were made unbearable, like slogging through a swamp, and even breathing seemed an effort.

I saw unemployed men in threadbare T-shirts and torn jeans lazing around on street corners under the midday sun. Everywhere I turned in Abidjan I was assaulted by poverty, filth, dust, and desperation. If this was the real Africa, I questioned whether I could cope. Quickly overwhelmed, I soon restricted my wanderings to a narrow corridor of road between my hotel and the AP bureau.

The more I discovered, the more I grew angry and disgusted at Africa's recent colonial experience, but I still knew little about African history. In my spare time at the bureau and during evenings back at the hotel I immersed myself in books about Africa's colonial roots, from slavery through the Boer War and Europe's mad scramble for African colonies, and on to the lingering economic dependency that remains today. I began to feel that sense of "white man's guilt" for what *my* people had done to Africa. Yet I still believed that, as a journalist, I had the power to make the world care about the evils being perpetrated in Africa.

After about a week of living in a ramshackle and cockroach-infested hotel near the AP bureau in Abidjan's Deux Plateaux district, I moved into the bureau, which was in fact a two-bedroom bungalow converted into an office. The walls were adorned with large, colorful maps of Africa. The living room, cluttered with desks and computers, was the newsroom. I lay awake nights on a mattress on the floor of my office and listened to the dot matrix printers screech and squawk as they churned out breaking news from around the world. In the evenings I watched rented movies or CNN on the bureau television and ordered Vietnamese food for dinner. An avid rice fan, I never adjusted to eating ground cassava, West Africa's primary carbohydrate staple. However, as a former French colonial city, Abidjan had become home to many migrants from other former French territories, including Lebanon and French Indochina, and the cuisine of these places was readily available. I ate most of my meals at my desk: breakfast was a strong cup of coffee with condensed milk and Nestlé's Quik instead of sugar. I skipped lunch most days.

After several weeks in Abidjan I was disappointed to learn that the social scene was limited. Unlike Vietnam, where most of the press corps had stayed put, most of the journalists and aid workers in the Ivory Coast were on the road much of the time.

I finally found a two-bedroom bungalow and moved out of the bureau with only the mattress that I had been sleeping on. About three weeks later, my furniture arrived from Vietnam. I spent several weeks decorating the bungalow. I enjoyed the large wrap-around porch, where I ate breakfast on Sundays. The yard was green and filled with trees; a looming mango tree offered shade for much of the backyard.

I converted the bungalow's spare bedroom into a home office with a computer and spare telephone line on which I could dial into the AP's computer system. The news business continues around the clock, and the copy editors in New York had a habit of calling in the middle of the night with questions about the stories my bureau had filed during the day. Rather than race off to the bureau at two in the morning, I could now just slip into the office beside my bedroom.

I had been living in my new house for about ten days when Glenn offered to take me to dinner at a local *maquis*— one of the popular outdoor restaurants found throughout West Africa. We climbed into Glenn's battered gray Land Rover and sped off through dusty streets. Poor lighting gave the streets an orange glow in the posh suburban Cocody neighborhood. Blocks before we reached the maquis I could already feel the heavy thump of reggae music in my chest.

"It's Alpha Blondy," Glenn said, explaining that he was the most popular singer in his native Abidjan. With songs like "Coup d'Etat" and "Boulevard de la Mort," Blondy was a champion of the anti-French movement in post-colonial Ivory Coast.

The Cocody maquis was in a sprawling yard covered in sand—like a beach parking lot, I thought—where rickety, weather-beaten tables and chairs were randomly arranged. An enormous waitress wearing a brightly colored wrap-around dress and matching hat came up to our table and took our order of ground cassava and chicken stew along with two beers.

I leaned back and smoked a cigarette while we waited for our food. When it arrived, it came in a chipped porcelain bowl with red flowers painted around the edges. The chicken stew inside was a sloppy brown concoction. Hunks of stringy chicken, still on the bone, lay at the bottom of the oily broth. The side order of cassava reminded me of the couscous I used to eat in my favorite Middle Eastern restaurant back in Toronto. I scanned the table for a fork and knife, but gave up when I watched Glenn dig in with his fingers.

After the meal and a couple more beers, we sat back to get to know each other. As a bureau chief I tried to meet my staff outside the office to break tensions over a few beers. Little did I realize the Ivory Coast's locally brewed Flag beer packed a wallop, magnified by dehydration from the high temperatures and dripping humidity.

Glenn and I tried to talk over the thumping music, but surrendered after an hour and headed home. Before turning in, I sat on the front porch of my house and lit a cigarette. The squawk of printers had now been replaced by chirping crickets and tree frogs in my yard. Basking in the glow of one too many beers, I thought, *I really love my job.*

I woke the next day with a splitting headache and a brutal hangover. On that same day I met David Guttenfelder, the AP's West Africa photographer, with whom I would forge an easy friendship. David was just back in Abidjan from Ouagadougou, Burkina Faso, where he had been photographing a youth soccer tournament. When we met in the bureau, David boasted about how he had passed out during a match from a malarial fever. The spectacle had been videotaped by the local television station and broadcast on the evening news. David had become an instant celebrity. "Now everyone recognizes me on the streets," he said.

At twenty-eight, David was a cocky news photographer from Waukee, Iowa. I took an instant shine to him, admiring his courage and skill as a combat photographer in places like Liberia and Zaïre. David had seen more death and destruction in his short tenure in Africa than most journalists see in a lifetime. As we chatted about Africa, David taught me the local handshake, which ends with a snap of the fingers. Nigerian troops on peacekeeping duty in Liberia had taught him that. Having studied Africa in college, David knew the lay of the land much better than I did. After graduation in the late mid-1990s he moved on to Dar es Salaam, Tanzania, to continue studying and to practice his Swahili. Shortly after arriving in Africa, David picked up some work as a photo stringer for the *New York Times* and the Associated Press. He was lauded for his coverage of the 1994 genocide in Rwanda and the ensuing refugee crisis in neighboring Zaïre. His skill eventually landed him a full-time job with the AP, which assigned him to West Africa.

David took me under his wing during our first few days together, showing me around town and recommending the best restaurants and nightclubs. Although he was just a few years younger than I was, David reminded me of myself when I had first gone overseas in terms of energy.

In preparation for the Pope's visit to Nigeria, we shared a taxi to the Nigerian Embassy to pick up our visas. We walked into press attaché Uche M'banaso's office at the Nigerian Embassy on a Monday morning in late February 1998. It was oppressively humid outside and the embassy's antiquated air-conditioning couldn't keep up with the heat. The hallways smelled of mildew and soggy newspapers. As I walked into M'banaso's office, I nodded to my colleagues already in the room.

Without shifting his eyes from the TV screen that dominated the room, M'banaso motioned with his chin that we should sit. For thirty minutes we waited quietly for our host to attend to our visa requests. Finally, he picked up a stack of applications and began calling out names. He rifled through the papers without saying a word. I strained to catch a glimpse of my approved application among the others.

"Guttenfelder," he eventually called out.

David stood and took his passport. He flipped through the pages to confirm that the visa was indeed stamped and valid. Blacklisted without explanation by the ruling military regime, the Associated Press had not been given a visa for Nigeria in eighteen months.

"Sullivan," M'banaso called out next.

"Mr. Sullivan is not here," I offered. M'banaso set Tim's passport and application aside and continued through the rest of the dozen or so applications. As he neared the bottom of the stack, I began to fidget anxiously. He read the name on the final application and set aside the heavy stack of papers with a swish of paper made top-heavy by passport photos stapled to the corners of each application.

"What about mine?" I asked, my voice frustrated and indignant. I was ready for the impending battle of wills even before M'banaso told me my application was not in the pile. Sweaty and irritated, I was in no mood for the political niceties required to sweet-talk my way into getting a Nigerian visa.

"What's your name?" M'banaso finally asked after an unnerving pause.

A thin film of perspiration had formed on my forehead. The salt stung my freshly shaved upper lip. The perspiration collected into beads of sweat that ran like warm tendrils down the side of my face.

"Ian Stewart," I said. "I'm the new bureau chief with the Associated Press."

"But the AP chief is Miss Tina," he said, referring to my predecessor, Tina Susman.

"No," I corrected undiplomatically, "she left three months ago."

M'banaso shuffled once more through the pile of uncollected passports and visa applications. I sat forward on my chair and hoped he would somehow pull my approved application from the stack.

"I don't see an application from you, Stewart," M'banaso said to me. "I'm sorry, but all the applications that have been approved have already come back from Abuja."

"Are you sure mine was sent to Abuja?" I asked.

"Yes, of course," the press officer answered with an irritating calmness that I took to be ambivalence. "All the applications that came to my office were sent in."

He paused and looked intently at my face. "I remember seeing your application," he said. "You are from Canada, aren't you?"

I nodded yes, but kept my mouth shut.

After about an hour of arguing, M'banaso finally relented. He picked up his phone and called for George, his assistant, who appeared in seconds with my application and passport in his hand. Without so much as a flinch of embarrassment, M'banaso announced, "I'll send this to Abuja today and we should get an answer about your visa in a month."

"A month?" I gasped incredulously. "But I have to be in Nigeria in a couple of weeks for the Pope's visit!"

Another half hour of debate passed, to no avail. Then I gave up and headed back toward the AP bureau.

Pope John Paul II was just days away from embarking on his second journey to Nigeria. The AP had mobilized correspondents, photographers, and TV crews from across Africa and parts of Europe. As bureau chief for the region, I was expected to coordinate the coverage, but now I panicked at the prospect of doing it from the sidelines. The only thing standing between me and this story was a seemingly immovable wall of Nigerian bureaucracy.

As I walked into the bureau, I was immediately informed that M'banaso had just called for me.

"What did he want?" I asked.

Saying nothing, the bureau's administrative assistant, Amba Dadson, simply shrugged.

I steeled my nerves to call the Nigerian Embassy and asked for M'banaso's office. He answered politely enough and then launched into the real reason for my visa problems.

"I wanted to take my family to Canada for a vacation last year," he began telling me, "but they would not give me a visa."

"I'm very sorry about that," I said, feigning sympathy and concern. My jaw was agape at the audacity.

*Barely a month in Africa and already I'm being black-mailed,* I thought while beginning to seethe.

"My children had their hearts set on seeing Canada," he went on. "Can you help me get a visa to Canada?"

I explained that I was only a Canadian citizen, which gave me no sway over the workings of the Canadian Embassy in Abidjan or its immigration machinations.

"But you are a reporter," he protested. "Can't you write an article or do something?"

After I had hung up the phone, I immediately called Frank Aigbogun and Gilbert Da Costa, the AP's part-time reporters in Nigeria. I explained the visa snafu and pleaded for their help. They directed me to call several officials, and, after a flurry of calls, I finally reached a sympathetic government bureaucrat in Abuja. He assured me he would personally see that I had my visa in time for my flight to Lagos.

The next day, M'banaso called me to inform me I could come to the embassy and pick up my visa.

"You called Abuja, didn't you? You should not have gone over my head," he said ominously. "I would have taken care of your visa."

I left M'Banaso's office with my passport, duly stamped and ready for my trip to Lagos the next month.

In the end, it would be my only trip to Nigeria during my stint as the AP's West Africa bureau chief.

DISGUSTEDLY, I EXPLAINED the blackmail ploy to David. He suggested we go to the beaches near Assini for a Sunday afternoon away from the city. David, his girlfriend Cassy, and I packed up their car with towels, a Frisbee, and a picnic lunch. David slipped a BoDeans cassette into the tape deck and cranked the volume once we hit the highway linking Abidjan to the picturesque town of Grand Bassam—the former French colonial capital—and then Assini. I could feel my blood pressure lower as we drove through the bucolic countryside. This was the Africa I had naively imagined: lush farmland dotted with simple villages unspoiled by foreign hands.

A ninety-minute drive east of Abidjan delivered us to the white beaches of Assini. For most of the day I frolicked in the water, or read about colonial Africa while sitting in the shade of a coconut tree. The breeze off the ocean was welcome relief after the steamy humidity of the city. For lunch, we gathered under a thatch-roofed gazebo and feasted on sandwiches and fresh salads. Africa was beginning to look better and better.

THE RELIEF FROM THE DAY at the beach distracted me momentarily from Sierra Leone—the lead story in the region at the time. In February, just days before my arrival in West Africa, ECOMOG troops and fighter jets had driven Sierra Leone's junta from the capital and were preparing to reinstall President Kabbah. David and I immediately began making preparations to head to Freetown to cover the mopping-up phase of the ECOMOG offensive and the inauguration of Ahmed Tejan Kabbah.

In the first week of March 1998, just two weeks after landing in Abidjan, I boarded a Ghana Airlines flight bound for Monrovia and Conakry in the Republic of Guinea. Once in Guinea, David and I immediately began searching for a charter airline willing to travel to war-torn Freetown. We finally hired a Lebanese crew that was willing to fly us to Sierra Leone's International Airport at the town of Lungi, just a few kilometers by boat or road from Freetown proper.

# 3

# "THE WORST PLACE ON EARTH"

DAVID AND I ARRIVED in Sierra Leone in early March 1998. Our plane flew low, skimming just above the lush mangrove waterways that edge much of West Africa's Atlantic coastline.

The international airport at the town of Lungi was bustling with preparations for President Ahmed Tejan Kabbah's official homecoming ceremony. We snatched our bags off the back of the Russian-owned twin-prop airplane that had brought us from Conakry, capital of the neighboring Republic of Guinea. We wandered over to the terminal building, where a smiling man in a dark blue uniform with red epaulets and embroidered government insignias greeted us. The customs officer welcomed us to Sierra Leone in Krio—a complex and charming language based on English, but peppered with expressions from other languages.

"How dee bodee now?" the officer blurted out in a rapid-fire staccato. Loosely translated, this means "How are you?"

46

I had been taught a bit of Krio before leaving for Freetown, so I answered, "Tank-ee Gah, dee bodee in dee clothes." ("I'm fine.")

The customs man took off the oversized blue cap that sat loose on his head. His hair, where it had not receded from his wrinkled forehead, was a thinning mesh of black, interspersed with small patches of white. He was a handsome man with an endearing smile, and I would learn that his gentle charm was no anomaly in this desperate land of misery and decay.

It was the dry season, but the customs officer's cramped quarters smelled of mildew and musty paper. On the wall behind his desk was a Coca-Cola clock. It tried in vain to tell the time; its arms had been broken off. The customs inspector sat in a battered gray desk chair, and its wheels squeaked as he pulled himself toward his desk. His head and shoulders disappeared behind a leaning stack of yellowed paperwork: neglected passport and visa applications from a time when people still wanted to come to Sierra Leone for cheap holidays, he explained with hasty embarrassment. David handed him our passports. The inspector gave them a cursory glance, then pulled a rubber stamp from the desk's top drawer and whacked an arrival stamp onto the visa pages. He tossed the documents back across the desk and stood to bid us farewell and a safe journey.

"Thank you," he said in English as we turned to leave. "Thank you, for coming to greet our president upon his return home."

SIERRA LEONE GOT ITS NAME—meaning Lion Mountain—
from early Portuguese explorers who thought the profile of
the region's shoreline mountains looked like a sleeping lion.
Modern Sierra Leone came into being at the end of the
eighteenth century, when slaves who had won their freedom
by fighting on the British side in the American Revolution
were given a fifty-two-square-kilometer parcel of land along
Africa's western coastline. It was mosquito-infested swamp-
land, and most of the original settlers died. However, other
ex-slaves arrived to keep the settlement alive. Sierra Leone
was a haven for freed slaves until it was taken over by the
British crown. It remained a British colony until 1961.

Western-style democracy and government were short-
lived in the newly independent Republic of Sierra Leone,
as infighting among ethnic groups undermined coopera-
tive development. A series of military coups and political
assassinations destabilized and impoverished the new
nation. Decades of corruption and political upheavals have
left Sierra Leone the "worst place on earth," according to a
United Nations Development Program Survey—worse
even than the Sudan, Ethiopia, Afghanistan, and Laos. Life
expectancy is thirty-eight years, while 164 of every 1,000
babies die in infancy. Sixty-nine percent of adults cannot
read or write.

In the late 1980s, Foday Sankoh, a nearly illiterate, low-
ranking army officer with Maoist leanings, founded an
insurgent force called the Revolutionary United Front
(RUF). Profoundly influenced by the philosophy and ideol-
ogy of Libya's nationalist leader Muammar Qaddafi—who

aspired to regional hegemony in West and North Africa—
Sankoh demanded free social services and genuine political
democracy. When the government failed to deliver, he
launched a guerrilla war.

The horrific nature of Sankoh's methods epitomized
everything evil. Under his leadership, the rebels degenerated
into a merciless fighting force more interested in terror
and revenge than social reform and change. Those who
resisted RUF rule were killed; women and girls were raped;
children were kidnapped and forced to become soldiers.

The RUF were helped to power in 1997 by a disgruntled
army colonel named Johnny Paul Koroma. Koroma,
sympathetic to Sankoh and the RUF, held a military post
through much of the 1990s in Sierra Leone's diamond-rich
Kono region near the border with war-ravaged Liberia. He
negotiated deals with the RUF that gave the rebels access to
the diamond mines in return for a share of the profits. At
the same time, Sankoh was forging lucrative business ties
with Liberian leader Charles Taylor. Taylor lent out his
country for use as a conduit through which to smuggle guns
and money into Sierra Leone. Selling Sierra Leone's
diamonds on the international market, Taylor laundered
the gem revenues for Sankoh in return for a hefty percent-
age of the profits.

In May 1997, Koroma staged a coup to depose elected
president Ahmed Tejan Kabbah and invited Sankoh's rebel
movement to help form a government. From May 1997 until
February 1998, Koroma and his rebel allies ran roughshod
over the capital, Freetown, and all of Sierra Leone.

In the mid-1990s, the West African Economic Community, or ECOWAS (comprising Nigeria, the Ivory Coast, Ghana, Togo, Benin, Guinea, Burkina Faso, Liberia, and Sierra Leone) established a military intervention force known as ECOMOG to help implement and enforce a peace accord in Liberia after Charles Taylor's rebels seized power. In 1997, the Nigerian-led and -dominated ECOMOG mandate was extended to Sierra Leone. In February 1998, ten months after Koroma's coup, the Nigerians launched air strikes on Freetown. Ground troops followed and drove Koroma's junta and the rebels from power. The capital was then secured for Kabbah's return to power. But rebels escaping to the countryside would run amok for weeks.

A SHIMMERING MIRAGE OF WATER danced off the baking black tarmac at Sierra Leone's International Airport. Palm trees at the edges of the runway swayed in the fresh sea breeze blowing off the nearby shoreline. Turquoise waves licked lazily onto white, sandy beaches. It was a postcard scene.

Suddenly a camouflage-painted Nigerian Alpha jet screeched overhead. The jet's turbines let out a deep-throated roar that echoed back onto itself and then was lost in the bush as it landed. A hulking C-130 transport plane from the Nigerian Air Force followed the Alpha jet. As the mammoth aircraft taxied to the terminal building, I stood near the customs inspector's office and watched. The C-130's rear hold opened and dozens of fresh young troops from Nigeria's commercial hub, Lagos, filed onto the tarmac, blinking and shielding their eyes from the blinding sun high in the sky. The soldiers lined up in a neat military formation.

For the ten months following Koroma's coup, Sierra Leone had been on a war footing. However, the troops arriving from Nigeria on this day were not here to join the jungle skirmishes that continued against the rebels upcountry. The new troops were coming to Freetown to herald Kabbah's return; they were here to be part of the military's pomp and circumstance. A brass band and color guard rehearsed the national anthems of Sierra Leone and Nigeria.

Even after Koroma's coup, troops loyal to Kabbah had been able to maintain control of the airport; they were reinforced later by ECOMOG, which used the airport as a staging point. Kabbah, who had fled into exile in neighboring Guinea, often shuttled back to the airport to meet with other ministers and advisors living in nearby Lungi. With a price on his head, Kabbah could go nowhere else in his country. From the sidelines, he had watched as ECOMOG battled to win back his country.

Power seized by military force is not new to Africa, but this was the first time that Africans had prepared a coordinated, multinational military campaign to restore power to a deposed but duly elected government. Yet Africa is a land of paradox. This altruistic operation was largely being funded and supported by Nigeria's dictator, General Sani Abacha, one of Africa's worst human rights abusers. Blind to this hypocrisy, my editors in New York now cajoled me to write stories about "Africa standing up for democracy," as one copy editor in New York naively put it.

*Bullshit,* I thought. This is one African military thug flexing his muscles to impress another military thug.

Although David and I were in Sierra Leone to cover Kabbah's return, we were also interested in covering the war being waged in the countryside between the ECOMOG forces and Koroma's rebel and junta coalition, which was worsening day by day. Before leaving Abidjan the week before, I had learned that Colonel Maxwell Kobe was the Nigerian officer in charge of ECOMOG ground operations in Sierra Leone. While David set out to find us some food and change our American dollars for leones, the local currency, I stayed behind at the airport to try and find Kobe. (At a 600:1 exchange rate, our pockets would soon be stuffed full of the ragged, filthy bills.)

Across the lounge I spotted a mature-looking man, perhaps in his fifties, with a goatee and a loose, oversized floral shirt. He wore cargo-pocketed army pants and had green rubber sandals on his feet. An assault rifle was propped up next to him. He leaned back in the seat— salvaged long ago from an abandoned Mercedes-Benz and converted into an airport lounge chair—and rested his feet on the rail of the veranda surrounding the entrance to the airport's VIP lounge. His gold-rimmed glasses slipped down his nose as he looked up at me nonchalantly.

I didn't know it then, but this was Julius Spencer, Sierra Leone's minister of information and a man who would play a key role in my life in the coming months. Young women flanked him on both sides. One wore a miniskirt and a tight, lime-green tube top. Her hair was chemically relaxed and dyed blonde. Her Day-Glo, three-inch platform shoes matched her form-fitting top. The other woman wore a long evening dress with spiked high heels. Her lips glowed with glossy red lipstick. Spencer finished the last bite of his army MRE (meal-ready-to-eat) and tossed the tin container aside. He looked at me, but showed no sign of surprise, as if a white man strolling up to him at the airport in war-ravaged Sierra Leone were commonplace—which it certainly was not.

I walked up to the veranda and leaned against the railing. "I'm looking for Colonel Kobe," I said casually, pulling my sunglasses away from my eyes and letting them hang from a black cloth strap around my neck.

"He's not here now," Spencer replied. He picked up his walkie-talkie and made a few inquiries. Finally he said, "He's at home taking a nap."

David returned after about an hour with two locally made soft drinks and a small package of cream-filled cookies. While we smoked my cigarettes and drank the sodas, Spencer arranged for a junior officer to take care of us while we waited for Kobe.

Another hour went by. A young officer in fatigues and a khaki-green undershirt arrived at the airport in a jeep. He told us to follow him. We trailed his jeep in the car David had hired while looking for the drinks. I watched intently as we drove through the airport grounds to the main gate. Soldiers in various stages of dress were everywhere. They sat in small clusters under the shade of trees by the roadside or lounged in the backseats of jeeps. Music—West African reggae—blared from a transistor radio beside the heavily armed guards who manned the front gate.

The guards at the gate stopped us until they realized we were with John, the young captain assigned to watch over us. Outside the airport, John made only a cursory attempt to find Kobe. We drove to the colonel's home in Lungi, but John waved us off even before checking whether Kobe was home. I was growing increasingly irritated as the heat in the car rose and my New York deadlines loomed.

*What does this guy think he's doing?* I cursed John in my head.

The young captain then led us down the road to the Lungi Airport Hotel. He told us we'd have to wait there until morning and then we could head upcountry with an ECOMOG convoy. David and I settled into our rooms in the hotel. There was no electricity, which meant no air-conditioning, and the rooms were sweltering. No electricity also meant no running water: no showers, no baths, and no chance to brush my teeth. Even after all my time reporting on conflicts, I tended to forget that hygiene is a luxury few can afford in a war zone. The toilet in my bathroom hadn't been flushed for days. It emitted an odor that made me gag.

I slammed the bathroom door shut and walked across the hall into David's room, where I collapsed onto the foot of the extra bed. Still adjusting to West African cuisine, my stomach was bloated with gas. A loud, prolonged fart escaped when I plopped down.

"Doorknob!" David said sharply.

"Huh?" I responded. David began punching my biceps relentlessly, until my muscles went numb. When he realized I didn't understand what he was doing, he eased off and explained.

"It's a game called Doorknob," he said. "I used to play it with my roommate in university."

The rules were simple: if one person farts in a room, he has to touch a doorknob before his opponent says "doorknob." Failing to do so leaves the opponent free to repeatedly punch the first person's arm until the victim can utter the magic word, in this case an extended version of "uncle": "Secretary-General of the United Nations Boutros Boutros-Ghali."

I reached into my breast pocket and pulled out my silver-topped pack of Marlboro Lights. I gave a cigarette to David and lit one for myself. We started swapping stories about our girlfriends and families back in the United States and Canada and we bragged about our past "heroics" on assignment in war zones. The time flew by as we sized one another up and laughed easily together.

At about six in the evening, John knocked on the door and handed us two MREs and two bottles of water. He told us he'd be back to pick us up around nine that night. I smoked a second cigarette and began exploring the MRE: grape Kool-Aid, Tootsie Pops, Pop-Tarts, and a disposable Bunsen burner to heat the chicken-stew entrée. We both knew this could be the last decent meal we'd eat for days; we savored every bite and continued to exchange stories.

When John arrived, he said he'd take us out for beers. He drove us in his jeep down the dusty road to downtown Lungi, a sleepy hamlet of half a dozen wooden shacks and a few abandoned, boarded-up shops. The night air was as stifling as it had been during the day. We pulled into a sandy lot beside a raucous bar. Behind the bump of reggae music, I could hear the mechanical churning of an electric generator—essential in a war zone to keep the tunes cranked, the beer cold, and, at this particular bar, the red, yellow, and green patio lanterns flickering. The bar was ringed with these familiar bright plastic lanterns, which evoked memories of the bars where I used to drink on summer weekends at a girlfriend's cottage back in Canada.

Most of the tables were filled with young Nigerian soldiers accompanied by their Sierra Leonean "wives." The influx of soldiers in Lungi had created an immediate demand for the existing, but previously little-used sex trade. David and I sat at the only free table and saved a seat for John. He quickly joined us with three Flag beers, imported from the Ivory Coast. He plunked the cans down in front of us. David leaned forward and confided to me, "I'm not much of a drinker."

"That's OK," I said, just loud enough to be heard over the generator and music. "Neither am I."

In Asia I had often drunk too much, but in Africa I had quickly learned that too much alcohol, particularly preservative-filled beer, did not mix with the heat. For most of the night, John kept a steady flow of cold beer coming to the table and the cans began to pile up. I don't know if he ever noticed as I surreptitiously poured half the beer into the potted fern next to me. But David had spotted me. His shoulders heaved once as he chuckled and flashed a sympathetic smile my way.

The night's revelry ended just after one in the morning. John drove us back to the hotel. Stumbling into the corridor walls, he guided us by flashlight to our rooms.

"What do you think?" I asked David after we were back in his room.

"I dunno." David shrugged his shoulders. "I mean, that guy John is pretty wasted."

"Yeah. I doubt he'll be in any shape to get going early in the morning," I said.

"Maybe we should go on our own," David suggested.

We were supposed to travel to Makeni to meet Miguel Gil Moreno, the AP television's West Africa–based cameraman. Miguel had been in Sierra Leone since the start of the ECOMOG attack in mid-February. David and I settled on a plan to go upcountry on our own to find the fighting and, we hoped, meet up with Miguel. For me, the night passed without much sleep. The little beer I had actually ingested was enough to give me bed-spins and a raging thirst in the morning.

By seven we sent for James, our driver. He arrived an hour late. We then debated with James about the safety of the roads we would take upcountry, and when we finally headed out at nine, the inside of James's vintage pea-green Mercedes was already like a sauna. We charted a course that took us from Lungi to Port Loko and on to Makeni.

Near that town, ECOMOG forces were still fighting RUF rebels on the run from the capital. For several hours we drove along the dusty clay road that links Sierra Leone's Freetown peninsula with the country's interior. We passed groups of disheveled refugees, belongings in hand, who waved happily at our car as they walked beside the road. It was just after noon by the time we reached Makeni and checked in with the Catholic missionary priests at the Pastoral Center. Eager for company from the outside world, the priests invited us to stay, and we set up there temporarily.

It was in this unlikely setting that I first began to learn the truth about the nightmarish war in Sierra Leone.

WHEN AHMED TEJAN KABBAH was elected president in 1996, his campaign slogan was "The future is in your hands."

The amputations began as a failed bid by Foday Sankoh to undermine the 1996 presidential elections. Employing the kind of twisted logic reserved for madmen and zealots, Sankoh reasoned he could stop the voting by cutting off every potential ballot-casting hand in the country. His logic was quickly endorsed and adopted by bloodthirsty factions of the Revolutionary United Front, which had begun to splinter. Some of the more brutal rebels put a macabre spin on the president's words, often telling their victims, "Go ask Kabbah for your hands back."

In a country with few resources and almost no intervention or help, it is almost impossible to estimate how many people have been maimed. But according to aid workers, it is safe to say the number is in the high thousands. In every town and village I visited in Sierra Leone, the evidence of the rebels' cruel orgy was visible on street corners, in school playgrounds, and inside churches. Everywhere I looked, somebody had lost an eye to a sharpened stick, or a hand, foot, arm, or leg below the knee to a machete. The rebels weren't killing people, I thought, as I composed my article on the RUF's maiming campaign, but they were destroying lives nonetheless, leaving their victims crippled and consigned to hobble through the rest of their lives.

Through much of February, RUF fighters—mostly teenagers with AK-47s—had overrun and terrorized towns in the country's interior, including Bo, Port Loko, Makeni, Kabala, and Magburka. The terror of the rebels' revenge had continued in these towns until columns of Nigerian soldiers arrived to liberate them. In the interim, villagers, relief workers, and missionaries became the hostages of the rebels, many of whom were little more than children kidnapped by the RUF. Trained as servants, sex slaves, porters, and, more often than not, soldiers skilled at maiming their living victims, children had become the unwitting and innocent henchmen of the RUF.

Father Victor Bongiovanni was a Jesuit priest at the Pastoral Center in Makeni who had witnessed the rebel invasion of the town and the liberation by ECOMOG troops during the first week of March. Immediately afterward, as Bongiovanni explained to me, it was as if a spell had been broken. As soon as the all-clear was sounded and the curfew was lifted, children emerged from their cubbyholes. At first, just a few ventured out from their hiding places in pantries and closets. Then, within days of the rebels' ouster from the town, hundreds of children, ranging from toddlers to teens, came out of hiding.

As Bongiovanni spoke to me in the courtyard of the Pastoral Center, a young boy he was counseling sat beside him. Masseh Mokangi was a nine-year-old with the biceps of a well-developed teenager. He wore tattered cut-offs and a grubby gray T-shirt with holes in the belly. While Bongiovanni relived the recent past, Masseh stared vacantly.

Then, as we sat in the shade of a sagging mango tree on a punishingly hot Sunday morning, Masseh spoke of horrors in a flat, empty voice, translated into English by Bongiovanni. With the awkward grin of a nervous child, he told me in halting, unemotional detail how he had been abducted as a small child by the RUF. At first he cooked for the rebels, washed their clothes, and carried their bags. As he grew stronger, he was taught how to kill, torture, and maim. In packs of several children, Masseh would wander the town streets where the RUF was in control. With a machete knife dangling at the end of his lanky arm, Masseh would ask his chosen victim "Do you want a long-sleeved or a short-sleeved shirt?"

Masseh shifted in his seat and began to make chopping motions with his right hand to illustrate his meaning. First he chopped at the wrist of his left hand (a long-sleeved shirt). Then his hand moved up to the elbow. And again he made a whacking motion. The answer to this young boy's macabre question determined whether he would chop his victim's arm off at the wrist or the elbow.

While I listened to Masseh's stories, Sunday hymns boomed triumphantly from the Pastoral Center's small wooden chapel about a hundred feet from us. There the residents of Makeni gathered for prayer and to give thanks. I wandered over and peered in through a window. In row after row, the pews were filled with people in their Sunday best. Some of the girls and women wore delicate pastel sun dresses or floral African wrap-around dresses. Some of the men wore pinstripe suits or casual slacks and dress shirts open at the neck. The majority of the congregation, however, wore ill-fitting, ragged, charity hand-me-downs. Tiny specks of dust swirled and floated in the long beams of subdued light that shone in through the stained glass windows. An organ led the hymns that praised Jesus for his guidance away from the darkness of evil.

I noticed a sad-eyed little girl in a pink sundress, sitting with her mother on the white cement steps of the chapel. She appeared to be about seven years old. With tears welling in her eyes, she looked down at the gauze bandages covering the stumps where her hands used to be.

Then she asked, "Mama? Will my hands grow back?"

The child's mother ran a strong hand through her daughter's hair. Her thick arms looked as if they could hug the world in their protective hold, but now she gazed helplessly at her small daughter and stammered for words that would not come. A bird chirped off in the distance, and the church's hymns continued.

"We'll wait to see what the doctors say," the mother finally offered.

I shut my eyes tight and held them closed to hold back tears that reporters aren't supposed to show. When I opened them again, I found I was staring with hatred at Masseh, sitting just a few hundred feet away.

Later that day, I approached the girl's mother to learn more about what happened to her. I found out that the child—Maria was her name—had actually been lucky, by the cruel standards of Sierra Leone under the domination of the RUF. She was alive; she still had two feet to walk on and both her eyes with which to see. Most young girls who were abducted by the RUF were raped repeatedly by their abductors and then hacked to death with machetes. Their bodies were discarded in the bush in some remote corner of Sierra Leone's countryside.

Maria had been kidnapped at the age of four, her mother told me. The child refused to tell her captors the whereabouts of her family: her mother and father, her two sisters, and her brother. The rebels flew into a rage and chopped off both of Maria's hands with an ax. For more than a year Maria's mother presumed that her daughter was dead. Then, in February 1998, fleeing rebels left her behind in Makeni. ECOMOG troops cleaned her badly scarred wrists and bandaged the stumps.

Later, I sat at my laptop, propped up on a chair in the Pastoral Center's dusty parking lot. I struggled to find words to tell this story. The more I had learned about Sierra Leone's rebel war, the more I had realized that it was a war against children: the amputees, the children of adult amputees, the children drugged and forced to carry out the amputations. Sierra Leone is a nation whose next generation has been destroyed. I knew that I needed to tell Maria's story without reducing it to melodrama, in a way that would spark some interest in Sierra Leone's conflict. As I thought about Maria's sad eyes looking at her bandaged wrists, my mind drifted back to the kindly, speckle-haired customs officer at the airport. All I could picture was his handless clock.

As I filed my story by satellite telephone, I noticed Miguel Gil Moreno's Mercedes approaching, kicking up a long tail of red dust. The driver Miguel had hired sat in the backseat, his face ashen and his eyes wide with fear. As he neared, Miguel gave me a wide grin. He seemed oblivious to the neat bullet hole in the center of the windshield.

Miguel stepped out of the car. He was wearing a pair of faded and torn jeans that hung off his emaciated hips, a gray T-shirt with a pack of cigarettes rolled under the right sleeve, and a stars-and-stripes bandana wrapped around his head. Watching Miguel work over the next several months, I realized he was driven by a religious fervor and dedication that led many people to believe he was an ideal candidate for the priesthood. But reporting was Miguel's calling in life.

Born and raised in a small town near Barcelona, Miguel had been trained as a lawyer, but soon tired of the day-to-day grind of legal writs and court formality. A passionate humanitarian, Miguel soon quit his law practice and moved to Bosnia, where he became a driver for foreign journalists covering that country's war to secede from the former Yugoslavia.

While in Bosnia, Miguel taught himself English and pestered his employers for tips on journalism. In Sarajevo, American war reporter Kurt Schork took Miguel under his wing and taught him the tricks of the trade. Before long, Miguel retired as a driver for other journalists and began freelancing for the AP's new television division. Eventually, Miguel was hired as a full-time cameraman for APTV. Based in West Africa, Miguel quickly acquired a reputation as one of the best war correspondents in the business, covering conflicts in the Balkans, Chechnya, Zaïre, and now Sierra Leone. A devout Catholic, Miguel took a personal interest in Sierra Leone, where the RUF had been harassing and kidnapping Jesuit missionaries.

David, Miguel, and I stayed in Makeni for several days, speaking to villagers and reporting on the atrocities committed by RUF rebels as they were driven out of the area. Kidnapped children spoke of rape and torture; some even told stories of how they had been instructed to kill their parents. Missionary priests described nights of terror and the psychological devastation of mock executions.

DURING OUR LAST NIGHT in Makeni, I lay awake on the hard cement floor of the Pastoral Center's courtyard, where the priests had let us sleep. I shooed away wave after wave of voracious, malaria-bearing mosquitoes. I listened intently to the incessant crackle of machine-gun fire, bouncing and echoing off the looming fronds of palm and banana trees. Pale moonlight cast weird shadows in the courtyard as it filtered in through the sagging palm leaves. At about two in the morning, I went to the satellite phone and called my parents in Toronto. I stared up into a velvet-black sky flecked with stars. I always found it comforting—it made me feel safe—to think that my parents could look up at the same stars from the other side of the planet.

"You'll never guess where I am," I whispered to my mother with boyish excitement in my voice. The gunfire continued to pop and crackle.

*The rebels have been forced from this town,* I thought. *But they're not far away.*

After hanging up from my call home, I stumbled in the darkness back to my sleeping bag on the floor. I curled up on the gritty ground, but I couldn't still my mind. Images from the past several days translated into words for stories I would write over the next day or two. I dozed fitfully to the ragged rhythm of David's snores until dawn.

In the morning, we jumped into our car and headed for Magburka, where the gunfire from the night before had originated. From the dusty, red country road we could still see thin wisps of gray smoke drifting up above the tree line. ECOMOG checkpoints lined our route. They stopped us at gunpoint to search for weapons, but once they realized we were reporters, they smiled and waved us onward. When we reached Magburka—a tiny community of three or four unpaved roads and a couple dozen clapboard homes— evidence of the RUF's destructive wrath smoldered before our eyes. Homes still smoked from an arson attack the night before. The contorted and charred bodies of victims lay beside the street.

I spoke with one young boy named Diallo, who had been forced to stand and watch as his mother and father, his older brother, and his sister were murdered the night before. The rebels were getting ready to retreat from the advancing ECOMOG troops, Diallo explained with the help of a friendly neighbor who spoke English. Shifting his weight from one foot to the other, Diallo told me nervously of four or five men who came crashing in through the front door of his house. At gunpoint, they ordered the whole family into the street. Frightened, Diallo ran out of the house behind his parents.

"They grabbed my older brother and began to kick him," Diallo told me. "They said he helped the Nigerian soldiers." I scribbled his words into my yellow notebook. The young boy's eyes darted apprehensively from my busy hands to his tiny, dust-covered toes.

The neighbor who had witnessed the attack continued the story and filled in the gaps for Diallo: "The gunmen took Diallo's brother by his elbows behind his back. They threw the young man to the ground. They kicked him in the face with bare feet until blood poured from his nose."

Diallo remembered when the rebels began to talk.

"You must laugh with your mother," Diallo shyly recalled, using the African euphemism "laugh" for "have sex with."

"If you don't, we will kill you," Diallo remembered one man saying.

"My brother refused. He begged for mercy," Diallo said, "but the rebel-man just laughed and put a knife to his . . ." With small, grubby fingers, Diallo motioned to his groin.

He explained that his mother told her older son to go ahead, to save their lives. With great hesitation and only after much convincing from his mother, Diallo's older brother had sex with his mother.

Sobbing uncontrollably, Diallo stopped talking. His little body quaked as tears poured over his round, brown cheeks. "The rebel-men all yelled and cheered," he finally continued.

When the two were finished, the rebels dragged Diallo's brother away. His body was found the next morning. His head lay by a tree trunk a few feet away. Diallo's mother was hacked to death with machete knives in front of her young son. His sister and father were also taken away. His father's body was discovered later that afternoon, in the bush on the edge of Magburka. Diallo's sister was never found, but she was presumed dead, village elders told me later that day.

ON MONDAY, MARCH 9, we headed back toward Freetown in time to check into a hotel and get set for Ahmed Tejan Kabbah's return—the biggest event in Freetown since the 1997 coup had sent the elected president into exile. Dignitaries from across Africa, including Nigeria's enigmatic and elusive Sani Abacha, were scheduled to attend the ceremony at Freetown's Siaka Stevens National Stadium.

We arrived in Freetown after dark and were forced to make our way through several military checkpoints. Along the downtown roads by the oceanfront, crews of workers toiled by flashlight to put the final touches on the city. They painted fresh white lines along the city's main roads; they cleaned long-neglected piles of rotting trash from curbs. In Kabbah's absence, Johnny Paul Koroma and his junta had turned Freetown into an anarchic city festering in its own filth. We reached the Cape Sierra Hotel, one of the few hotels still functioning. As soon as I got to my room, I sat down to begin composing the background for the story I would file the next morning.

I woke just before dawn on March 10. In the distance I could hear the thumping of a marching band. The day's festivities had begun. David and the AP's Freetown stringer, Clarence Roy-Macaulay, set out to take photos of the day's celebrations. In order to be close to a telephone to file the story quickly, I waited back at the hotel. Hunched over a small transistor radio, I listened to Freetown's FM 98.1 for word of Kabbah's arrival. A helicopter thumped overhead and I sprinted to the window to catch a glimpse of it as it passed over the hotel and headed toward the soccer stadium. I turned up the radio and listened as the sound of the helicopter faded from my window and grew in volume on the airwaves. The helicopter set down just outside the stadium and the crowd roared ecstatically. The band played and the military honor guard snapped to attention. "The people of Sierra Leone have suffered for too long," Kabbah told them. Vowing the RUF would be destroyed, the president went on to promise peace and stability in his country.

I typed the first few paragraphs of my story and filed it to the Abidjan bureau with instructions that it be relayed at once to New York and all points worldwide. Then I stretched out on the bed—I began to notice the heat in my room. Sometime in the morning, the air-conditioning had cut out and the temperature was quickly rising to unbearable. I stood and moved to open the window. In the courtyard of the Cape Sierra Hotel, five Nigerian troops lounged in the sunshine, M-16s lying in the grass beside them. I looked and watched them celebrate their victory with smiles and high fives.

The RUF were on the run, but the number of rebels confirmed killed or captured by the ECOMOG force was miserably low. I knew that since 1996, the RUF had repeatedly been defeated and written off as finished, only to come back. I hadn't been in Africa long, but after Afghanistan and Cambodia, I knew war had a way of reinventing itself.

# 4

# THE STRONGMAN AND THE POPE

BACK IN MY BUREAU IN ABIDJAN, I had to shift gears quickly from reporting on the horrors of war to balancing my annual budget and managing my staff of reporters. Of particular interest to my editors in both New York and London was the Pope's upcoming visit to Nigeria. I was not particularly enthusiastic about covering the story, since I knew it would be assigned to the AP's more senior reporters, including Paris-based special correspondent Mort Rosenblum and Rome-based Vatican correspondent Victor Simpson. I grumbled about the assignment and my role as an administrator, ensuring that all stories were adequately covered. It promised to be a bureaucratic nightmare.

The story of Pope John Paul II versus Sani Abacha had all the makings of an epic battle of wills, not to mention its potential to further inflame hostility between the majority Muslim population in Nigeria's north and its southern Christian community. Nigeria was one of Africa's most corrupt, crime-ridden nations, and its leader, Sani Abacha, was the very antithesis of the pontiff. Abacha, an army officer who had seized power by force, had a record of human rights abuses second only to Uganda's former "Big Man," Idi Amin.

To cover the Pope, David and I would have to fly from Lagos to the Nigerian capital, Abuja, and then on to Enugu, all on airlines barred for safety reasons from landing in the United States and Britain. Then we would make a final four-hour drive, over potholed roads frequented by bandits, to Onitsha, where the Pope would beatify a local priest during Sunday mass.

I had learned long ago that travelers' horror stories tend to become more exaggerated with every recounting. But the tales that emerged from Lagos were terrifying even to the most seasoned traveler. According to the rumor mill, customs officers routinely fleeced tourists at the airport of every last penny. Passports were said to vanish in the hands of immigration officers. But worst of all, street crime was said to be so bad that just leaving the airport was risking one's life. In the end, all the fussing over security and dangers in Lagos was for naught. David and I were waved through customs and immigration with little more than a cursory glance, and we set out for the Sheraton Hotel in the Ikeja District a few miles away.

It was already dark by the time our taxi reached the hotel. Still, the city dripped with a heavy curtain of humidity. Power outages had left the streets blackened; the soft orange glow of candlelight danced out of windows. Dust whipped across empty, potholed streets and I saw only the occasional pedestrian skitter past.

Behind the Sheraton's reception desk a portrait of a grim-faced Sani Abacha, the quintessential army strongman, gazed out at the world from behind dark glasses. I stared back at the unsmiling general—and then checked into a $500-a-night room. (Throughout my year in Africa, I struggled with a gnawing unease at living in such ostentatious luxury in the midst of abject poverty. But in my mind I justified it as a means of getting my job done, which called for working phones and reliable electricity—available only in high-priced hotels.) Despite the cost of my hotel room, it smelled like a gas station. In fact, my strongest impression of this brooding city was the ever-present odor of diesel fuel that permeated everything: my clothes, my hair, and my bags.

Before leaving Abidjan, I had put together a research file of story ideas and background. In addition to the general news story about the papal visit, I hoped to gather enough material to write feature articles on the anniversary of the Biafra civil war, on the still-simmering Muslim-Christian divide, and on Nigeria's desperate poverty despite tremendous petroleum resources.

Later that evening, David and I met with Mort Rosenblum, the AP special correspondent based in Paris. One of the news agency's top journalists, Mort had covered the civil war in Nigeria in the late 1960s. He was now back to add some continuity, as well as knowledge of the region, to our coverage of this enigmatic and elusive country. Pope John Paul II's visit wasn't in itself a huge news story, but it was a great excuse to get reporters into Nigeria, an otherwise politically hermetic nation.

Over dinner and several rounds of $15-a-glass Chardonnay, Mort regaled David and me with a monologue about his days covering the Biafran civil war. Puffing on his ever-present pipe, the impish, bespectacled foreign correspondent recounted how he had smuggled copy past censors and checkpoints. Getting copy past government censors was just half the battle in those days, he explained. Before the advent of the portable satellite telephone, the real trick was getting copy back to the editing desk in New York.

Mort explained what Nigeria was like in its first years of independence from British rule and made me more aware of the economic and social hurdles Nigeria and all of Africa have faced since the 1960s.

Rooted in the arid north, the land-owning Muslim Hausa-Fulani tribe were (and are) the dominant ethnic group in Nigeria. In southwestern Nigeria, near the commercial hub and former capital, Lagos, the Yoruba dominate. Although politically weak, the Christian Yoruba derive their influence from their commercial and economic preeminence. Further west, the oil-rich southern Niger delta region is the traditional homeland of another ethnic group, the Ibo. Also predominantly Christian, the impoverished Ibo have long felt marginalized by Hausa-Fulani political control.

For the sake of political simplicity, the British forced all three groups to live under one national banner, favoring the Hausa-Fulani. But less than six years after independence, the chaos began, with a military coup led by an

ethnic Ibo. In retaliation, Muslims from the northern
Hausa-Fulani began an orgy of destruction in the south.
Thousands of Ibo Christians were killed, countless homes,
businesses, and churches were razed. Within six months, a
counter-coup led by a Hausa-Fulani member took over
the government.

Enraged by the widespread killing of Christian Ibos,
Chukwumeka Odumegwu Ojukwu, a prominent Ibo army
officer declared independence in May 1967 for the Republic of Biafra—a large swath of Nigeria's lucrative oil-rich
territory in the southeast. For three years, federal troops
pummeled the secessionist Ibos, destroying entire cities,
including the Biafran capital, Enugu. Mort Rosenblum
was there at the time, writing stories about refugees and
fire fights and the famine that came after war. More than
a million people were killed or died of starvation before
the Ibo rebels surrendered to government troops in 1970.

Petroleum companies, including Shell, Mobil, and
France's Elf, paid close attention to the war that ravaged the
Niger River delta region. Many oil firms even took sides,
supporting either the breakaway rebels or the federal
government (depending on whom they believed would
retain control of the oil fields). The resulting funds
prolonged the disastrous war and raised the death toll.

Mort's stories tantalized me with a fascination and
empathy for Africa; he rekindled in me that same love affair
for journalism I had experienced when I first went overseas.
It seemed to me that evening that Mort exemplified the

kind of life I would want to look back on in the years to come.

AFTER A BRIEF FLIGHT from Lagos to Abuja, Mort, David, and I set up shop at the Sheraton Hotel in Nigeria's political capital. I fiddled with the air-conditioning thermostat for about twenty minutes in my room before calling the front desk to change rooms. I slung the shoulder strap of my satellite phone around my neck and grabbed the strap for my laptop computer. I then hefted my blue backpack over one shoulder. Crammed with unnecessary extras, it weighed a ton.

The hallway overlooked an open-air courtyard filled with lush jungle plants and exotic, squawking birds. Unsteady from the extra weight of the bags and saturated with sweat, I staggered the few hundred yards toward the bank of elevators. When the elevator finally arrived, I stepped in and stood next to a heavyset man with sandy blond hair and a goatee. A television camera hung from his arm, which did not surprise me, since the hotel was crawling with journalists covering the papal visit.

"How's it going?" he asked me, in an unmistakable New York accent. Irritated by the heat and humidity and the frustration of having to lug my bags from room to room, I didn't bother to answer.

WITH MORE THAN A DOZEN AP photographers and reporters in Nigeria for the Pope's visit, I decided we needed to coordinate our reporting plans. In order to cover such an important story—one that would also be reported by CNN, the BBC, and the *New York Times*—the AP had sent numerous "spot" reporters to the scene to cover the daily, or breaking, news, along with "enterprise" reporters who would write longer, descriptive stories about related topics such as Nigeria's oil industry, its human rights record and religious freedoms, and profiles of the Pope and Sani Abacha. As we made up the assignments, I drew the short straw and was assigned to write about the crowd attending the Pope's Sunday mass in Onitsha, along with photographer Jean-Marc Boujou. We set out for the airport on Saturday morning, despite the thick shroud of sand that had engulfed the city overnight.

I sat in the domestic Nigeria Airways jet staring out the window as the sandstorm blew in over the airport at Abuja. At first just the tip of the wing was swallowed up by the soupy, gray wind. Then the tarmac disappeared from view. My stomach was knotted with anxiety at the prospect of flying in what looked like zero visibility. *They can't actually fly in this,* I thought. *This is insane.*

But the engines of the cramped DC-10 roared and the jet began to move forward on the runway. I clutched the armrest so tightly that my fingernails left grooves in the hard plastic. The flight from Abuja to Enugu in eastern Nigeria takes only thirty minutes in the air, but the flight that day seemed to last a lifetime. As we descended into Enugu's sleepy little airport, I continued to stare unblinking into the blanketing sand outside my window. I couldn't even see the ground approach. The bump of our rear landing gear touching down was sudden and unexpected. I slumped back into my seat. My shirt was drenched with sweat made clammy and cold by the plane's air-conditioning.

Later, I checked into a crowded and crumbling government-run hotel in Enugu and made arrangements for a driver and car to take me to Onitsha in time for Pope John Paul II's arrival. As we sped along the highway between Enugu and Onitsha, we zipped past a row of aging men in wheelchairs who waved politely as we drove by. I asked my driver who they were.

"Veterans of the civil war, sir," he answered.

"Biafra?" I asked.

"Yes, sir," he answered. I decided to return on Monday morning to interview the veterans after the Pope's visit was complete.

ON THE WAY TO ONITSHA, I made a side trip to the sleepy town of Aguleri, where legend and the faithful hold that a priest named Cyprian Michael Iwene Tansi performed miracles many years ago. The Pope was coming to Nigeria to speak out against human rights abuses committed by Sani Abacha's regime, but he was also scheduled to beatify Tansi, a move that could clear the way to sainthood for the Nigerian priest. To qualify for beatification, a board of Vatican experts must certify that the candidate performed at least one miracle.

A dusty, remote village of a dozen or so wooden houses and a church, Aguleri would probably never have made it on the map if not for the work of Tansi's pious and soft-spoken brother, Godwin. I sat on the front stoop of Godwin's modest clapboard home and watched intently as the old man remembered his brother, the miracle worker of Aguleri. Neighborhood children crowded in around us to listen once again to the stories that were already part of Aguleri's folklore.

"If you call his name when you say your prayers—" Godwin began, in halting but perfect English. A true story-teller, he paused for effect before continuing. "We know those prayers will come true."

For hours, Godwin Tansi sat on the stoop, and the stories dripped off his tongue, becoming more fantastic as the day wore on. Although Father Tansi had died in 1964, legend held that a young girl dying of cancer touched the wood of the priest's coffin.

"Within days, the cancer was gone," Godwin said, waving his brother's heavy wooden crucifix through the air to emphasize the word "gone."

The children squealed with delight, oohing and ahhing as if mystified by some trick or sleight of hand. Like one of them, I sat wide-eyed with Godwin until the afternoon waned. A natural skeptic, I doubted the stories, but as a reporter I knew they'd make for great copy.

I ARRIVED AT THE ONITSHA public fairgrounds the next morning just before seven, and the temperature had already reached 39°C. A crowd of about 100,000 people had converged on the fairgrounds in hopes of catching a glimpse of the aging pontiff. As the hour of the Pope's arrival approached, I climbed up on the stage and looked out onto an endless sea of faces. I had never seen so many people peacefully assembled in one place. Though I am not a deeply religious person, I was awestruck to see in this crowd genuine love, warmth, and community. Parents cradled their infant children, young couples held hands; choir and altar boys brought cold water to the elderly spectators in the crowd. Love flowed from thousands of hopeful souls.

I stood under the punishing sun and scribbled the scene into my notebook, wiping the sweat from my brow with the back of my wrist. Then my knees began to shake, and darkness crept in at the corners of my eyes. I woke up about ten minutes later, looking up at a Nigerian nurse wearing a large silver crucifix around her neck. She was fanning me with an official papal visit program that featured photos of Pope John Paul II and Sani Abacha on the cover. She advised me to drink more water.

"You need to be careful under this sun," she said.

Unsteady, I rose from the cot in the blue-plastic-tarpaulin medical tent. I sheepishly thanked the nurse, drank the jug of water she handed me, and wandered back out into the sun.

The Pope's white helicopter circled overhead. Its blades kicked up a storm of dust and sand that stung my eyes and turned my green pants a patchy shade of beige from my knees to my ankles. The crowd roared with delight as the then-seventy-seven-year-old Pope descended and climbed into his protective, glass-encased "Pope-mobile." The vehicle slowly rolled through the massive crowd, which parted effortlessly to make way for the leader of the Roman Catholic world. A red awning lined with gold trim sheltered the pontiff from the sun's unforgiving glare.

I worked the crowd like an eager young reporter, buzzing from group to group to gather quotes and prepare my material for Victor Simpson, the AP's Vatican correspondent, who would write the day's main story. The Pope performed the beatification ceremony for Father Tansi and delivered a brief sermon for Sunday Mass.

"Respect for every human person—" he mumbled, nearly slurring into his microphone. He stopped and closed his eyes. "—for his dignity and rights, must ever be the inspiration behind your efforts to increase democracy and strengthen the social fabric of your country."

Battling the oppressive heat, the Pope slumped in his chair as large standing fans blew fresh air across his face. The crowd remained silent, hanging on his every word. This frail old man in flowing white-and-gold robes was going to take on Sani Abacha, Africa's notorious military dictator. It was a classic story of good versus evil. As a journalist, I relished its prospects. I entitled my analysis that was transmitted on the AP's wire "Strongman and the Pope."

The story began: "If peace and harmony are Pope John Paul II's message to Nigeria, he's found a tough audience in this country of purges, summary executions and iron-fisted rule."

The next and final day of his visit, the Pope met with Sani Abacha and discussed human rights. He requested the release of sixty political prisoners and journalists. But Abacha made no reference to the request during remarks made at a ceremony to mark the Pope's departure.

SANI ABACHA ASSUMED POWER in 1993 in a bloodless coup. As his first official act in office, Abacha suspended Nigeria's constitution, dissolved all government departments, and replaced civilian state administrators with his military cronies. He jailed more than seven thousand dissidents and critics in his five years in power. The country's judicial system was handed over to the military, which in turn established a network of kangaroo courts that bowed to the whims of the dictator.

Abacha's misrule enfeebled the country: by 1998 at least 80 percent of Nigerians lived in poverty, occupying the shantytowns that surrounded every major city and town. During my visit to Nigeria, I discovered most people lived without clean water, reliable electricity, or basic health care. By contrast, Abacha lived in a world of ostentatious wealth in Abuja, a new capital developed at a staggering cost—like many African leaders, Abacha had moved the capital to his hometown to benefit *his* people. Under Abacha, Nigeria's $4.45 billion in gross oil exports did little to ease the crippling poverty of most of its population.

Abacha remained an enigmatic leader, shying away from the glare of publicity. When seen in public, he was often in large dark sunglasses, which he used to conceal the tribal markings etched into the skin on his cheeks, a rite of passage prescribed for young men when they reach puberty.

AFTER THE POPE'S DEPARTURE, I shifted my focus to the feature articles I had planned to do during my two weeks in Nigeria. I met David and we set off to interview the Biafra war veterans I had seen on the highway between Enugu and Onitsha. They were easy to find: they lined the roads and begged from their makeshift wheelchairs for handouts from passing motorists. Like broken toy soldiers cast aside by a petulant child, the Biafra war veterans wouldn't let their compatriots forget what had happened those many years ago.

Francis Joku was once a foot soldier in the Biafran People's Army. He was on patrol one afternoon in the spring of 1968 when he triggered a land mine that blew off his left leg below the knee. His right leg was so badly mangled by shrapnel that surgeons amputated it at the knee as well. Thirty years later, Francis sat with his daughter under a thatched banana-leaf shelter by the highway and told me his story.

"None of us can walk," he said, pointing a finger at the dozen or so fellow veterans on the other side of the highway.

Using the common term for Biafra, Francis summed up his feelings about the war and his shattered dream of independence for the Ibos: "We're cripples, like Iboland."

With a grunt to punctuate his effort, he leaned forward in his rusting wheelchair made from spare bicycle parts. He rubbed a hand over the callused stumps where his shins used to be.

David sat with Francis's eight-year-old daughter and examined one of the war veteran's prosthetic limbs—donated by a foreign-aid agency, not the government, Francis quickly pointed out. A car roared past, kicking up a choking cloud of red dust along the side of the road. A bundle of Niara notes, the local currency, was hurled out the window and spread into the air like a twinkling burst of fireworks. Francis's daughter, in a yellow dress that she had put on backward, scurried to the roadside and began gathering the money, stooping to snatch up each loose note (worth pennies) as they scattered in the breeze stirred up by the car's wake.

DAVID AND I PLANNED to head next to the Niger delta region so that I could begin reporting on Nigeria's squandered petroleum potential. Graft, government inefficiency, and plain old-fashioned greed are the primary problems. Nigeria is the sixth-largest oil-producing nation in the world, earning approximately $563 million in oil revenue profits in 1997. Approximately $200 million of that was earmarked for the upkeep of Nigeria's oil refineries, but it just vanished one day without explanation. All but one of Nigeria's refineries fell idle through disrepair. And still, the people lived in squalor.

Before visiting the oil fields, we had arranged to meet with a television cameraman named Myles Tierney in the area's hub city, Port Harcourt. Myles planned to do a television report on Nigeria's oil industry, and it made sense for us to work together and share resources. We arrived at the Sheraton Hotel in Port Harcourt late in the evening and called up to Myles's room.

I watched a muscular, sandy-blond-haired man with a goatee cross the lobby toward us. *That's the guy from the elevator in Abuja,* I thought to myself. *I wonder if he'll remember me.* With a broad smile, Myles shook David's hand. David quickly introduced me as the bureau chief for West Africa.

"Welcome to Africa," Myles said with a wry, knowing grin. He shook my hand and held my right upper arm with his left hand, giving my biceps a squeeze. I felt Myles was sizing me up from the moment we met. He stood only a few inches taller than I did, but he loomed larger than life. Dimpled and confident, he had a smile that could charm women and warlords alike. His laughter boomed and filled a room. His brawny, tattooed arms often shadowboxed at the air or toward some unsuspecting colleague.

Myles was thirty-three when I first met him in Nigeria. He was based in the AP's East Africa bureau in Nairobi, Kenya, but he often traveled on assignment to West Africa. I was immediately in awe of his apparent self-assurance and command of the endless difficulties that shadowed all journalists working in Africa. Although actually born and raised in SoHo in lower Manhattan, Myles spoke with the brashness of a Brooklyn native, and he told most of his friends and colleagues (me included) that he had grown up there.

For several days we traveled around the Niger delta region, which simmered with anger and unrest. Oil executives were routinely kidnapped, and sectarian violence annually claimed hundreds of lives. We were taken on a helicopter tour of the Ogoni homelands—it was too dangerous to go by road, we were told.

To get a better look at day-to-day life in the region, I spent one evening on Bonny Island, home to some of Shell Oil's largest operations in Nigeria. The sun had begun to set, but the sky continued to flicker with a Halloween-orange glow. Gas flares just offshore lit the night sky. I was stunned to see little if any working infrastructure.

We visited the Shell Oil headquarters. Myles and David bubbled with enthusiasm, snapping photos and filming my interviews. While on the bus that took us from the Shell headquarters back to our hotel, I complained to Myles about my visa snafu back in Abidjan.

"That jerk was trying to extort a Canadian visa out of me," I complained bitterly.

"Relax, man," he responded. "Take it easy. You just have to learn to grease the wheels a little."

Sitting in the cramped bus seat in front of me, Myles turned my way, his heavy arm slung over the back of his seat. He explained how he had brought a box of chocolates to Irene Idundun, the chief press officer in Abuja, to ensure he would get access to future news events in Nigeria.

"You have to learn how to operate in Africa," he said to me.

"You mean bribe officials with candy," I said, my voice cutting with sarcasm. As a purist, I considered it a cardinal sin to bribe government officials with gifts, no matter how insignificant, which lent an air of impropriety to the relationship and tainted one's reputation with other government and political opposition sources. Credibility, I believed, was one of the most important things a foreign correspondent had to rely on.

"Stop busting my chops," Myles snapped back. "That's how it works here. If you don't like it, go back to Vietnam."

BACK IN ABIDJAN, I SETTLED into a routine of writing my features about Nigeria and editing the reams of copy flowing in from the AP's stringers all over the region. Over time, African capitals and leaders became familiar, as did each country's recent history (known as b-copy), which was a basic requisite in news stories. And sometimes the stringers were our lifelines.

On June 8, I got a call from a colleague at Voice of America in Washington, D.C.

"What's going on in Nigeria?" he asked me.

"I don't know. Why? What are you hearing?" I answered.

"There are rumors flying all over the place that Abacha is dead," he responded.

*Shit,* I thought. My heart immediately began to flutter with the fear of having missed a big story.

"Let me check on it and I'll get back to you," I finally said. I sprinted to the newsroom.

"You heard anything about Abacha being dead?" I blurted out. Glenn stared at me with a stunned expression on his face. "Well, that's the rumor. Let's start trying to confirm it," I ordered.

I ran back to my office and began phoning our stringers in Nigeria. After fighting with the faulty phone connections of West Africa for about twenty minutes, I finally reached Gilbert Da Costa in Nigeria's political capital, Abuja.

"Gilbert, what's going on there!" I snapped. "Is Abacha dead?"

"I don't know yet. The presidential compound has been closed off and is surrounded by troops."

"Didn't ya think that was worth telling me?" I barked. I lit a cigarette with shaky hands and blew the smoke at the computer screen in front of me.

"I was waiting for confirmation of Abacha's death first," Gilbert answered politely.

"Never mind, never mind. Just call me when you get more," I said, hanging up the phone.

"Glenn, get Frank on the line!" I shouted from my office.

Half an hour later, Glenn called my office. "Frank's on line one," he said of our stringer in Lagos. I dashed back out to the newsroom and snatched up the phone.

"Frank, is he dead?" I said, skipping our usual conversational pleasantries.

"We think so," Frank said. "His family says his body is being flown to his hometown for the funeral tonight to observe Muslim customs."

I closed my eyes and took a deep breath.

"Frank, I need better than 'We think so.' This is a very big story. If you're wrong, we'll all be working as garbage men next week. Do you understand?"

"Yes," Frank said. "I'm almost positive he's dead."

I hung up the phone and debated whether to go with the story. "Ah, fuck it!" I said out loud in the newsroom. "Let's go for it."

I sat at a free computer in the newsroom and tapped out a one-line urgent bulletin. I pressed the transmit button at 11:51 A.M. on June 8, 1998. The AP broke the news to the world:

"Nigeria's General Sani Abacha dead of cardiac arrest, family, friends say."

I slouched down in my chair and caught my breath. My heart rate slowly dropped from an incessant pounding to a more relaxed beat. I wandered out to the bureau's front porch and plopped down on the rattan couch. I lit up a cigarette and began to consider what I had just done. My breathing once again sped up, along with my heart rate. *What if we're wrong?* I thought in a fit of panic.

I returned to the newsroom and flipped the television on to CNN. The top story was Abacha.

"Nigeria's dictator Sani Abacha is dead, the Associated Press reports," the announcer said.

*Shit, why haven't Reuters or AFP matched us?*

I skulked back to my office and flipped on the BBC World Service for their hourly radio newscast. The top story once again was Abacha.

"Sani Abacha is dead, the AP is reporting," the announcer said.

I had to wait for more than an hour for Reuters, the AP's primary competitor, to confirm the news and "match" our story. For a week I stuck by the bureau, editing copy about Sani Abacha's death. I wrote several analytical articles about the impact it would have on Nigeria, the region, and indeed all of Africa. Finally, Bill Kole, then the AP's Amsterdam bureau chief, arrived to relieve me.

Although there was the occasional adrenaline rush of this kind at the bureau, it never took long for me to want to get back on the road. In May, I had been in the Congo to cover the anniversary of self-declared president Laurent Kabila's first year in power. In June, right around the time of Abacha's death, reports from the Portuguese news agency trickled into the bureau that army officers in Portugal's former colony of Guinea-Bissau had staged a failed coup. For hours that country's capital was pummeled with rocket and mortar fire, and then a full-out civil war erupted in the tiny country. We had no stringer in Bissau, the capital, and would be at a terrible disadvantage covering that story.

*Here we go again,* I thought. I packed my bags. I was off to my second African war zone. On and off, the Guinea-Bissau war would last most of the year and leave hundreds of civilians dead and thousands homeless.

**5**

# AFRICA'S FORGOTTEN WAR

BEFORE I MANAGED TO GET into Guinea-Bissau, I met up with David in neighboring Senegal, where he had been covering the evacuation of foreigners from Bissau to Senegal's capital, Dakar. From there we headed to Zinguinchor—a tourist town near Guinea-Bissau—and spent a week exploring the sealed border in search of a way into Guinea-Bissau.

Vowing not to skip yet another promised vacation with his girlfriend, Cassy, David left to return to Abidjan. Within a day or two, Brennan Linsley, a photographer based in the AP's East Africa bureau in Nairobi, Kenya, arrived to replace David. I had never met Brennan, but we got along immediately. An easygoing young man from the American East Coast, Brennan had soft, curly blond hair. Wearing baggy shorts and an oversized T-shirt, along with canvas sneakers and loose white socks, Brennan looked a bit like a cover model for a skateboarding magazine. He certainly did not fit my image of a hard-driven news

photographer. He carried with him a small pocket encyclo-
pedia of artwork, within which were small reproductions of
works by Matisse, Renoir, Gauguin, Kandinsky, and Bacon.
Brennan's book was a godsend against my own encroaching
boredom during the weeks I spent on assignment in
Guinea-Bissau.

On June 24, 1998, we hooked up with a Guinean
reporter named Alain, who offered to help us cross into his
country and would work as our guide and translator.
Starting before dawn, we drove most of the day to a remote
southeastern corner of Senegal. Then we rumbled along a
dusty dirt road for half an hour until we came to the
border with Guinea-Bissau. An old length of tree trunk
shaved of its bark and painted with yellow and black stripes
was laid across the dirt road to indicate the frontier. I
handed Alain the two hundred dollars he had requested
earlier. He got out of the car and spoke briefly to the
Senegalese troops at the border. One soldier made a
cursory check of our luggage. I spotted Alain handing the
two hundred dollars to the second soldier. We were waved
through.

"We can enter my country this way," Alain said. "But we
can't leave. We'll have to find another way back to Senegal."

While still in Senegal, I had met several Portuguese journalists who said they would be heading to Bafatá, where a
colonial-era hunting lodge was the only place to stay,
because it had running water and electricity. We instructed
our driver to take us there, and two hours later, we pulled
up at the lodge, which turned out to be a collection of small

two-bed cabins and a main reception building housing the restaurant. The snarling heads of wild boars and jackals lined the white stucco-plastered walls of the reception building. There was also a dusty collection of stuffed guinea fowl and other birds.

Brennan and I shared a cabin and settled into a routine that we followed for the next two weeks. Waking around dawn, we would rouse our driver and instruct him to head south along National Highway 7, away from the relative safety of Bafatá toward Bissau, the capital city, which was still under heavy artillery fire. We'd spend an hour or two gathering material for that day's story, and then we'd turn around and drive the two hours back to Bafatá to file. It was on one of these trips about a week into the assignment that we stumbled onto the tiny hamlet of Cumere.

The heat was rising inside the blue Mercedes. I opened the window a crack to cool off, but it felt as though I had thrust my face into a convection oven: my eyes ran dry from the blasting heat. Alain turned in his front seat to face me in the back.

"*C'est chaud ici,*" he said to me.

Not sure what he meant, I smiled shyly and shrugged. Within my first few weeks in West Africa, I learned that the term "hot" could be either a measure of temperature, or a way of describing the intensity of war. The first weeks of Guinea-Bissau's civil war were very "hot." By the time we arrived, things were calming down: artillery and rocket attacks on the capital now lasted only minutes as opposed to hours.

My face stinging from the hot air, I closed the window and turned to watch the postcard scenery sweep past. Guinea-Bissau's midland plateau is a lush, emerald landscape of rice and peanut farms. My mind wandered back to Vietnam and its stunning physical beauty. The moment I had left the Far East for Africa, I had begun to regret it. Here in Africa I had found the adrenaline rush I sought, but I was beginning to suspect that the serenity of Southeast Asia was more to my liking than the nonstop conveyer belt of war and suffering in Africa.

As the road curved around a hill, my eyes were drawn to a thick cement structure perched atop it, overlooking the flat landscape for many kilometers in all directions. Narrow slits were cut into its sides.

"It's a—" Alain began and then trailed off. "Oh, how do you say it in English?"

"*Ah oui.* A medicine . . . no. A pillbox."

The bunker was a dead ringer for the fortifications I had seen in Vietnam, built by the French around Hanoi, Saigon, and other key cities during the colonial era. I wondered whether the European colonial powers had compared notes on what methods worked best to subdue the so-called natives.

Although Portuguese explorers were among the first to colonize Africa in the sixteenth century, their influence was quickly overshadowed during the late-nineteenth-century scramble by France, Germany, Great Britain, and Belgium.

Unlike other continental powers that used their colonies to extend influence, wealth, and prestige, faltering Portugal became heavily dependent on the income it derived from colonies such as Guinea-Bissau. Reluctant to surrender its access to raw industrial materials, Portugal held on to its African colonies until the bitter end. Years after much of Africa had gained independence in the early 1960s, Guinea-Bissau, Angola, and Mozambique had to fight for their autonomy.

In the late 1960s and early 1970s, the Party for Independence in Guinea and Cape Verde, or PAIGC, terrorized the countryside, ambushing government convoys and destroying colonial farming operations and palm-oil-bottling facilities. When Lisbon finally capitulated, it left Guinea-Bissau a tattered and underdeveloped shambles. The PAIGC rebels never fully disbanded; decades later they would regroup and take up arms against what they considered a corrupt government backed by Portugal.

AS WE THUNDERED DOWN National Highway 7, we passed small bands of rebel soldiers. Their threadbare fatigues, flip-flop sandals, and frayed straw cowboy hats diminished the menace of the old carbine rifles that each guerrilla clutched in his hands. They smiled and waved as we rocketed by, leaving a long column of reddish-brown dust in our wake.

It was as if the rebels were off for a walk through the fields on a brilliant sunny day instead of patroling a war zone for infiltrators. We finally came to the last checkpoint before Bissau. A beautiful young woman, wearing a police officer's uniform and flip-flop sandals, stood up from her red plastic stool and stepped from the gravel shoulder into the middle of the road, aiming her AK-47 at our windshield. As we approached, Alain rolled down his window and explained to her that we were journalists trying to reach the capital to report on the growing insurgency. She told us she had joined the rebellion against President João Bernardo Vieira because he had failed to live up to the ideals of the PAIGC and its rebel *camaradas.* The heavy thud of artillery fire rumbled from Bissau. I kept a close eye on that direction and finally spotted a cloud of thick black smoke billowing up above swaying palm fronds.

Figuring I could sweet-talk my way past the guard, I handed my point-and-shoot camera to Brennan and asked him to take a quick snapshot of us together. The top of her head—covered in neat rows of tightly wound dreadlock braids—came to about the height of my chin. The strap of her AK was slung over a shoulder, and the weapon, large for her petite frame, almost touched the ground. After the picture was taken, I gave her my kindest smile and motioned with my chin down the road in the direction of Bissau, as if to ask "Can we go now?"

She laughed sweetly like a shy schoolgirl, but again shook her head and motioned with the rifle barrel that we should head back the way we came. As we got back into the car, I asked Alain if there was another way to get close to the capital to see what damage the artillery had done. He suggested a back road that would take us near the capital.

"Great! Let's go," I said.

We sped down the side road, passing clusters of refugees, as they trudged wearily through the sluggish midday heat. They were fleeing wave after wave of artillery and rocket fire. Into torn burlap sacks they had crammed all they could carry—dented tin cooking pots and pans were stuffed in beside firewood and twisted cassava roots. One woman in a bright, multi-colored dress balanced an infant on one hip, a sack of belongings on her back, and a rolled-up foam mattress over her free shoulder. I stopped her and asked Alain to inquire why she carried the mattress. Couldn't she sleep on a blanket? Her lips curled into a smile as Alain translated my questions. She shook her head.

"It's not for sleep," she said, the infant squirming in her arm. "It's to use as shelter in case we get caught in the fighting again."

Sleep had become the exception in this West African country. Along national highways and in crowded towns away from the fighting, it sometimes seemed as though the entire population of Guinea-Bissau had become zombies plodding through their days, aiming only to survive, at least until the next day. They continued on this journey for weeks and months in the summer of 1998.

At the end of the back road lay Cumere, a village a few kilometers across a river inlet from Guinea-Bissau's capital. It was a sleepy hamlet of half a dozen clapboard and corrugated steel homes, now seemingly abandoned by all but the rats that scurried by our feet as we crunched across the gravel paths. The silence was punctuated only by the whining buzz of a bumblebee; daily shelling from Bissau had driven the birds away. Then, out of the corner of my eye I saw a shadow move. Heart racing, I prepared to run. A queasy flutter of panic coursed through my chest as the shadow took form.

Coming out from under the shade of the looming baobab and cashew trees was a lone figure wearing tattered, soiled clothes. This ghost apprehensively approached us, his hands raised above his head.

*"Bom dia,"* he finally shouted in Portuguese.

Alain spoke with him, asking about the hamlet, its residents, and why he was still here despite the daily onslaught of shells and rockets.

Eyes wide and desperate, Gbadne Quade explained he was alone in Cumere. Most everyone else—including his sons, their wives, and his grandchildren—had fled when the war erupted on June 7. A few people hit by shrapnel were killed along the hamlet's gravel footpaths. But, gaunt and frail, Gbadne was too old to run. Only the need for food had overcome his fear of the daily shelling from nearby Bissau's artillery batteries and brought him outside.

"Yes, I'm afraid, but the only thing I'm feeling now is hunger," Gbadne told Alain, who translated the old man's words into French for me. As he spoke, Gbadne's glazed eyes stared lifelessly over my shoulder toward our car. Brennan stood to the side and began taking pictures of the old man.

The shelling had actually been aimed at a nearby army base controlled by mutinous soldiers, said Gbadne, pointing through the trees to a barracks disguised behind camouflage netting and razor-wire fence. Looking around, I saw that indiscriminate artillery fire had razed several homes. They lay in crumpled heaps, like piles of kindling by a fireplace. Day by day, shell by shell, the war was destroying a little bit more of Gbadne's world.

"I'm just here to pick my apples," he said, absently scratching at a sore on his arm.

While interviewing him, I squatted behind a tree as a safeguard against shrapnel if another artillery barrage began. I was scribbling the last of Gbadne's words when I first noticed the chugging throb of an engine in the distance. Alain said it was a Senegalese patrol boat just offshore. Every day the patrol boat fired on Cumere to keep the base's renegade troops off balance.

"Shouldn't we get out of here?" I asked.

"It's OK," Alain said. "They only fire in the morning and evening."

I relaxed a little and began to put my notebook back in my blue waist pouch. Then came the distinct *pop* and *whoosh* I remembered from mortar fire in Afghanistan and Cambodia. My heart froze and my mouth ran dry. Alain's eyes widened.

"Come on," he said urgently, tugging at my arm. "Let's get out of here."

We jumped to our feet. I hurriedly shook Gbadne's hand and sprinted after Alain. I turned once as I ran, and saw Gbadne wave, the shredded sleeve of his black shirt flapping loosely like ends of a mop. Pangs of guilt tugged

at me as I abandoned the old man, once again leaving
him alone with his despair. Guilt gave way to anger and
frustration. With barely enough money to take care of
Alain and myself, I knew I could not take Gbadne along
with us, but would my reporting really help him? And
would it be in time?

AS I RAN QUICKLY TO CATCH UP with Alain, my right
foot kicked something. Without stopping to check what
it was—I assumed it was a rock—I ran another pace or
two. I don't know what it was—instinct perhaps—but I
suddenly stopped to see what I had kicked.

I froze in the middle of the road and slowly looked at my
feet. I almost retched when I saw I had kicked a "toe-
popper" land mine—the kind that are scattered over the
surface of roads or paths. It had skittered in front of
me, but I still stood rigid, panting to the point of hyper-
ventilation.

Paralyzed with fear, I couldn't move until, once again, I
heard the muted *fump, fump, fump* of mortar shells leaving
their cannons. Several more rounds had been fired, and
they would be landing in seconds. I finally snapped out of
my frozen state of terror and ran for the car.

"How long does it take for a shell to travel from there to
here?" I yelled to Alain, who was now well ahead of me.

"About a minute. Maybe ninety seconds," he yelled back
without breaking stride.

Alain and I dove into the car, which fortunately had been
idling while I conducted my interview. I watched out the

back window until Cumere and Gbadne were no longer within sight.

To this day, I wonder what happened to Gbadne. I like to think he's still quietly picking his apples and waiting for his family to come home. I pray that's what happened.

ONE AFTERNOON WE RETURNED early from our outing. Wearing only boxer shorts and socks, I lay on my bed, skimming through an old copy of *The Economist*. Brennan, also in boxer shorts and a tank top, lay on his bed looking through his pocket guide of art.

Out of the corner of my eye, I saw a flicker of movement. Instantly, I turned my head to see what had moved, but there was nothing. For several moments I stared intently at the floor near the closet door. Nothing. But a second later, I spotted a three-inch-long red insect—it looked like a hybrid between a spider and a scorpion—darting out from under the closet door.

I looked at Brennan and paused for his reaction, but his nose was still buried in his art book.

"Did you see that?" I asked, sounding a little more panicked than necessary. "What the fuck was that thing?"

"What the fuck was what?" asked Brennan, not really paying attention to me.

"That spider thing. It was humongous. And red."

"Where?" Brennan asked skeptically.

I motioned with my chin toward the spot on the floor where the thing had scurried, but it was already back in the closet.

"I don't see anything. Maybe you're imagining things."

With that, the red insect scurried back out of the closet. This time, Brennan caught a glimpse of it.

"Holy shit!" he blurted out. "What the fuck *is* that thing?"

I reached to the side of my bed and grabbed one of my hiking boots from the floor. I watched nervously as the insect sped toward my bed. Instinctively, I hopped up to my feet on the shaky mattress. The bed creaked with my unevenly distributed weight. Brennan did the same as the creature ran under his bed. We stared at the floor, waiting for the insect to make its next move.

"Kill it," I said to Brennan.

"Shit, no, man. *You* kill it."

I hurled my boot under Brennan's bed and the insect ran out. It quickly moved toward my bed.

"Shit!" I yelled, bounding over to Brennan's bed. The mattress sagged toward the floor under our combined weight. The red bug stopped in the middle of the floor and turned toward us.

I grabbed a spare curtain rod from the corner near Brennan's bed. Intending to nudge the insect toward the corner of the room, I moved the pole toward its head. The creature reared back on its hind legs and spread its front legs around the pole.

"Yipes!" I squealed, dropping the wooden rod to the floor.

The insect darted to the wall. I finally mustered my courage and gingerly stepped down to the floor. I picked up the pole and began to corral the enemy toward a corner. Brennan jumped off the bed and walked out of the room.

"And just where do you think you're going?" I barked, my eyes focused on the insect.

"Hang on, I've got an idea," Brennan said as he left.

"Well, hurry. He looks angry."

Outside the room, I heard Brennan cutting something. He returned carrying a large plastic Coke bottle, the bottom half of which had been cut off. The bottle was now flat at one end with its open spout at the top—for air. Brennan inched his way toward the cornered creature.

"Keep that pole steady," he cautioned me. "I don't wanna die of a spider bite in Guinea-Bissau. When I say 'now,' you pull the stick away."

I waited as he inched closer and leaned toward the red thing.

"Now!"

I pulled the pole back. The thing began to run, but not before Brennan clomped his homemade Coke-bottle trap on top of it. It desperately tried to scamper up the sides of the bottle, but found it too slippery.

"There," Brennan said as he held the bottle tight to the floor. "Go find a big rock we can use to hold this thing down."

I ran outside and searched the area near our cabin for a rock large enough to rest on the Coke bottle's spout. I returned in a moment with a large, flat rock about the size of my foot. For most of the afternoon, Brennan and I sat in our underwear around the red insect and stared at it through the veiny imperfections of the clear plastic bottle.

"Look at that," I said. "You can see it breathing."

We watched the red creature try to climb the sides of the bottle. We sat and watched, until I finally went to the lodge staff, who released the red bug to scurry away into the nearby fields.

REFUGEES HAD OVERWHELMED Mansôa, Bafatá, Canchungo, and Guinea-Bissau's other towns soon after fighting broke out in the capital. Some 300,000 people were on the move, depleting meager food reserves and crippling the country's tenuous medical infrastructure.

I met Adao Bodjam in Mansôa. An infant boy, just a few months old, Adao haunted me for the rest of my stay in Africa. Adao's grandmother, Isabel Djata, sat helplessly beside her young grandson. Her leathery hand engulfed the fragile fingers on his left hand. She stroked them gently for comfort—the child's and her own.

Adao was one of many hapless victims I met in Guinea-Bissau during its brief but catastrophic war. His mother was killed by a sniper's stray bullet in the first few days of street fighting in Bissau. Adao stopped feeding, refusing formula, milk, and even breast milk from a wet nurse. The quick onset of malnourishment was worsened by dysentery, said his doctor at the small makeshift clinic in Mansôa. He told me Adao could die at any time unless he received some nutrition. Too weak for intravenous feeding, the baby was receiving saline liquids to ward off a more immediate death from dehydration. A naso-gastric tube was taped to his button nose.

I stood in the dirty little room, clutching my notebook like a shield in front of my heart. I looked at this beautiful little infant dying in front of me. Tears welled in my eyes as I scribbled the doctor's words onto my steno pad.

"What can be done to save this baby?" I asked, struggling to contain my rising emotions. I felt disgusted with myself for even asking that question. More and more, I felt like the journalistic equivalent of a rubbernecking motorist slowing to get a better look at a bloody crash site.

"He needs plasma to regain strength," the doctor said. "But we have none; we haven't had a shipment in months."

I looked at my feet with pity and cast a glance at Isabel, who looked away quickly.

"I wish to see the day when I can watch him running and playing soccer with the other boys," she said, staring at the wall, as if she could envision her grandson dashing across a soccer field.

"I'm so sorry," I said, even though Isabel spoke only Portuguese. I placed a hand on her shoulder and looked at her pained face.

I stood back as Brennan began taking photographs of what would turn out to be the last moments of this baby's life. Suddenly I became aware of the room. Mansôa's only hospital was a dilapidated, cinder-block clinic with fifteen rooms. There was no electricity and few supplies, except for those stolen or bought on the black market. Clean sheets were unattainable luxuries;

air-conditioning in the 40°C heat of a West African summer was sheer fantasy.

Isabel's gnarled hand rhythmically traced a circle around her grandson's motionless head. Flies that had gathered at the corners of his wide eyes zipped away from Isabel's hand, only to return at once. Adao's withered, exhausted face had become the face of death of an old man; the skin was taut, stretched over awkwardly large cheekbones. He lay still, resigned to his minute-by-minute slide toward death. His unblinking eyes stared straight into my own.

I looked away quickly, unable to bear the sadness. When I looked back, the infant boy's eyes remained fixed on me. He spoke no words, but his eyes appealed for my help; I felt as if he were pulling me closer to him. Was he trying to find the strength to live? Or find the courage to die?

SUBDUED, BRENNAN AND I TURNED and left Adao's room to tour the rest of Mansôa's demoralizing little hospital. The sun beat down on my head. Sweat ran down my face and my shirt was sodden with it.

Before leaving, we quietly entered the room next to Adao's. Inside, an eighteen-year-old woman named Sabado Tchame was giving birth. There were no heart monitors, no forceps. There were no maternity-ward instruments of any kind, apart from a hospital bed with heel stirrups. Sabado stared stoically at the ceiling as two nurses massaged her belly, trying to coax the baby out. Sweat rolled down her forehead, while a trickle of watery blood from her vagina streamed down the rusting legs of her bed.

After about ten minutes that seemed like an eternity, a healthy baby girl emerged into the world and let out a wail to announce her arrival. The infant's skin quickly transformed from a gray-blue pallor to a rich, healthy brown. Overwhelmed by the unfair juxtaposition of life and death at the clinic, I began to cry.

Sabado lay motionless on the bed, her once distended belly now flat and relaxed. She breathed heavily, panting to overcome the strain of labor. Flies buzzed around her head. After being weighed and having her lungs cleared of fluids, Sabado's new baby daughter was laid on her mother's bare breasts.

Feeling awkward and intrusive, I shyly went to Sabado's bedside and asked her how she felt about her daughter's future now that war had engulfed Guinea-Bissau.

"You have no choice where you are born," she said, still out of breath. "But at least I want my child to grow up in a place of peace."

WE RACED BACK TO BAFATÁ to file our copy and photos. Back at the hunting lodge, I saw an aid worker with whom I had spoken at the Mansôa clinic. A pediatrician working with the Belgium-based Médecins sans frontières, he took me aside and told me that Adao had stopped breathing shortly after our visit.

For the next several days, my heart felt frozen, numbed by the sadness of the place. I felt as if my body were detached from my mind. I could see and hear, but I felt nothing. Apart from a handful of Portuguese reporters and the BBC's Mark Doyle, Brennan and I were the only foreign journalists in Guinea-Bissau. Despite my own increasingly dark mood, I was determined to tell the world about Adao and Gbadne and the many other nameless victims I met in that troubled country.

JUST BEFORE NOON about a week later, I spotted a white 4x4 SUV on the dirt road that led to the Bafatá hunting lodge. I assumed it must be Myles Tierney, since we had been awaiting his arrival for several days. His jeep kicked up a long reddish cloud that left a cinnamon dusting of powder on the elephant grass beside the road.

His driver pulled into the lodge's parking lot, and Myles began unloading what looked like an army's worth of gear. There are two kinds of journalists in the world: notebook-toting print reporters, and heavy, gear-laden television reporters. I resented Myles's intrusion on the story that Brennan and I had cultivated and worked tirelessly to cover with little or no recognition. At the same time, while I don't love television journalism, I enviously recognized its power and influence.

A great many more people get their news from TV than from reading newspapers or magazines. It's a harsh truth that die-hard print reporters like me must face and accept. It's also one of the primary reasons the Associated Press diversified into television news in the early 1990s.

Myles and his cameraman Khaled Kazziha moved into the cabin next to the one in which Brennan and I were staying. While Myles and Khaled unpacked, I sat at my laptop and continued to struggle over the stories of Adao and Gbadne. Then, frustrated by writer's block and the growing realization that I was suffering from burnout, I wandered into Myles's cabin. Unlike my own sparse pickings, it looked as if Myles had come to Guinea-Bissau prepared for a party. Copies of *Playboy* and *Hustler* lay on his floor. Sitting at a table where he had set up his satellite phone and a television editing deck, Myles offered me a shot of Jack Daniel's. Always a free spirit, he had quickly changed out of his jeans and work boots and slipped on a pair of plastic flip-flop sandals. A green and blue sarong from East Africa was neatly wrapped around his waist.

Myles downed a quick shot of Jack Daniel's with a frown; he squinted as the liquor burned the back of his throat. Forgetting that he had offered me a drink, he stood and began to rummage through his bags. He collapsed on the bed with a thud and lit a cigarette, then, propped up on one hand, he handed me one. I leaned against the doorframe and smoked it slowly. The nicotine sent a wave of cool calm through my overheated brain.

"So, what have you guys been doing?" Myles asked.

*Getting a suntan, you asshole,* I thought. I blew a long column of smoke out of my mouth. I didn't say a word. I was teetering on complete exhaustion and battling a week-old cold, and I knew enough not to confront Myles with my smart-alecky remarks.

Brennan walked in at that moment and described our daily excursions to Bissau and then back to Bafatá to file.

"Four hours of driving and one hour of reporting," Myles huffed. "Well, that's not going to work for us."

I felt resentment rising like bile from my stomach.

Later that evening at the hunting lodge's communal dining hall, François Leblanc, another doctor from Médecins sans frontières, took me aside.

"Is the report on the BBC true?" he asked me.

"I'm sorry, I don't know," I said, pausing for a moment. To myself I thought, *Which report? What did it say?*

"I heard it this afternoon," he said in his thick Belgian-French accent. "There was news that an airplane from Senegal bombed the city of Canchungo."

I nodded, acting blasé as if it were old news. But my heart raced. Had we been beaten by the competition?

"I should get back to a story I haven't filed yet," I said, politely excusing myself from François. As soon as I was out of his sight, I sprinted back to the cabin.

Because foreign correspondents must cover such enormous swaths of territory—often on their own and with limited resources—they typically rely on news tips from local media and very often from their competitors. The BBC and the *New York Times,* both with extensive networks of correspondents, are among the most reliable sources of news leads.

I tuned my short-wave radio to the BBC's World Service. The newscast would come at the top of the hour. The host began with the headlines: "An air attack on a town in Guinea-Bissau leaves dozens dead and wounded. . . ."

Later, the announcer introduced the full report: "Our

correspondent Mark Doyle reports from the capital
Bissau. . . ."

*Wait a minute,* I thought. *If Doyle's in Bissau, how can he
know what's happening in Canchungo?*

Still, whether fact or fiction, if it's on the BBC or in the
*New York Times,* it was my job to "match" the story or at the
very least confirm it. I took Myles and Brennan aside after
dinner and told them about the report.

"Well, we've got to check it out," Myles said. Brennan
agreed.

In the morning, we met by Myles's car. Both Myles and
I vied for the front passenger seat.

"Get in back, man," Myles said.

"No way. I'm a bureau chief," I answered, half jokingly.

"Screw that."

"No, seriously, I get carsick," I lied, preferring not to
reveal my mild claustrophobia in crowded cars.

Myles acquiesced and sat in back, complaining the whole
trip. Once settled, we headed down National Highway 7
toward Mansôa and then beyond to the small provincial
town of Canchungo. We drove six hours, with Myles and
Khaled bickering most of the way about how best to protect
their cameras against the jolting shocks of the bumpy road.
Exhausted and irritated, we pulled into Canchungo's main
square. Alain went into the local information ministry
office, now controlled by the rebels. He explained what we
had heard on the BBC and asked if we could have a soldier
show us the damage done by the bombs.

"Yes," he was told. "We were attacked by an airplane."

My heart raced as Alain leaned into the car window and relayed what he had been told. A soldier in a jeep led the way through Canchungo's streets, down a narrow back alley and up to a small cluster of homes. Our suv stopped behind the jeep. We all looked around.

"This can't be the place," I said. "Where's the crater? There's no damage, no burned-out homes. Nothing."

But the soldier strolled back to our car with the owner of the house in front of which we had parked. "This man can tell you what happened," the soldier said.

We followed the man down an uneven, muddy path that led to the farm field behind his house. We must have been quite a sight for the people of Canchungo: a column of white men, laden with our equipment, marching into the back field. I scribbled details of the scene into my notebook as I walked and stumbled. Brennan snapped photos (of what, I'm not sure) while Khaled moved precariously over the mucky terrain, his camera balanced on one shoulder.

The man leading us spoke quickly in Portuguese as he pointed here and there.

"The first one landed here," Alain translated for us. "The other one was over here by this tree."

I looked at both spots and strained to see any sign of an explosion. Typically, a bomb blast explodes out, sending slivers of jagged, red-hot metal into the vicinity. The shrapnel usually tears through the walls, destroys trees, and rips through human flesh and bone.

"Tell him I don't see anything," I said to Alain.

The man marched us over to the cashew tree and pointed out several deep gouges close to its base. There was even one sliver of metal jutting out of the trunk.

"Ask him what kind of airplane it was," I urged Alain.

"He doesn't know, but he heard a propeller."

I ruled out a Senegalese air strike, reasoning that with one of West Africa's better air forces, Senegal would not send a propeller-driven aircraft to bomb the town of Canchungo.

"What kind of bomb was it?" I asked Alain.

"He thinks it was a mortar, or hand grenade dropped from the plane."

"We heard that many people were killed or hurt. Is that true?" I asked.

"No, but two of my guinea fowl were killed," the farmer said.

We all eyed one another. At the top of the page I scribbled "a rumor of war" and then closed my notebook. Khaled lowered his camera and Brennan put his cameras back into the car.

"Oh great. I can see the headline now," I said sarcastically, gesturing with my hands to portray the spread of a banner headline: "Two guinea fowl perish in daring night-time air raid on Canchungo."

We chuckled, thanked the man for his tour, and piled into the car. We were pretty quiet during the ride back.

BY THE BEGINNING OF JULY I was back in Abidjan, once again editing stringer copy and writing up feature articles

I hadn't had time to write while on the road. A major story broke in Nigeria when Moshood Abiola, the jailed president-elect, died of a heart attack, and for twelve days straight I worked fifteen-hour days, editing copy and writing explanatory articles on the changing political landscape of Nigeria.

But when I had time to think again, I realized that after just five months in Africa, the relentless scenes of death and destruction were making me question whether I was serving any purpose as a reporter. I had always justified my role as a journalist by saying to myself that I could do some good by reporting to the world what was happening in forgotten places like Guinea-Bissau, Cambodia, and Sierra Leone, but the AP's subscribing newspapers weren't using many of my articles. I was pretty sure it wasn't the quality of the writing or reporting. It was the subject matter: the world just didn't care about faceless wars on the other side of the globe.

I had returned to Abidjan emotionally bankrupt. Adao and Gbadne haunted me. And further back, Maria and Masseh and Chea. Too many suffering faces and being the helpless onlooker. Everyday minor frustrations, such as Abidjan's traffic or spilling food on my shirt, sent me off on a swearing tirade.

One night at about three in the morning, the air-conditioning unit in my bedroom began to rattle. The clatter woke me from a dream about handless African children wandering through my house asking to be fed or dressed. With wide, appealing brown eyes they looked up at me and begged me to help them. I went to give them money, but quickly realized they had no hands with which to take the coins.

As I shook off the dream I climbed out of bed and stumbled in the humid darkness toward the air-conditioner. Dressed only in boxer shorts, I sat on the marble floor beside the wall unit and began pounding it with my fist until my knuckles bled.

"Stop!" I bellowed. "I can't help you. Just stop."

After that, I began taking more time off work, fearing I was on the brink of a complete psychological breakdown.

Then, army officers in Kinshasa staged a failed coup d'état to oust Laurent Kabila, the increasingly unpopular rebel-cum-president of the Democratic Republic of Congo. Within days of the coup attempt, David and I were on our way to the former Zaïre to cover the story.

# 6

# FROM KURTZ
# TO KABILA

IN MY EARLY MONTHS IN AFRICA, I had been eager to visit
Kinshasa and get a glimpse of the country that had so thor-
oughly mesmerized me as a young man through the novella
*Heart of Darkness.* As it turned out, I would make two trips
to the Democratic Republic of Congo while I was in Africa,
in May 1998 and again in August. The first trip had
elements of farce; the last was a nightmare I will never
completely escape.

In mid-May 1998, the Congo's self-declared president,
Laurent Kabila, marked his first year in power. David
Guttenfelder and I traveled to Kinshasa to cover the anniversary and write a series of features on the renamed
Democratic Republic of Congo. One year before, Kabila
had marched his insurgent fighters into Zaïre's capital,
Kinshasa, and toppled the thirty-two-year-old dictatorship
of Mobutu Sese Seko. The change from Mobutu to Kabila
sent an already unsettled and volatile region into a chaotic
tailspin in 1997 and 1998. Mobutu's had been a remorseless

reign of corruption, oppression, and despotism, but it had been stable—a source of certainty in an otherwise shaky part of Africa.

Everyone expected that Kabila—a onetime socialist guerrilla who likened himself to Bolivia's Ernesto "Che" Guevara—would promote Pan-African nationalist doctrines. The world was promised and awaited democratic elections. Congo and the world are still waiting. In Kabila's Democratic Republic of the Congo, the world anticipated a newfound respect for human rights and economic responsibility. Neither has materialized. In fact, Kabila's first order of business was to abolish all organized political opposition, gag the country's independent press, and chase off nosey UN war-crimes investigators, making their job next to impossible by throwing up bureaucratic hurdles every step of the way.

WITH JUST TWENTY MINUTES' NOTICE, Laurent Kabila called a news conference at the Presidential Palace—an ornate edifice of long white halls and glittering chandeliers built by the colonial Belgians.

At first, Kabila had shunned the material trappings of the presidency. But eventually he had taken up residence at the palace. He had also traded in his battered army jeep for a shiny new black Mercedes limousine.

Two hours after the press conference was to have begun, Kabila—wearing an open-necked floral shirt à la Nelson Mandela—finally burst into the red-carpeted corridors of the building. Hidden within a huddle of boy-faced, rifle-toting soldiers, Kabila glanced nervously from side to side. The ceiling-high French doors to the conference room swung open. Kabila, still in the center of his scrum of camouflage-clad bodyguards, strode confidently into the white-walled room with his chest puffed out like a peacock's. The first two rows of foldout chairs were filled with neatly groomed cabinet ministers who stood as a group and began applauding Kabila's entrance. Dozens of camera flashes popped. Blinding halogen light danced through the room in every direction.

Bemused, I sat watching this spectacle. The initial bustle in the chamber settled, leaving the room filled with the lone static hum of Kabila's microphone. I opened my notebook and checked that my tape recorder was running. Finally, Kabila spoke.

"Africa must take its destiny into its own hands," he said in slow, deliberately punctuated French phrases. As if choreographed, the cabinet ministers stood together and applauded. It was at least a minute before they settled back down and the press conference resumed.

For more than two hours, Kabila held court with the assembled Kinshasa press corps—a mix of local African reporters and foreign correspondents from Europe and North America. At first, the latter scribbled notes and prepared to file their dispatches, but as time wore on, they began to fidget, periodically checking their watches to see if they had missed their deadlines back home. Many began to lose patience with Kabila's rhetorical declarations.

After a lengthy sermon on African independence and a scathing attack on corporate neo-colonialism, Kabila concluded his diatribe with one last meaningless bit of propaganda. "We are not going to continue to be fooled by those who have always dominated Africa," he pronounced.

In unison, the ministers stood once again. They howled with delight at Kabila's defiance.

My notebook was already filled with more anti-West quotations than I could use and I had quit taking notes an hour earlier. Finally, Kabila announced that he would take questions. I always hated the pushy aggression of press conferences, but when forced to I could hold my own with the pushiest of them. When Kabila pointed to an attractive French radio reporter who had already asked several questions, I ignored his selection and spoke over the woman's voice.

"Mr. Kabila—" I began in loud English that was hastily translated into French (for the other reporters, not for Kabila, who speaks fluent English).

"—when you came to power, you promised elections. It has now been a year. Do you still plan to hold elections? If not, will you still call your country the *Democratic* Republic of Congo?"

Remaining in their battleship-gray seats, the congress of ministers hissed and jeered like members of parliament from a rowdy opposition party. Kabila raised his hand and scowled sternly. A hush fell over his cronies.

Kabila paused to strike a thoughtful pose. Then, right on cue, camera flashes began popping. Kabila's large shadow shuttered back and forth on the back wall, bouncing with the shifting angles of light. He shifted his bulk forward and tugged with a meaty hand at one of his chins. Finally, he let out a dismissive laugh and beamed with the mischievous smile of a child who knows a secret, but refuses to tell.

"The problem here isn't democracy," he said, pausing for effect. "The problem here is stability."

THE KNOCK ON MY HOTEL ROOM DOOR was sharp and sudden, startling me. I peered apprehensively through the peephole. Postwar Kinshasa was a place of intense paranoia, suspicion, and intrigue. I had been in Kinshasa only a few days, but already my reporting had irked the moody president. Kabila's envoy in Washington had protested to the AP that my reporting was casting his regime in a bad light. But it was not President Kabila's notorious secret police at the door; it was a friend, Claude Kamanga Mutond.

Claude was a well-known Congolese radio personality and the AP's part-time reporter in Kinshasa. He had the raspy, booming voice of a hard-smoking radio news jockey. A gentle, gangly man with long arms and spindly legs, he usually wore neatly pressed clothes and smelled faintly of Chanel for Men. But on this Sunday in early May, Claude seemed oddly agitated. His face was awkwardly distorted, stretched wide by the fish-eye view through the peephole.

"Ian. *C'est moi,* Kamanga," he said in a forced whisper through the heavy wooden door. (After Kabila came to power, Claude had dropped his French first name and begun using Kamanga, his African name, in public.) I pulled open the door. Claude held out his hand and greeted me with customary Congolese formality. Then I saw that two men were with him: a squat, round-faced man in jeans and a floral shirt, and beside him a taller man in dress slacks and a white T-shirt who stood stiffly with his arms folded across his chest. His black loafers were neatly polished, but his pants were rumpled and baggy.

Claude quickly introduced the men as former officers in Kabila's ragtag army of rebels that had overthrown Mobutu the previous year. Decommissioned and unemployed, they now wanted to talk, Claude explained. I ushered them quickly into my room. The two officers took a seat on the couch, while I sat at the desk by the balcony's sliding glass door. Claude stretched out on the bed and flicked on the television to watch CNN. Always adept at spending other people's money, he called room service and ordered coffee, fresh fruit, and croissants for breakfast.

For two hours we talked, sometimes in little more than a whisper. It became clear that these men had witnessed Kabila's senior commanders orchestrate the massacre of some two thousand ethnic Hutu refugees during their campaign to depose Mobutu. The name James Kabari kept coming up. At one point, the stout officer leaned forward. He slurped at his coffee and wiped his upper lip with a white linen napkin. His face grew stern. He weighted his elbows onto his knees and looked me square in the eye:

"Kabari ordered large holes to be dug in which to dump the bodies," he said in a hushed voice. I could barely hear him over the hum of the hotel's central air-conditioning.

LAURENT KABILA HAD BEGUN RECRUITING his army of rebels in eastern Zaïre in 1995, around the time that neighboring Rwanda was still reeling from the fallout of the Tutsi-versus-Hutu carnage. Since Kabila had seized power, the country had been rife with rumors that his troops had systematically killed hundreds, maybe thousands of ethnic Hutu refugees who were living in camps in eastern Zaïre after they fled Rwanda.

As with so many other African countries, the Rwandan civil war had roots in the colonial period, when the Belgians had fueled an ethnic rivalry that would ultimately erupt into the 1994 genocide. Over time, the Belgians' preferential treatment for the Tutsis had become overt and ingrained. Tutsis attended the best schools, got the best jobs, and were paid better than their Hutu counterparts. By the time of Rwanda's independence in 1962, a seething hatred pervaded the country. Hutus began butchering Tutsis. And Tutsis slaughtered Hutus. In 1994, an estimated 800,000 Tutsis were shot, beaten, or hacked to death with machetes by their Hutu neighbors. Thousands upon thousands of Tutsis sought asylum in the Democratic Republic of Congo—then still Zaïre—and other neighboring countries.

However, Tutsi rebels from the Rwandan Patriotic Front continued to battle the government in a long-simmering civil war. By July 1994, the Hutu government in Rwanda was clearly at risk of collapsing to the advancing rebels. Fearing reprisals at home, more than a million Hutus fled across the borders to Zaïre, Uganda, Tanzania, and elsewhere. The vast majority went to eastern Zaïre. Mobutu Sese Seko reluctantly cleared the way for the Hutu refugees, ostensibly aligning his government with the Hutus of Rwanda. Now both Tutsis and Hutus—groups who no longer considered each other human—were living as refugees in Zaïre.

When rebel leader Laurent Kabila set his sights on ousting Mobutu, he used Mobutu's apparent favoritism toward the Hutus to coax Tutsis into his ranks. Kabila recruited hundreds, perhaps thousands, of Rwandan Tutsis. Among them was a prominent officer named James Kabari, whom Kabila would later appoint as his army's commander-in-chief. First as Zaïre and later as the Democratic Republic of Congo, Central Africa's largest country had become a powder keg waiting for a spark.

FOR MONTHS FOLLOWING KABILA'S VICTORY in May 1997, the United Nations had hounded the new Congolese regime for clearance to investigate alleged wartime massacres and atrocities. As I sat with Claude and his two army sources, I bristled with excitement at the prospect of breaking a major story about Kabila's Congo. I called my editors and told them I had *the* story that would confirm Kabila's complicity in the massacre of Hutu civilians during the 1997 war. My editors were skeptical. They wanted more substantive proof from credible sources before they would file the story on the wire.

Later that same afternoon, Claude and I climbed into his white SUV and began a winding three-hour drive through the crumbling streets of Kinshasa.

"Do you know where you're going?" I finally asked after the first hour, my exasperated voice cutting with sarcasm.

"Of course I do," he snapped back in French. "It's only ten minutes from your hotel."

Claude eyed his rearview mirror nervously and glanced back to me with wide eyes.

*"Merde!"* he said. "I just can't lose them."

In the passenger's side mirror, I caught a glimpse of a black Mercedes-Benz sedan several cars behind us. I slumped down in my seat out of view, my stomach churning.

"Oh yeah," I said, feeling foolish for my hastiness.

After circling through the foothill suburbs near the University of Kinshasa southeast of downtown, Claude was finally satisfied that our tail had given up and turned away.

We headed back downtown and drove past the Inter-Continental Hotel. A few blocks away, we drove down a narrow side street congested with little shops and throngs of pedestrians. We parked the car and Claude led me to the offices of the "African Zone Alliance for the Defence of Human Rights." We marched up a flight of dank cement stairs and down a dim hallway. Claude led me into the director's office. It was a small, dingy workspace with water-stained walls and peeling paint. A ceiling fan whirled lazily overhead, pushing the humid air around the cluttered room. The top of the director's desk was stacked with teetering piles of reports from Amnesty International, Human Rights Watch, and the Canadian Centre for Democracy and Human Rights. Claude introduced me to the director, who was also his close friend. We shook hands and sat. He introduced himself as "Etienne," which I knew from Claude was a pseudonym.

Etienne wasted no time. He rose from his chair, walked behind his desk, and shut the door to his office. Sitting cross-legged in a rattan chair, Claude waited in the corridor.

"We are about to release a report about the massacre of Hutus by Kabila's forces last year," Etienne told me under his breath.

At once, he handed me a preliminary copy of the report—a joint project with various worldwide human rights groups, including Amnesty and Human Rights Watch.

"This won't go public for several weeks," he said. "But you are here so you can have it now. Just please don't use my name."

I agreed. (My discretion made no difference; I found out after the fact that Etienne was arrested and imprisoned, held incommunicado, for a week after my story appeared in newspapers across North America and Europe.) Bidding him farewell, I tucked the report under my shirt and left with Claude. All the way back to the car, I kept glancing furtively over my shoulder. We quickly returned to the hotel; I could make Sunday newspaper deadlines if I filed my story right away.

The top paragraph summed up the key element of the story:

"A top military aide for Congolese President Laurent Kabila knew about the slaughter of thousands of Rwandan

Hutus during [the Democratic Republic of] Congo's civil war and did nothing to stop it, a report by four human rights groups says."

After filing my Kabari story, I spent several days wandering the streets of Kinshasa. For once, I had the rare chance just to visit an African country and see how it was rebuilding after a war. Sadly, I discovered that the Democratic Republic of Congo wasn't rebuilding at all. Kabila had replaced one form of totalitarianism with another.

Kinshasa, formerly Leopoldville, remained the shambles it had become under Mobutu. Fly-swarmed shoulder-high hillocks of rancid garbage lined street corners. Rats darted between the piles. Rutted streets lay in crumbling disarray from neglect. A construction crane erected in 1990 sat idle.

Every day, under an unrelenting sun in a cloudless sky, hundreds of young men gathered outside the State Bank of Congo building (they call themselves *Le Parlement des Peuples*). There they debated the fate of their nation and how to change their own miserable lot in life. With an unemployment rate among young men as high as 75 percent, Kinshasa was a breeding ground for discontent and anger. I could see it in my first few days in the city. Every time I went to talk with the crowd, men in tattered clothes swarmed me. They shoved their hands toward me, grabbing my shirt and tugging at my notebook. At first I thought they were begging for food or money, but I quickly learned they wanted their grievances heard by the outside world; on scraps of paper or bits of napkin shoved into my pockets, the destitute of Kinshasa had written out their appeals to the world. It was then that I realized that Kabila was leading his country toward another war. His slow economic start and undiplomatic demeanor had quickly given rise to new opponents rooted in the ethnic animosities he had exploited.

"Nothing has changed the way we expected," unemployed schoolteacher Mpoyi wa Mpoyi told me. "The people aren't happy. There are no jobs, and we have no rights."

WEEKS BEFORE LEAVING ABIDJAN for Kinshasa I had read an e-mailed press release from the United Nations Children's Fund that discussed the lasting psychological problems children in the neighboring Republic of Congo would face after having witnessed bloodshed and carnage in their city streets during that country's brutal civil war.

Brazzaville, the capital of the Republic of Congo, and Kinshasa, the capital of the Democratic Republic of Congo, are twin cities separated only by the Congo River. I nagged David to take an afternoon off from Kinshasa and come with me to Brazzaville to report on the plight of that city's children. Finally he agreed.

We stood at Kinshasa's "Beach" port terminal, waiting for the ferry that would take us to Brazzaville. Hundreds of people jammed the queuing lanes cordoned off with rusting, paint-chipped steel railings. The barriers made no difference. The longer we waited in line, the further we drifted from the front. At the Beach, whole families with all their worldly possessions crawled beneath the steel railings.

They looked at David and me, the only white people in the line, and shrugged half apologetically. Young adults gawked in wonder. Around us, little groups of children ran around squealing with excitement.

"*Muzungu! Muzungu! Muzungu!*" they cried in chant-like rhythm—the Swahili word for "white man." "Hey, Muzungu! Me American too."

The sun beat down on our heads. I had taken a shower an hour earlier, but already I was beginning to reek of dried perspiration. Near the docks, piles of rotting banana leaves filled the air with a foul stench, mingling with the fetid odor of human feces that collected at the openings between the dock's narrowly spaced cement pilings. The heat and the smell, along with the jostling crowd, began to exhaust my overwhelmed senses. After thirty minutes under the hot sun, David finally snapped.

"Come on!" he barked at me. "We're going."

He grabbed my arm and we began shoving past the families who had pushed their way into the line. Some protested, wagging fingers and muttering something in the local language, Lingala. Others just stood and watched. We bought our tickets, shoved our way through customs and immigration, and headed down the long ferry dock. To get from the end of the dock to the ferry's gangplank, we had to pick our way over a series of pirogues—wooden dugout canoes—that had been tied together as an extension of the dock. Weighed down by my heavy blue backpack, I gingerly stepped over the gunwales of one boat and eased into the next. When an outboard motorboat whined past, kicking up a small wake that splashed into the pirogues, the whole unsteady bridge began to dip up and down. The $4,000 satellite phone hanging in its case from my shoulder began to slip. I spun to grab it and began lurching toward the dirty water. David grabbed my arm from behind and steadied me back into the canoe.

Finally, we climbed aboard the ferry.

Belching out long columns of black exhaust smoke, the rusted, timeworn paddleboat struggled against the powerful flow of the Congo River's muddy waters. It was a frustrating battle, as the ferry seemed to keep losing ground. When the captain periodically pushed the throttle forward, the nubbled metal decks vibrated, tickling the soles of my feet through my hiking boots. A frothing broil of white water churned up behind the boat's paddles.

Taking a long swig of the overpriced Heineken I had bought at the "Topdeck Snax Bar," I squinted against the sunlight glinting off the water in stabbing dagger points. With beer in hand, I stood at the ferry's railing, absentmindedly picking at the flaking white paint. I stared into the waters below. My mind wandered with the hypnotic flow of the water.

*I wonder if this is how Joseph Conrad felt?* I thought. Like Conrad, I had first come to Africa months before my thirty-second birthday. Also like Conrad, I had quickly become disillusioned and horrified at man's inhumanity to man. Conrad had witnessed at a nascent stage the lesson European colonialists were teaching their indentured African workers. With brutal proficiency and ruthless abandon, Europe demonstrated to Africa that self-serving greed outweighed all else.

*Heart of Darkness* remains as valid today as when Conrad first wrote it as a criticism of what he saw in the Belgian Congo. But it wasn't just Congo where Europeans were busy teaching dirty little lessons to Africans. All over the continent, colonialists clamored for land, wealth, and imperial prestige. Running roughshod over Africa's cultural heritage, ignoring tribal distinctions, divisions, and enmities, Europe's colonialists hacked, butchered, shot, and ravaged their way across the continent. But deaths alone do not measure Europe's legacy in Africa. The true measure of that is found in the value system introduced and perpetuated in Africa today.

Money pours into Africa, but increasingly it winds up in the hands of corrupt military regimes or vicious rebel militias such as Angola's UNITA rebels and Sierra Leone's Revolutionary United Front. Over and over, I was stunned by the West's treatment of Africa as little more than a source of raw material. I witnessed European diamond dealers continuing to buy gems in the Democratic Republic of Congo and Sierra Leone even though it was common knowledge that diamond revenues helped fund rebel wars. I also watched North American and European petroleum firms operating in the Niger River delta and elsewhere in Africa defiling the environment for the sake of an uninterrupted supply of crude oil. I watched rubber tappers in Liberia collect raw rubber-tree sap for pennies a day so that major automobile manufacturers had a steady supply of tires for their vehicles. All over Africa, commerce and profit reign supreme. Our consumer culture perpetually sends a message to corporate and political African leaders alike: the West's luxury and comfort comes before the human rights of African citizens. Hasn't that been our message to Africa all along?

BACK ON THE BATTERED old blue-and-white ferry, I looked up from the Congo's waters and caught my first close-up glimpse of Brazzaville. For the troubled Republic of Congo, 1997 was a year of war. Pockets of rebel fighters had battled from street to street in the final days of the war, and Brazzaville was devastated. Entire neighborhoods had been razed by artillery and rocket fire. Brazzaville's one and only skyscraper—an impressive steel-and-glass structure that was home to the state-run oil corporation—had been shattered. Long streaks of black soot lined the building's sides where flames had licked from blown-out mirrored windows. I saw entire city blocks in ruins, with slabs of concrete strewn in every conceivable contortion.

For decades, Marxist dictator Denis Sassou-Nguesso ran the Republic of Congo according to the strict dictates of the Kremlin and Marxist-Leninist doctrine. Although the country was rich in oil and other natural resources, he led it into numbing poverty to please his Soviet benefactors. But that came to an abrupt end when the Soviet bloc collapsed. Sassou-Nguesso then traded his hammer and sickle for a pinstriped suit and decided to give free enterprise a whirl.

In the country's first free elections since the end of French colonial rule in 1960, Sassou-Nguesso was soundly defeated and driven from the presidency—the only job he'd ever known. It didn't take long for the one-time army officer to assemble a rebel militia known as the Cobras. Crying election fraud, Sassou-Nguesso embarked on a war to reclaim what he considered his rightful place in power. Eventually he clawed his way back to the presidential palace, but the price for Brazzaville and the whole of the Republic of Congo was staggering. Tens of thousands of people were killed, soldiers and civilians alike. Virtually the whole of Brazzaville's population fled to the countryside or across the Congo River to avoid the daily onslaught of rocket and artillery fire. Young men suspected of sympathizing with one or the other side simply disappeared during the night. Wives lost husbands, children lost parents, and a city lost its soul.

ONCE WE HAD DOCKED, David and I began exploring the city with the AP's part-time reporter and translator, Louis Okamba. I quickly learned it wasn't just the city that had been deeply scarred. We wandered about a block or two, climbing over concrete rubble still blocking the sidewalks. I told Louis I wanted to write a story about the psychological impact of the war on Brazzaville's inhabitants, particularly the children. Louis knew just where to go. In Lingala, he instructed our taxi driver to take us to the School of the Martyrs. A public grade school in downtown Brazzaville, the School of the Martyrs had been pinned down for weeks in the middle of street fighting.

The cab stopped at the side of a busy street in front of a sandy yard. I looked across the lot.

"Louis, why are we stopping here?" I asked.

*"C'est ici,"* he answered.

I got out of the taxi and began to walk up toward a wall still pockmarked with bullet scars. The wall's outer edge was blasted away and crumbling. Steel reinforcement rods jutted out of the broken concrete like twisted branches on a dying tree.

Over the din of the nearby street, I heard the squealing laughter of children at play. I approached the battered wall and turned the corner to look inside a walled playground. When the children spotted me, they fell silent, as if a large wool blanket had suddenly muffled them. A chill ran down my spine—the kind you get when they say somebody has just walked over your grave.

As I slowly moved across the sandy lot, I could feel dozens of young eyes trained on my back. The children watched quietly as I passed them and headed toward the principal's office. One bold little boy made eye contact with me.

"Bonjour," I said, forcing a smile.

The children held their silence until I had passed by. As I rapped at the principal's door, I heard *"Mbotay,"* Lingala for "hello."

The principal, Jeanne Bitousa, answered the door and agreed to an interview. We stood in the open-air corridor by the playground. After a few minutes the children resumed their play.

"When I walked into the playground, the children all went quiet," I told the principal. "Why is that? Are they still traumatized by the war?"

Bitousa nodded knowingly. She straightened the front of her brightly flowered frock. She pointed to the spot where I had entered the playground.

"That's where Mrs. Tsongo was shot." Mrs. Tsongo was a beloved fourth-grade teacher, Bitousa explained, clearing her throat. "She was leaving the school during a lull in the gunfire."

As Mrs. Tsongo approached the wall by the road, at the same spot where I had entered, "Suddenly gunfire exploded!" Bitousa said, waving her right hand.

One bullet ripped through Mrs. Tsongo's heart. She fell onto the sandy lot beside the wall and quickly bled to death. Another teacher met the same fate soon afterward, Bitousa told me. The school was closed after the second shooting death. It had remained closed until the war ended, at least in downtown Brazzaville.

Bitousa took me on a brief tour of the School of the Martyrs. In one classroom, I met twelve-year-old Etou Loubaki. His wide eyes gazed up at me. I asked Bitousa if I could talk to Etou outside the classroom, away from the other children. She agreed and we walked back out into the bright sunlight. Etou's skin looked very dark next to his white school shirt and beige shorts. His hair was clipped short, leaving his scalp exposed to the sun. His feet were bare, toes wriggling in the sand. With the principal standing by, I asked little Etou about Mrs. Tsongo.

"When I came back to school, I asked about Mrs. Tsongo—" he said distantly, his voice fading to a whisper. He looked down at his feet as if he might find the strength there to keep talking. "They told me she was dead," he finally finished. There were no tears, no anger. Etou seemed devoid of emotion, frozen in a moment of time that had betrayed his young heart.

"There were bodies all along the road," he offered absently.

Later I moved from classroom to classroom. Most were empty except for woven mats on the floor to sit on. A few classrooms had a large desk and chair for the teacher. Stray bullets had shattered most of the blackboard slates. Lewd wartime graffiti remained on many of the classroom walls, left by government soldiers who had used the school as a temporary base. But the physical damage to the school paled by comparison to the psychological wounds inflicted on its pupils.

After concluding my visit at the School of the Martyrs, I asked Louis to direct the taxi driver to the offices of the United Nations Children's Fund in Brazzaville. While still in Abidjan, I had read a brief UNICEF report about a study on war's long-term psychological impact on children. Preliminary figures showed that most of Brazzaville's 450,000 children had witnessed killings, brutality, and rape during the country's four-month civil war. It was a war characterized by torture, random killing, and even ritual acts of cannibalism. Of the two thousand children who had been interviewed by UNICEF by the time I visited, about 90 percent displayed symptoms of post-traumatic stress disorder (PTSD) related to the war. (It was the first time I had ever heard of PTSD. I had no idea that soon I too would be displaying symptoms of the disorder.)

But in Brazzaville as elsewhere in Africa, it wasn't just what the children saw. In many cases, it was what they did, or were ordered to do. As in Sierra Leone, the larger Democratic Republic of Congo, and elsewhere, many children in Brazzaville had been recruited as fighters by both sides of the conflict.

Sitting in her neat and air-conditioned office, Dr. Dominique Serrano-Fitamant, a consulting child psychologist with UNICEF, explained the devastating effects of trauma on children.

"You're just fourteen and you're goaded into killing people, or told to help hold somebody down while they are raped or maimed or killed," she said. "How do you then go on to lead a normal life?"

Most of Brazzaville's children display some or all of the classic PTSD symptoms: eating disorders, sleeplessness, aggressiveness, emotional withdrawal, and incoherent speech patterns.

"We aren't just talking about a few cases here," Serrano-Fitamant said. "This is an entire generation, and the long-term consequences could be devastating for the country."

I headed back to Abidjan and returned to a routine of editing stringer copy, while awaiting the next big story.

# 7

# TU VA LA GUERRE LÀ?

LESS THAN THREE MONTHS after my first trip to Congo, several army officers in Kinshasa attempted a coup d'état to oust Laurent Kabila. This had been triggered when Kabila, responding to rumors of a coup plot, dismissed Rwandan army officer James Kabari as his military's chief of staff. In late July Kabila had expelled hundreds of Rwandan Tutsi soldiers who just the year before had fought to help him depose the dictator Mobutu Sese Seko.

It was just before dawn on the morning of August 3 when machine-gun fire had erupted through the Camp Kokolo army base in southwestern Kinshasa, about eight hundred meters from Parliament and blocks from the city's downtown core. Artillery fire followed soon after. Within hours, it was clear that Kabila's patchwork alliance of military support was in open revolt.

At the same time, 1,900 kilometers east of Kinshasa, through thick banana mangroves and uninhabitable primeval forest, troops of the 222d, or Zulu, Brigade in Bukavu, South Kivu's provincial capital near Rwanda, had declared war on Kabila. In an understated fashion, the commander of those units declared the rift between Kabila and the army: "[We are] not in agreement with the president," Major Ilunga Kabambi told journalists at the time.

Within days of the coup attempt, David and I were scrambling to find a way back to Congo. There were plenty of ways out of Kinshasa, the panic-stricken capital, but fewer and fewer ways in. Waiting to see how serious the coup attempt was, I was slow to act on the story, leaving few airline options available for flights to Kinshasa. Each day, my assistant, Amba Dadson, walked into my office and read off the list of airlines that had canceled or suspended service. In New York, meanwhile, my editors were growing impatient for copy. David and I finally arranged to take a Sabena flight to Brussels, where we could still make a connection to Kinshasa.

THE COMPACT TOYOTA TAXI sagged under our weight as David and I plopped into the backseat. I rolled down the window. Humid evening air washed across my face as we sped down the street. We zipped down rue des Jardins, the main avenue bisecting Abidjan's suburban community of Deux Plateaux. In minutes, we were on the Charles de Gaulle Expressway, Abidjan's answer to the Daytona speedway. Like a small insect weaving between blades of grass, the taxi zigged and zagged in and out of traffic all the way to the airport. I was always aware of the risks when flying on substandard African airlines, but nothing scared me quite as much as the hair-raising, death-defying race to the airport in an Ivorian taxi.

Our driver, Saïd, looked over his shoulder and into the backseat. He flashed us a gleaming white smile. I braced for disaster as he continued to drive at the same breakneck speed while peering over his shoulder at us instead of the road. A truck overloaded with long stalks of sugarcane rumbled past on the hazy airport road.

"Where are you going?" Saïd asked in French.

"We're going to the Congo," I answered in rusty, grade-school French.

"Ah!" he blurted out in a slangy pidgin French. *"Tu va la guerre là?"*

*"Oui,"* David responded in about the only French he was really sure of. *"On va la guerre là."*

"—Oh God, Africa. My God. This is Africa," the driver muttered.

We continued along the gritty, industrial airport road, past shantytowns of cardboard-box homes and crumbling tenements of clapboard walls and corrugated steel roofs. The bright stare of high-beam headlights glared back at us through the taxi's grease-smeared windshield. Cocoa processing factories line the road that leads to Abidjan's Houphoüet-Boigny International Airport. One of the Ivory Coast's few claims to fame, apart from having some of the deadliest riptide beaches along West Africa's coast-lines, is its global hold on the cocoa market. The govern-ment says 40 percent of the world's cocoa supply comes from the Ivory Coast. During the drive to the airport, I always found it an uneasy juxtaposition—surrounded by abject poverty in this lower-income part of Abidjan and yet washed over with the sweet, tantalizing aroma of fresh chocolate.

The aging bug-like orange taxi pulled up to the departures section of the airport's terminal. As always, just getting out of a taxi meant a fight to get past the shoving throng of overeager porters. Stony-faced, I usually ignored the persistent offers from these desperately poor airport servants. Typically, the porters offered more than just baggage cartage; they could proffer cigarettes, chocolates, chewing gum, and women, though not necessarily in that order. Another common curbside service among the porters was foreign currency exchange. David and I hefted our bags on our own and struggled through the pushing crowd of helpers. We made for the entrance, past gun-toting, khaki-uniformed gendarmes who checked tickets, passports, and billfolds before bidding entrance to *their* airport. Five or six hundred CFA (West African francs), worth about one U.S. dollar, usually expedited the process. We wandered in and headed for the Sabena check-in counter, lining up behind two European executives in the business-class line—a decadent luxury for cash-strapped wire service reporters who normally fly economy.

From desperate poverty in West Africa you are swiftly transported to luxury and decadence with a European airline's business-class service of steak entrées, chilled champagne, and first-run films. After eight hours of pampering, we arrived in Brussels and sought out our connecting flight to Kinshasa. The Belgian woman at the Sabena Airlines transfer desk took our tickets and checked our passports for visas. She paused for a moment to give us one last good look.

"You do realize," she said, "this is our last scheduled flight to Kinshasa?"

We both nodded yes.

"I mean, we won't be sending another plane in if the fighting continues," she added for emphasis.

The Brussels National Airport is modest by comparison to many in Europe, but it still has its share of posh duty-free boutiques. For about $700 here (about five times what an average Congolese makes in a year) you can buy a new Tag Heuer watch, Louis Vuitton luggage, or a couple of obscenely over-priced designer silk scarves from Hermés. Next to the stacked cartons of duty-free cigarettes, shops offered boxed bars of pricey Belgian "Gold Coast" chocolate—the expensive profit-driven end product of the Ivory Coast's primary cash crop. Although it is the driving force behind the Ivory Coast's economy, it also encourages a flourishing trade in modern-day slavery. Unable to feed and clothe their children, parents in Mali, Burkina Faso, and other nearby West African countries sell their children as indentured slaves to work on the vast cocoa plantations in the central plains of the Ivory Coast near the border with Mali.

SABENA FLIGHT SN 557—an Airbus A320—slowly lifted away from the runway. In seconds, Brussels disappeared behind a thick curtain of cloud cover. It's very quiet in business class at 35,000 feet—a good place to do some thinking. For hours I pondered and second-guessed and fretted over what we were getting ourselves into. David broke the tension of my self-absorbed musings when the flight attendant showed up to take drink orders. Unsure of his French, David confidently ordered, *"un jus de pomme de terre, s'il vous plaît."* For the next six hours I needled him about his linguistic gaffe.

Coming in over Central Africa in the wee hours of the morning is a scary airborne prospect at the best of times, but during a civil war it's downright heart-stopping. First we circled in low over Brazzaville, the capital of the neighboring Republic of Congo.

Usually, when you fly in over a city after dark, the landscape is illuminated by hundreds of thousands of street lights, office-building lights, and homes: a Christmas tree spread over the ground to help you establish geographic bearings. Descending over Brazzaville on a moonless night, we might just as well have been coming down over the moon. Only a scattering of dim yellow lights was visible. Otherwise the landscape was an eerie dark blue that only vaguely hinted at texture—hills, roads, homes, and the banks of the mighty Congo River dividing the twin capitals of Brazzaville and Kinshasa. It was worse over Kinshasa; the city was still under a dusk-to-dawn curfew and no lights were permitted within city limits.

The plane bumped down on the rutted airstrip, jolting me from my daydreaming gaze out the porthole window.

I hesitated as we descended the steps to the tarmac. The air was cool and fresh, much easier to breathe than the

steamy, thick air of West Africa. It was pitch black outside
the terminal building, except for the fluorescent blue glow
from the sign of the airport's name over the terminal:
"Aérogare-Ndjili—Bienvenu." We pushed through immigration. The last time I had been in Kinshasa, it had cost
me $500 to "import" my laptop and "sat" phone. I expected
the worst now, with the city in the throes of a nascent civil
war. But our passports were stamped quickly and we were
ushered through to the baggage carousel. David was slowed
by a customs inspector who tore through his camera bag.

David quickly made arrangements to get us onto the
Inter-Continental Hotel's shuttle bus to downtown. It cost
$100 for the two of us, but that included the price of
armed protection and the cost of bribing our way through
the many checkpoints on the way into town from the
airport. As it turned out, we were stopped only once, at a
checkpoint in the eastern suburbs of Kinshasa. Three
young soldiers—boys with guns—circled the shuttle bus
filled with journalists from Africa, Europe, and North
America; there were also one or two intrepid executives
from European gem companies and a handful of returning
Congolese travelers frantic to get home to their families.
One of the boy soldiers climbed on board through the
front door. He strolled ominously down the darkened aisle,
eyeing each passenger. Tensely he clutched his rifle. His
uniform smelled of topsoil and diesel. His face was etched
with deep scars—marking his rite of passage into
manhood. David looked at him and in fluent Swahili said,
"What are you looking for?"

The soldier chuckled apprehensively and replied in Swahili. I don't know what he said to David, but he turned, walked away, and left the bus. We drove off and I began to grill David about his knowledge of Swahili. I knew David spoke the language, but I had had no idea how fluent he was. I decided it was time to stop teasing him about his potato-juice blunder during the Sabena flight.

By the time we arrived in Kinshasa in early August, Kabila had already whipped his capital city into a frenzy, thirsty for blood. Martial law had been imposed. Suspected rebel sympathizers or collaborators were being rounded up and jailed without court hearings or formal charges.

I SAT ON THE EDGE OF MY BED in room 1218 at the Inter-Con. The sun was dimming to a luminous orb of orange hovering low in the sky. While waiting for my room-service club sandwich, I spoke by satellite phone with Tim Sullivan, who was back in Abidjan. I had turned off the television's volume, but a dizzying array of images flickered across the muted picture tube. Kabila appeared on the screen and began pounding a fist into his open hand.

*What is he saying?* I wondered. *Is something happening?*

I cut short the call with Tim and leaped from the bed, cranking up the volume on the aging Zenith just in time to catch the tail end of Kabila's sentence: "—in the southwest of Congo!" he said, emphatically hammering his fist in his open hand with each phrase.

Moments later, *poof!* The lights in the hotel went off.

You're never aware of how much noise electric appliances

make until the power goes off. The air-conditioner fan ground to a halt and the antiquated television screen imploded into a single brilliant spot of light in the center of the picture tube. Only the fluorescent light from the bath-room continued to shine. The backup battery had kept my laptop running, but the computer was well past its prime and I knew the battery wouldn't last long. The whole room turned an eerie shade of icy blue as the sun's light finally disappeared below the horizon. I hoped there was enough left to enable me to save the story on my screen. I did so and re-read it on my screen. The wall and mirror behind the desk glowed from the computer's backlit screen. The day's lingering heat in the room began to overtake the dwindling remnants of the air-conditioning. Beads of sweat formed on my forehead and my shirt became saturated. I stripped down to boxers and a T-shirt. I could easily slide open the glass door leading to the balcony, to let in the evening air, but that would also invite an onslaught of malaria-carrying mosquitoes into my room. I decided to suffer the heat and get on with the article I was writing.

I gathered together the long cables that linked my computer to the sat phone and both pieces of equipment to the now-dead electric sockets. I carried the precarious stack to the bathroom and set up a makeshift office on the counter. The hotel's backup battery system was enough to keep electricity flowing to the bathroom lights, the wall's razor socket, and the elevators. Risking an electric shock, I jammed a pencil into the wall socket to release the safety catch. I plugged my multi-plug extension cord into the wall and waited. Nothing blew up. The computer and satellite phone once again hummed with life. I sat on the closed lid of the commode and began tapping away at the laptop on the marble countertop. My sweating thighs stuck to the plastic toilet lid. I stared into the mirror that ran the length of the counter.

*So this is the glamorous life of a war correspondent,* I thought. *Too bad your friends can't see you now.*

It wasn't perfect, but my makeshift office got the job done. The sound of distant gunfire snapped me out of my reverie.

*Has the city fallen?* I thought. *Oh shit! What am I missing?*

With Howard French, the *New York Times* correspondent, in the next room and several Reuters reporters just two floors below me, my competitive spirit for this story was fierce. I ran to the balcony and peered out. The foothills of Mount Ngaliéma that edged Kinshasa's western outskirts were dotted with small orange fires; otherwise, the city was black and quiet.

Sometime after eight in the evening, the AP's Kinshasa stringer, Claude Kamanga Mutond, arrived at the hotel to report on what he had learned about the blackout. We set off in his white Toyota Tracker with pink and aqua-blue racing stripes. When it became clear there was no street fighting, we went on a tour of Kinshasa's downtown district to get an idea of what was happening.

It was like some post-apocalyptic nightmare. Kinshasa

residents had poured into the streets and many people were huddled around fires glowing in upturned oil drums. The dancing flames and shadows twisted and contorted their faces. Lit from below, they looked like Halloween jack-o'-lanterns. Many people wore tattered clothes; most had no shoes, except the lucky few who owned plastic flip-flops. Angry-looking groups of people gathered around transistor radios. No longer trusting their daily diet of propaganda from Kabila's state-controlled media, the public mostly relied on short-wave broadcasts from overseas for news on the war against an army of rebels backed by Rwanda and Uganda.

One man threw up his arms and shouted, *"C'est faux! Ils veulent nous nous tromper!"*

The British Broadcasting Corporation had just confirmed what Claude had already told me: that the Inga power station about 125 miles southwest of Kinshasa had fallen to the rebels. We cruised the streets, stopping occasionally to gather man-on-the-street reactions to this latest development.

We drove slowly down Kabinda Avenue on the south side of the core downtown district. The street was thick with humanity. A haze of dust particles flickered and swirled in the beams of our headlights. People stared and glowered into the car; many shook fists at my face through the window. After an hour or so, Claude drove me back to the hotel where I went through my notes and clarified scribbled quotes so I could read them later when I needed them for a story.

• • •

OVER THE NEXT FEW DAYS, tension in Kinshasa worsened
as foreign embassies began evacuating their personnel. The
French, the Belgians, the Dutch, and then the British
pulled out. The Canadians and the Germans and finally the
Americans left. Chartered flights lifted off from Ndjili
Airport on an almost daily basis, heading for Yaoundé, the
capital of Cameroon, or Libreville in nearby Gabon. With
all the foreigners leaving, it became easier for the government to blame the West for the Congo's latest problems.
About a week after the power went off in Kinshasa, we had
shifted to the Belgian-owned Memling Hotel across the
street from the French embassy.

On Saturday we hopped into Claude's car and set off on
a brief outing to gather material for the day's story. We
slowly cruised along June 30th Boulevard, heading west
down the empty road. Suddenly the boulevard—all four
lanes—was jammed with pedestrians. In front of us were
the backs of hundreds of marchers. Since they were facing
away from the car, I couldn't read their banners and placards. The crowd chanted rhythmically, thrusting fists into
the air in time with the slogans, but I couldn't quite make
out the words. By the time I realized this was a rally by
university students demonstrating against foreigners in
Congo, it was too late. I had already been spotted.

"*Ici!*" a young man shouted at the top of his lungs. "*Il y
a un étranger, ici!*"

In unison, dozens of students wheeled around. They
swarmed the car in what seemed like the blink of an eye.
They berated me, calling me a "French pig" or "American

imperialist." I held my Canadian passport up to the front windshield, hoping to speak rationally with the crowd. I quickly learned that mobs don't reason.

One young man blind with rage reached through the side window. He grabbed my shirt by the collar and began to tug me toward the open window. My heart raced. I shouted frantically, "I am Canadian! You have the wrong person!"

I spoke only English since I was afraid French would reinforce their suspicions I was from France. I wondered to myself if they would know the difference between a Canadian and an American. Or would they simply lump us all into one indistinguishable lot of greedy Westerners?

More hands reached in, grabbing my arms and ripping at my hair.

Fearful of looking sympathetic to a foreigner, Claude sat and watched dispassionately. Before I knew what was happening, I was out the window and on the ground. I looked up at the clutch of seething faces staring down at me. My panic gave me the strength to struggle to my feet. Hands reached at me from everywhere, grabbing and poking. I was shoved and pushed from every possible angle. A thick gob of spit hit my cheek and oozed down my face. A fist flew wildly over my head—I'm sure it purposely missed my face; he was too close to me to miss. I heard fabric tearing and watched as the buttons from my shirt popped off in neat succession. My shirt flapped open. A leafy tree branch held by a protester slapped me in the face, scratching more than hurting, but it scared the hell out of me.

*I'm dead. I'll never get out of this,* I thought.

The crowd's shouting continued, growing more frantic and disorganized: a thousand voices churning, spilling and pouring over one another until they became a single throbbing drone. I reached into my back pocket and pulled out a wad of U.S. dollar bills. I flung it over the heads of the crowd and instantly—as if doused with ice water—the crowd dispersed and scrambled for the money. I took my chance to slip away unnoticed, walking cautiously to avoid redirecting attention my way. As I wandered down the street back toward Claude's car, I spotted a police officer and soldier, both of whom had been watching my assault. Now they joined the frantic mob, scratching and fighting for the loose dollars.

Once I was safely back in Claude's car he turned around and we headed in the other direction. He took an hour-long drive to get me back to the hotel without coming near the protest again.

Near the hotel and a few hundred yards from the Army of Victory Church was Kinshasa's main soccer stadium—where in 1974 Muhammad Ali had rumbled with George Foreman. Now there was a new kind of rumble at the stadium: hundreds of young jobless men gathered to join the army and get a paycheck.

An out-of-work grade-school teacher, Edmund Mboyo, stood apart from the crowd of zealous recruits. He held a crumpled sheet of paper—a black-and-white photocopied diagram of an AK-47 assault rifle. The army doesn't have enough guns to go around, Mboyo told me. They handed out pictures of the rifles to reassure the new recruits that real guns would soon replace the paper weapons.

With most of his key military officers now fighting on the rebel side, Kabila had scrambled to assemble an army to defend his capital. Most of his new conscripts were among the 75 percent of young men in Kinshasa without jobs. Choking on clouds of dust rising up under dozens of feet marching to a beat pounded out on empty jerry cans, hundreds of young men gathered to train for Kabila's army. This outpouring of support had little if anything to do with love for Kabila or even of country. For most, this was a business prospect.

Mboyo walked toward the group of recruits and watched as they were put through basic training drills. He tucked his paper gun in his back pocket and quietly turned away.

"We're happy to be soldiers," he said, out of earshot of the recruiters, "but the way to win this war is to pay your soldiers."

DAYS BEFORE TROOPS FROM ANGOLA and Zimbabwe arrived in western Congo to rescue Laurent Kabila's government, the rebels had marched to the capital's eastern outskirts. During the last week of August, Kinshasa's residents went on a witch-hunt for Tutsis, people associating with Tutsis, and even people with the angular facial features that distinguish Tutsis from Kinshasa's majority Bantu population. It still isn't known exactly how many Tutsis died in August, but it is suspected that hundreds were killed by the mobs and troops.

The dead were found in rivers, in garbage heaps, and down back alleys. By early September, there were few if any Tutsis left in Kinshasa. Brigades of loyal troops and police officers rounded up thousands of suspected Tutsi sympathizers.

"A humanitarian objective," is how Interior Minister Gaetan Kakudji described the round-up.

So it isn't surprising that when the rebels—many of whom were indeed Tutsi—arrived in eastern Kinshasa, they were hunted down, denounced, and killed by lynch mobs on the streets. It didn't hurt that Kabila was on state radio imploring the people to destroy the enemy "with spears or arrows, with hands, guns, and sticks."

A SCRAWNY NINE-YEAR-OLD dressed in rags, Domain Luminda was one of thousands of homeless children living on the mean streets of Kinshasa. On a sunny Saturday morning in late August of 1998, I watched from a distance as he picked his way past the smoldering bodies of two dead rebel soldiers. Covering his nose with a bare hand of tiny fingers and a weathered, leathery palm, he tried in vain to filter out the thick stench of burnt hair and flesh rising in long, gray wisps of smoke from one of the freshly scorched bodies. The child looked down at the corpse. His deep brown eyes fixed, as if he were in a trance. The corpse's glassy, lifeless eyes stared back. The dead man's face was frozen in a grimace of agony.

I had been interviewing Domain and his two friends for a story on street kids in Kinshasa when a truck filled with government troops bumped and rumbled down the city's potholed June 30th Boulevard. The battered olive-drab truck screeched to a halt when three men, assault rifles in hand, dashed across the four-lane avenue. Scrambling over one another like Keystone Kops, the troops in the truck leaped off the tailgate and took to the street. One soldier, a young man with fair skin and pants too big for his emaciated waist, pointed his Kalashnikov at the fleeing rebels. The sound of one shot rang through the abandoned neighborhood, that crack of gunfire ricocheting off empty homes. One of the suspected rebels fell heavily in his tracks. The blue plastic flip-flop from his left foot flew up into the air as his rifle clanked against the pavement and skidded forward. He lay motionless as blood seeped into his clothes and pooled beneath his chest. More shots crackled and popped as the two other rebels scurried into the shadows.

Domain and his two buddies slipped behind a mango tree, its twisted gray trunk wide enough to hide all three children. Farther back, I looked on from behind a brick wall. The boys watched in fascination as half a dozen government troops set off on foot to catch the two fugitive rebels who had ducked down a side alley. Sporadically, gunfire continued to echo through the residential neighborhood.

Two other government troops stayed behind to collect the corpse from the street. One fellow took the dead man's feet; the other grabbed an arm by the wrist. The body sagged in the middle, its rear end dragging along the pavement, but the free arm waved like a ghost's, bobbing up

and down as if beckoning to the hidden boys. Swinging
the body back and forth to gain momentum, the troops
gave one final heave and let the limp figure fly into the
back of the truck with a heavy thud. The blood-saturated
shirt squished and splattered when it hit the steel floor of
the flatbed. Domain and his friends remained small
behind the tree. Holding their breath, they watched with
wide eyes.

Off in the distance, long before I could see them, I heard
the screams of the captured rebels. They wailed for mercy,
alternately cursing their captors, vowing revenge, and
pleading for their lives.

They saw it coming.

From the back of the truck, another soldier—the apparent platoon commander—pulled two tires and a jerry can
of gasoline. Panic seized the captives. They squirmed, and
one broke free. He didn't run, but froze to glance over his
shoulder at his compatriot. Several soldiers held the second
rebel down on the ground. The commander brought the
tires forward. He raised one over his head and unceremoni-
ously shoved it down snug over the head and shoulders of
the prisoner. Bound with the tire and still held down, the
man let out a hair-raising cry of terror that reverberated
through the street. He sobbed uncontrollably.

The commander did the same to the second prisoner,
who was still paralyzed with fright. When he shouted,
another government soldier shoved a filthy rag from his
back pocket into the captive's mouth. The rest of the
soldiers backed away as the commander raised the can and

doused the men with gasoline. The commander pulled a
red, flip-top pack of cigarettes out of his breast pocket. He
drew out a slender Marlboro. Then he struck a match.
Inhaling slowly, he lit the cigarette and exhaled a long
column of gun-metal-blue smoke. As if looking for
witnesses or an audience, he glanced from side to side and
tossed the lit match at the captives.

The gasoline burst into a raging ball of orange fire that
quickly engulfed the two men. In agony, they screamed,
crying, pleading, and wailing. They shouted until they were
breathless. The fire took hold of the tires and burned
cruelly. Their work done, the troops climbed back into the
truck. Ignoring the bloody mess, they sat near the corpse.
With a clattering racket, the truck drove off as the captives
squirmed frantically, attempting to roll onto their sides to
extinguish the flames. Within seconds, they stopped,
succumbed, and fell still.

Not daring to budge, the boys still looked on. For twenty
minutes the flames burned until nothing remained of the
tires except for the steel-belted loops that encircled the bodies.

When the flames had receded, Domain led the way.
Emerging from behind the tree, he stepped cautiously
toward the dead men. One was little more than a charred
skeleton, his clothes and flesh burned away. The temperature
from the fire on the rag in his mouth had so heated his skull
that it cracked and blew open like a sealed can of beans
heating on a stove element. The shattered skull lay in large
ivory-white chunks near Domain's feet. The fire had spared
the head of the other captive. Half his face was untouched

by the flames. Most likely he died of asphyxiation long before the flames could have done their job. The dead man's open eyes were brilliantly white against his charred skin. His mouth was fixed in a contorted scream. Hours later, smoke continued to curl up from the wide-eyed corpse, and motorists slowed to gawk at death on their street corner. Pedestrians veered well clear of the bodies. Through much of the afternoon, Domain and his friends pensively circled the dead men from a safe distance. It was as if the boys were standing guard.

"I'm scared," said Domain. "I've never seen a dead man before, but I want to see it."

A MONTH AFTER I RETURNED to Abidjan from Kinshasa, I was still struggling to shake the images of death and killing that shuttered through my mind's eye during the day and when I slept. Rebels writhing in fiery agony; a soldier plunging to his death from a bridge; and innocent children caught in the midst of it all. To function on a daily basis I pushed the scenes to the back of my mind. But they came out in different ways on their own. I became tenser and more short-tempered than usual. A car horn honking sent me jumping out of my seat at the bureau; my heart would begin to pound in my chest, my mouth would run dry, and my hands would shake. In fact, any sudden noise became for me a machine gun firing or a mortar shell exploding nearby. I lived my life in a constant state of readiness, like a cat always ready to pounce. I started chain-smoking in an effort to calm my frayed nerves.

When Glenn McKenzie once presented me with a story he had written, I barked at him, "What the fuck are you doing?" Having simply done his job, Glenn looked at me, bewildered. I stormed out of the bureau and got into my jeep; I drove around the city for the remainder of the day. I felt lost in my own world of misery and self-pity. As the days went by, I closed myself off from other people, knowing that I would just snap at them too and irreparably harm all my relationships. I didn't understand what was happening to me. I refused to talk about Kinshasa with anybody except David.

Early one evening I walked out to the plastic picnic table on my patio. The cool breeze rustling through the palms of the coconut trees was a refreshing change from the stifling heat of the midday sun. Then I opened a small set of watercolors my father had given me years earlier. I sat in the plastic blue chair at my table and relaxed with a cold beer as I began to paint.

I mixed up a dark, grayish-black mix of paint and swept my brush across the paper, making what I thought would form the bold outlines of a map of Africa. Painting in swirling motions I continued to fill in the outline until I saw two eyes staring back at me. Almost detached, I watched as my brush moved across the page, making strokes that seemed beyond my control. A mouth with white teeth formed in what I had assumed would be southern Africa on my map. I began to feel faint, but I kept on painting. I went inside to grab another beer and a small bowl of peanuts. When I returned I stared at my creation and shook with anger and fear. Without meaning to, I was painting the burning victims I had seen in Kinshasa weeks earlier.

I abandoned my original idea for the painting and simply went with the emotional outpouring that flowed from within. Perhaps I could purge the horrific images from my mind and dreams if I moved them from my head and onto the watercolor painting. I added a ring of fire around the haunting apparition on my page. Red, orange, and purple licks of flames danced around the head and neck, just as I had seen in Kinshasa. I stared at the hapless victim. I imagined the heat of the flames on my face. I heard the two men screaming, wailing, and pleading for mercy.

"Shut up!" I shouted into the empty yard. "Leave me alone!"

THROUGH MOST OF SEPTEMBER and much of October I stopped going to the bureau except to handle the administrative duties of my job as a bureau chief. I even had my assistant bring paperwork to my house. I could no longer cope with the endless stream of violence and bloodshed I had confronted in West Africa. I couldn't maintain my role as the professional observer. I knew I was a bystander who could do nothing to help, nothing to curb the bloodshed. I scorned my earlier naïveté in thinking my stories might change anything. On several occasions I started to write to my supervisors in New York to ask for a transfer to another, more peaceful bureau, but always I decided against it, fearing it would be viewed as an admission that I couldn't cut it as a war correspondent. In the end, that admission of failure scared me more than having to wade back into another war zone.

In mid-October I headed off to Vietnam for a month-long vacation that I thought would let me relive those days when I was happy as an AP journalist. It felt like a last-ditch attempt to salvage my career. On the way, I stopped off in Bangkok for a couple of days to meet up with old friends and to begin looking for a new job. I contacted friends from *Time* and began inquiring about whether the magazine was hiring. There might be an opening in New Delhi, I was told. I put together a package of my writing samples and a résumé and sent it off to *Time*'s Hong Kong office. I began to hope I might find my way out of Africa without having to admit to the AP that I had failed to cope.

Once I got to Hanoi, I was flooded with remorse for having left in the first place. On almost every day of my vacation, I met up with an old friend or colleague. While they spoke of the same old boring stories and marveled at how exciting my life in Africa must be, I would listen politely, but with growing agitation. *You don't know what you're talking about,* I'd think. *And you're lucky you don't.*

I visited my old bureau in Hanoi and spoke to the new bureau chief about how long he planned on staying. I reasoned that maybe I could come back to Hanoi and pick up where I had left off. It was the last place I could remember being happy.

It was mid-November when my vacation ended. I headed back to Abidjan. With every hour that brought me closer to the Ivory Coast, I could feel my chest get tighter and my patience grow shorter.

I returned to work feeling a little more rested than when I had left, but I promised myself I'd avoid wars to keep my sanity intact. In the end, *Time* did not want to hire me, and I gave up looking, figuring I'd just quietly ride out the remainder of my three-year posting in Abidjan. However, my resolve weakened quickly when the lure of more travel presented itself.

In early December I headed down to Cape Town, South Africa, to attend a conference of the AP's bureau chiefs from Africa. This was followed by a trip to Mali to cover its vaccination program, and a detour from that to an Organization of African Unity (OAU) conference in Burkina Faso. I would try to search out positive stories. But no wars, I vowed, no more wars.

ON MY LAST NIGHT IN CAPE TOWN, after the AP conference, we had all gone out for an elaborate dinner of endive salad, ostrich steaks, and South African merlot. Afterward, I sat up late in the hotel bar with Terry Leonard, the AP's South Africa bureau chief. After one too many vodka-and-tonics, we discussed the many dilemmas journalists face when covering war. Since he was a much more senior journalist than I was, I hoped Terry could help me with my inner turmoil, nightmares, and mood swings. I no longer believed I was doing any good as a journalist in war zones. I'd do better to quit and become a relief worker, I said.

Terry tried to encourage me, reminding me that aid workers and the world would never know about Africa's tragedies unless we were there to report the news.

At the end of the conversation I took a final sip of my drink. The ice cubes rattled in the bottom of the glass. I leaned toward Terry, took a drag of my cigarette, and said, "My problem is that I just don't want to send anybody into a war zone. What if they were hurt or killed? I just couldn't live with myself."

I know now that this was largely a front for the truth—I was an adrenaline junkie getting high on the thrill of going to war zones and I didn't want anybody else taking my fix. Wars were mine; I was guarding them like a heroin addict protecting his stash. It didn't matter what promises I made to myself about keeping away from the front lines; my addiction seemed stronger than my dread.

At the OAU peace conference, Sierra Leone's president Ahmed Tejan Kabbah had appealed for help in containing the increasing hit-and-run attacks by the Revolutionary United Front in his country. Indeed, there were reports of RUF rebels pushing toward the capital, Freetown. When I returned to Abidjan, I began to monitor the situation in Sierra Leone on an hourly basis.

# 8

# INTO "THE WHITE MAN'S GRAVE"

LIKE VINES HANGING FROM A TREE, long strands of glittering silver tinsel dangled over the man's outstretched arms. His festive bunting swayed in the breeze made by the passing cars along rue des Jardins. Wearing faded jeans and a threadbare orange tank top, this African Santa Claus sported mirrored sunglasses that hid his eyes, lending a bug-like quality to his face. It was 29°C under a merciless sun, but Santa's head was snug under a cheery red stocking cap replete with fur trim and a white pompom. His chin was covered with a thick beard of dirty cotton balls clumped together with glue. On the way home from the bureau I spotted Old Saint Nick and pulled over to buy a string of tinsel for my tree.

At my home in Deux Plateaux, I tried my best to celebrate Christmas, but a year's worth of death and carnage had robbed me of my Yuletide spirit. I listlessly shopped for a small plastic tree and draped it with a string of multi-colored lights, but when I surveyed my handiwork the effect was more Fu's House of Chow Mein than Kringle's North Pole Emporium.

On Christmas morning before work I wolfed down a quick plate of scrambled eggs and a bowl of rice (a lingering habit from my time in Asia) and then tore open the gifts my parents and sister had sent me: a travel alarm clock, a couple of videos (which I never found time to watch), and a small stuffed Santa Claus, his head peeking out of a red stocking squeezed into the corner of the cardboard FedEx box. The box smelled faintly of peppermint sticks and Christmas potpourri. Amid the bits and scraps of wrapping paper strewn across my floor—a Rudolph here and a Grinch there—I let my mind wander homeward to Christmas with my parents: evenings in front of a roaring fire at the house in Nova Scotia, while waves pounded the shoreline.

I roused myself from my reverie and decided to give my parents a call. I chatted briefly with everyone, exchanging holiday greetings. But my heart swelled with homesickness.

"I'm thinking of coming home for Dad's birthday," I told my mom. My father's sixtieth birthday was coming up on January 6. My mother and sister had planned a small but significant family dinner party. I felt I should really be there, but shortly after I hung up the phone around noon, it rang, this time with a call from the AP bureau in London.

"We just heard from Clarence," I was told. "He wants you to call him immediately."

Clarence Roy-Macaulay, the AP's Freetown stringer, often

called London (which was easier to reach by phone than Abidjan) to alert the desk that he had urgent news to report.

*Everything's urgent to Clarence,* I grumbled to myself. Nevertheless, I went into my office at the back of the bungalow, to make the call.

"Ah yes. Hello, sir," Clarence said with the proper formality of an African who had grown up in a British colony. "I've just interviewed Sam Bockarie. He says the RUF will overrun Freetown by New Year's Day."

I asked Clarence for more details and scribbled the notes onto a loose piece of foolscap lying on the desk.

"OK, thanks, Clarence. Let me go and get this on the wire right now."

"Merry Christmas, sir," Clarence said as I hung up.

I jumped into my black Suzuki Samurai and sped the two kilometers from my house to the bureau, where I sat down at a newsroom computer and quickly tapped out a story from Freetown, under Clarence's byline. I then headed home and spent a restless night thinking about Sierra Leone and the mayhem that would ensue if the RUF actually retook the capital. I thought of how the rebels had been jeered and harangued, beaten and lynched by hundreds of angry villagers when the RUF was ousted from Freetown in February 1998. If the rebels came back now, just ten months later, they'd be out for revenge. I dreaded a massacre in Sierra Leone similar to the carnage in Rwanda, or an African repeat of Pol Pot's Cambodian nightmare.

Two days later, I was back in the bureau finishing up

expense reports for my December trips to Mali, Burkina Faso, and the bureau chiefs' conference in South Africa. The phone rang. It was Myles calling from Nairobi. His voice faded in and out through the crackling static of the colonial-era trans-African phone line. He said he was mulling over whether to come to West Africa to cover the threat of renewed war in Sierra Leone.

"I dunno," I said. "I can't believe the RUF will get past the Nigerians."

Over the next several days, however, the rebels pushed their way to the outskirts of Freetown, their tenacity surprising everyone, me included. Just as I had feared, they left a fresh path of killing and maiming in their wake.

A few days before New Year's Eve, Myles and Brennan arrived in Abidjan. Brennan was filling in for David, who was in the United States visiting his ailing grandmother in Iowa. Although all commercial flights to Freetown had been canceled, Myles and Brennan kept working at finding a charter airline that would take us to Sierra Leone's capital. Everyday, Myles, Brennan, and I would pack our bags into two taxis and head off to the airport in the hope of finding a flight chartered by aid workers, but we had no luck. Even the daredevil charter pilots were refusing to go. And each day when we couldn't find a flight, I felt as if I'd been issued a reprieve.

I didn't say anything to Myles or Brennan, but I dreaded the thought of going to Freetown. A feeling of doom was gnawing at my stomach. Maybe I still needed my war zone adrenaline fix, but it wasn't getting me high any more. I'd already made up my mind that Sierra Leone would be my last assignment for the AP in West Africa. I would request a transfer once I got back to Abidjan.

WHEN DAVID RETURNED to the office after his trip to the United States, he could see the aggravation and tension in our faces. Since there were no flights in the offing, he suggested that we take a few hours off and spend the afternoon at a local go-cart track run by Lebanese expatriates. David, Brennan, Myles, and I all met at the track, where we donned helmets and climbed into souped-up go-carts and vented our pent-up frustrations on the track. It was about the fifth lap when I watched Myles roar past me on a sharp hairpin turn. He looked over his shoulder and flashed his trademark grin while giving me the finger. Feeling like a kid, I laughed myself silly that afternoon.

After the races, we drank beers and retold our racing stories with bravado, as if we had each just won the Indy 500. For that afternoon Sierra Leone was forgotten. But reality came back quickly the next day, January 6, 1999—my father's sixtieth birthday. Brennan headed back to Nairobi, while Myles chased down a rumor that Reuters TV and several print reporters had managed to charter a plane to Freetown. Myles's competitive instincts kicked in and he resolved to get us to Freetown. I no longer cared about the competition. *Good. Let Reuters have the story,* I thought.

Myles gave me the number for the charter airline carrying Reuters and instructed me to call them to see if we could also squeeze aboard the flight. I went to my office and sat staring at the phone. Thirty minutes passed before Myles poked his head through the doorway.

"Did you get 'em?" he asked like an excited kid. "What'd they say? Can we go?"

"The lines are busy," I muttered, looking away so my eyes wouldn't betray my lie.

"Damn! Keep trying."

After another half hour, I gave in. Picking up the phone, I dialed the number for Air Ivoire and asked about the Reuters charter flight.

*"Ils sont déjà partis,"* I was told.

I sighed in relief. My luck had held for another day.

Feigning a crestfallen look, I delivered the news to Myles and David, who were in the newsroom playing a computer game while phoning around for alternative transportation to Freetown. Then I returned to my office and began unpacking my bags. An hour later, Myles bounded in.

"Get your bags. We're going! We've got a flight," he said energetically.

We gathered up our bags, including Myles's large trunks of television equipment, hailed two orange taxis, and sped off for the highway. Since we had done this every day for the past week only to be turned away at the airport, I was skeptical that we'd actually get on a plane bound for Freetown.

THE LANDING GEAR on the white Beech King Air folded into the plane's belly with a mechanical clunk as the aircraft cleared the coconut groves at the end of the long runway.

The turboprops whined as we steadily climbed above the thin, hazy clouds hovering over Abidjan. We settled back in our seats for the ninety-minute flight that would take us around the southernmost part of the great bulge of Western Africa—over the Ivory Coast and Liberia and then north up the coast to Sierra Leone.

"So, what do you think it's going to be like?" I asked hesitantly. Saying nothing, David looked at me, shrugged, and then turned to gaze distantly out the window.

"This one could get pretty bad," Myles said. "These fuckers are insane, man."

Then, as if compelled to bare his soul, or confess his sins, Myles began a tell-all monologue: childhood secrets, his love life, and his run-ins with the law back in the United States, including a brief stint as an inmate on drug-related charges at Riker's Island in New York. Myles talked about being a tough kid growing up in New York. He told us how he got tattoos at Riker's to stave off beatings from the bigger inmates. He lamented a difficult relationship with his estranged father and spoke adoringly about his mother, Hanne, a bohemian spirit and artist who had raised him through good and difficult times. Hanne was clearly the inspiring force behind Myles's love of life.

As I listened, I wondered why he felt the need to pour it all out this way. I looked questioningly at David, but he merely shrugged again. Much later, it would occur to me that Myles, too, might have had a premonition about the ill-fated Freetown assignment.

The plane banked hard to the right, making a 180-degree

turn along the coast. The choppy ocean below twinkled with sunshine. When we descended, the lush green carpet below resolved into the finer detail of palm trees, mangroves, and thick jungle foliage containing every imaginable shade of green. As we neared our final descent, the co-pilot emerged from the cockpit.

"The tower is refusing to give us landing rights," he said.

*Yes!* I thought.

"They want to know who you are. What should I tell them?"

*Nothing. Let's just turn back,* I suggested hopefully in my head.

"Tell 'em we're reporters from America," Myles answered.

My racing heart slowed and my spirits sank as I realized the airport authorities had accepted Myles's answer. The airplane's rubber tires screeched in protest as we touched down on the hot tarmac. The smell of diesel and cordite was thick over the airport, caught up in the fine cloud of dust that swirled over the town of Lungi. David and I quickly unloaded our bags as Myles chatted with the pilot.

"Just checking to see if he'd come back to pick us up if things get messy," Myles explained later, with a grin on his face. I was never quite sure whether or not he was serious.

The airport terminal building was swarming with Nigerian soldiers and civilian refugees trying to catch an evacuation flight out of the country. Myles, David, and I stood in line with a group of other journalists, including the BBC's Mark Doyle and the crew from Reuters that had arrived about an hour before us. The same gray-haired immigration officer I had met in March the year before took our passports and stamped us into the country. I noticed that his armless clock was missing from the water-stained wall.

"How dee bodee now?" I asked.

He smiled politely, but did not answer.

A Nigerian Alpha jet thundered in for a landing, its engine thrusters growling into the palms that sheltered the airstrip from the nearby ocean. The jet taxied slowly toward the terminal building where the long, sagging blades of a Russian-made Mi-8 helicopter were beginning to turn slowly. The helicopter's gyros built to a high-pitched whine until the propeller blades began to beat, *thump, thump, thump,* against the humid sea air. Once airborne, the helicopter gracefully lifted its nose gear from the tarmac and hovered over the end of the runway. I watched as, tail high in the air, the helicopter roared off toward Freetown, several kilometers across the ocean inlet that separates the Lungi peninsula from the capital.

BY EARLY AFTERNOON, six or seven foreign reporters, now including Agence France-Presse correspondent Michèle Leridon, who had arrived on the Reuters flight, were gathered together at the airport to seek out lodgings for the night. It quickly became apparent that we would only get as far as Lungi on this day. I didn't know it at the time, but January 6 was the day RUF rebels came storming into Freetown, overrunning Nigerian positions and destroying everything in their path. They called it "Operation Kill Every Living Thing."

Mark Doyle knew of a hotel near the airport where we could stay until we managed to get to Freetown. We crammed into several cars and sped off to the Lungi Coco Beach Hotel and Resort. David and I shared a room while Myles took the room next door and set up his portable editing suite. I wandered over to his room and watched as he began reviewing the video footage he had shot at the airport—troops in formation, jets screaming in for landing and roaring out on takeoff. He had also filmed clusters of refugees unloading from the Mi-8 that was running evacuation flights almost around the clock. As we watched the footage, the helicopter's thumping roar grew louder and louder. I realized it was hovering just offshore, a few hundred meters from Myles's window. Having grown up with images of the Vietnam War, I was captivated by the mystique of helicopters—their power and dragonfly grace. I dashed out to Myles's balcony and watched the enormous aircraft kick up a whirlwind of sand and dust. A fine mist of water swirled up from the ocean surface as palm fronds whipped back and fourth in the gusty wind. Myles stood by my shoulder, filming the helicopter as it moved nearer to the beach.

David and I stayed near the hotel most of the day, while Myles returned to the airport to ask the Mi-8 pilot if we could hitch a ride to Freetown during one of the evacuation runs.

It was just past eleven at night when I set up the satellite phone's dish on the balcony. I moved quietly to avoid waking David. I sat cross-legged on the balcony floor and dialed my parents' number in Toronto.

"Hi, Mom. It's me. Is Dad home from work yet?" I shooed a swarm of mosquitoes and gnats away from my face.

"Hello?" my father answered. "Oh, hi, Ian."

"Hi, Dad. I just wanted to give you a quick call to wish you a happy sixtieth birthday."

Laughter burst out in the background.

Holding the phone's handset away from his mouth, my father rebuked his guests. "Shhh," he hissed. "It's Ian. He's calling from Africa."

"Where are you, son?" he asked me. "You calling from Abidjan?"

"I just got to Sierra Leone this afternoon," I answered reluctantly. I had always avoided telling my parents when I was going to a war zone. "I'm at the airport still trying to get to the capital."

My father was silent. I could hear his sister Heather laughing. I pictured the dining room table where we had celebrated so many birthdays and anniversaries before.

Finally my father's voice came back over the phone.

"Just promise me one thing," he said. "Promise me you won't go to Freetown."

I didn't respond.

I WOKE WITH A HEADACHE the next day, the result of too much beer and far too many cigarettes over dinner the night before. The sun was especially blinding on the morning of January 7, except offshore, where a thick haze

hovered a few feet over the water on the beachfront—
looking like a world seen through orange-colored cheese-
cloth. We headed back to the airport the next morning and
I began gleaning as much of a story as I could.

*This isn't so bad,* I thought. *I can report the story from
here.*

I interviewed villagers from the town of Lungi, many of
whom had been in Freetown just days before the RUF
offensive. I managed to buttonhole James Jonah, a cabinet
minister, who admitted the rebel offensive "came as a
surprise." For the latest developments in Freetown proper,
I tuned my Walkman to the state-controlled FM 98.1. For
most of the morning I cobbled together bits and pieces of
the story to file back to Abidjan, where it would be
retransmitted to New York and London. One thing had
become tragically obvious: raping, murdering, and looting
rebels had overrun Freetown, while the ECOMOG West
African coalition force charged with defending the
government was panicked and in disarray.

Standing in the sun outside the airport terminal building, I picked up the handset of my sat phone and dialed
the number for Sam "Mosquito" Bockarie, the rebel
commander leading this latest RUF offensive. In fact I had
already interviewed him several times during my first
twelve hours in Sierra Leone.

"Mr. Bockarie's line. This is Martin. May I help you?"
The voice had the prim accent of an Oxford scholar.

"Hi, Martin. It's Ian Stewart from the AP again. Is Mr.
Bockarie there?"

"One moment, Mr. Stewart. He's speaking to the BBC in London right now."

Squinting against the bright sun, I waited and watched as more Alpha jets took off toward Freetown on air strike missions. After a moment or two, a large white United Nations helicopter settled down on the tarmac. Two UN military observers dressed in smart full uniforms stepped off the aircraft, followed by several men in suits and dark sunglasses. Finally, President Ahmed Tejan Kabbah himself stepped onto the tarmac and walked toward the airport's VIP lounge, his white robes flapping in the breeze. The military attachés—an Indian and a Pakistani major—approached me.

"Sir. We are in most urgent need of your telephone," said the Pakistani officer.

"Hi, Ian. I'm Bockarie," said the voice on the other end of the line.

"Mr. Bockarie, I'm very sorry. Can you hold on for one second?"

"Yes, OK."

I held the handset away from my face and spoke to the Indian and Pakistani officers. "I'll let you have the phone in about five minutes. I'm just interviewing Sam Bockarie right now."

"Mosquito?" the Indian said with a look of impressed astonishment. He eyed his Pakistani counterpart, who reacted in a similar fashion.

"Ask him if he'd be willing to negotiate a ceasefire," the Pakistani eagerly said to me.

"Ask him if he'd like to speak with President Kabbah," the Indian said.

I asked both questions, but Bockarie dismissed the proposals without discussion. "We are not going to allow ECOMOG to bomb our people and kill our people any more," he said defiantly.

After the phone interview with Bockarie, one of Kabbah's aides approached the small gathering of journalists. "The president will hold a press conference after lunch in the VIP lounge," he said.

*Great,* I thought. *If the president is here and willing to give press conferences, I'm better off here than in Freetown,* I reasoned. But in my heart I knew that the real story—the story I had come to Africa for—lay with the bodies in the shattered streets of the capital.

Around lunchtime, the cluster of reporters and photographers from AFP, Reuters, the BBC, and AP met in the abandoned departure lounge at the Lungi airport. We all sat on the blue plastic seats by the wall. I sat at the far end and gave a bemused chuckle at the brightly colored tourism posters on the walls.

"Discover Sierra Leone Tours: sponsored by Hotel Sofitel," advertised one large yellow poster trimmed with idyllic palm trees. A resort poster touted beachfront property, guides, car rentals, and a spa replete with sauna and swimming pool.

*Who the hell would come here for a vacation?* I wondered. I thought back to one of my favorite books, P. J. O'Rourke's *Holidays in Hell.*

Myles showed up a few minutes later with a big tray of food—an overflowing bowl of rice and a plastic bowl filled with greasy chicken stew. A small Sierra Leonean man—an airport porter now out of work—shuffled in on Myles's heels, carrying a large red cooler of cold soft drinks and beer. We all began to eat. I cracked open an Orange Crush and grabbed a spoon. Having skipped breakfast that morning, I was ravenous. I slopped a large dollop of stew down the front of my baggy, green pants and onto my prized yellow Foreign Correspondents' Club T-shirt.

After lunch, Myles and I explored the cavernous airport building. Like two mischievous kids, we tromped around as if we owned the place, climbing over the luggage conveyer belts and pretending to man the customs booths.

"Anything to declare, sir?" I asked in an officious baritone.

"Just this bomb," Myles chuckled in reply. After a moment of goofing around with the customs officers' rubber stamps, he wandered off.

"Yo, Ian!" Myles called out to me, his voice echoing down an empty corridor. "Check these out."

I found him in a small office that had once served as an airport medical clinic. Myles was sitting in a rusting old wheelchair, the rubber from its wheels almost worn off. An equally decrepit chair sat beside him. Grinning broadly, he looked up at me.

"Race ya!"

"I'll kick your ass, man," I taunted him, lowering myself into the creaky chair.

We wheeled across the large black-and-white-checked

floor tiles until we were back at the departure lounge. Everyone had gone back outside except David, who took a turn in my wheelchair and then snapped photos of Myles teaching me how to pull a wheelie.

After lunch, we were summoned to the president for the promised press conference. Armed guards led the small corps of reporters to Kabbah. On the front steps of the VIP lounge—the veranda where I had first encountered Julius Spencer in March 1998—Myles spotted the ECOMOG commander, General Timothy Shelpidi, and asked him how we could get to Freetown.

"Nobody's going to Freetown just now," Shelpidi said.

"What about on the Mi-8?" Myles suggested helpfully.

"You can talk to the pilot, but I don't think you should go in right now," Shelpidi said.

Inside the dimly lit but well-air-conditioned VIP lounge, Kabbah laid out the situation in Freetown. The eastern and central parts of the city had been overrun. The State House had been captured and set on fire. ECOMOG forces now controlled only the Aberdeen peninsula in western Freetown. Kabbah lashed out at the indiscriminate violence of the RUF. Rebels had been randomly killing civilians and ECOMOG troops alike. They had torched scores of homes and other buildings.

The president told the small assembly of reporters that he had met with Foday Sankoh, the Revolutionary United Front's condemned leader. Sankoh was still awaiting his execution for treason, and most people believed the January 1999 RUF offensive had been orchestrated to free the rebel patriarch before the government carried out the death sentence. Kabbah said Sankoh would call on his troops to halt the attack.

"We both agreed to the need to stop this carnage and destruction of our very limited infrastructure," Kabbah said.

After the press conference, we regrouped outside. Myles wandered over to the crew of the Mi-8. I watched him chat with them while I called Tim Sullivan in Abidjan to dictate Kabbah's quotes for an updated version of the story I had filed in the morning. From a short distance, I watched Myles shake hands with the pilot.

*Shit,* I thought. *He's got us onto the helicopter.*

Tim interrupted my train of thought.

"Is David around? New York is looking for him. Can I talk to him for a minute?"

I motioned to David to come and take the phone. David snapped a couple of pictures of me on the phone in front of the Mi-8.

Myles smiled eagerly as he walked over to us. "OK," he said. "They'll take us now."

*God dammit!* I thought. *I'm staying right here.*

But, like David, I scrambled to get my gear together, collecting my blue backpack and my laptop and my sat phone. We piled into the helicopter's dank hold and sat on canvas seats along the sides of the aircraft. It had been ferrying load after load of refugees out of Freetown, and the helicopter's belly reeked of sweat and fear. Michèle from AFP, Mark Doyle from the BBC, and the Reuters crew followed us in through the rear drop-down door. A heavy-set soldier in khaki-green fatigues and long, flowing silver hair stood in the side doorway. He gripped his M-60 machine gun as the helicopter's gyros spun, building to a high-pitched whine as they turned.

Mark looked at me.

"Are you sure about this?" he asked.

*Fuck, no,* I thought, my head eagerly nodding yes.

Mark undid his seatbelt and scampered for the door. He looked at me one last time and shouted over the din of the helicopter's rotors.

"You're crazy, you know!" He jumped out to the tarmac and was gone.

INSIDE THE HELICOPTER, the thumping rotors produced a deafening roar that made conversation impossible. I sat pensively and watched Myles and David photograph Freetown's low-rise skyline as we thundered across the ocean inlet that separated Lungi from Freetown. We zipped along just two hundred meters above the ocean surface. Waves and lurking shadows flew past, giving the aquamarine water a sinister appearance.

All along Freetown's eleven-kilometer waterfront, fires burned in the aftermath of an arson campaign by the RUF designed to force the city's population into the streets. Plumes of acrid black smoke hovered over the beachfront near the water. As we got closer, I recognized the smell of burning rubber tires mixed with the campfire aroma of burning wood. Freetown had become a massive bonfire around which the child and teenaged rebels danced and howled, firing their assault rifles into the air and hurling bricks at windows and shuttered buildings alike.

In a storm of dust, the helicopter settled to the ground, using an empty soccer pitch near the Mammy Yoko Hotel in Freetown's Aberdeen peninsula. I stood in the rear of the craft and grabbed bags and cases of television gear, tossing them to David, who pitched them out the door to Myles. I had stalled as long as I could.

*This is it,* I thought. *I can just stay on board and fly back to Lungi or stay here and do my job.*

"You coming?" I heard David shout at me over the still-throbbing rotors. He motioned to the door with his head and jumped the few feet to the ground below. I followed right after him.

The three of us stood and watched as the gunman, whom David and I had nicknamed Cocheese, gave us a wry grin and waved as the helicopter slowly lifted away. David stared vacantly into the distance where the Mi-8 had headed. Its thumping grew faint and finally the air fell still and quiet.

"I wonder if he was saying 'good luck' or 'you're fucked'?" David said.

As Myles began gathering our gear, a Sierra Leonean in green fatigues walked up to us from the nearby parking lot of the Mammy Yoko Hotel. Waving his AK-47 at us, he shouted, "Who are you? What you doing here? You have to leave!"

"Whoa, man," Myles said, raising his hands to show we were not hostile.

The man approached, introducing himself as Muhammad, a Nigerian lieutenant with ECOMOG. I knew this was a lie, since his uniform was missing the ECOMOG insignia. But I wasn't about to question a man in a war zone pointing an AK-47 at my chest at point-blank range. I later learned that Muhammad was an officer with the Freetown paramilitary police force.

"I have no authorization for you to be here," he said. "You are going to have to leave."

"How?" I asked. "You want us to swim back to Lungi?"

"I'll radio for the helicopter to come back," he said, raising his walkie-talkie to his mouth. It crackled with static electricity as he spoke into it. His words were quick, though I couldn't make them out since he had turned his back while speaking.

"Hang on, hang on a minute," said Myles. "Can't we work something out?"

*Shut up, Myles,* I thought. *Let's just get out of here.*

Muhammad walked off with Myles trotting along beside him, offering a cigarette and lighting another for himself. David and I waited with Michèle and the two Reuters staffers, Jeff, a Kenyan-American television producer, and Clothaire Achi, an Ivorian photographer from the Abidjan bureau. After about ten minutes, Myles and Muhammad returned, walking arm in arm.

"It's all set," Myles said encouragingly. "Muhammad's going to get a car and take us all to the Cape Sierra, where he'll help get us rooms."

We piled into three cars and headed off to the Cape

Sierra, where once again David and I shared a room. I watched as Myles discreetly slipped several hundred dollars into Muhammad's hand.

Later that afternoon, Myles, David, and I set out to interview some people from the shantytown near the Cape Sierra. Since it was well within the Aberdeen district controlled by ECOMOG, it was a safe way to get color and quotes for my story. Out in the parking lot, Myles found a young man named Sharif who agreed to drive us the few hundred meters down dirt roads to the shantytown.

An Alpha jet screamed as it flew overhead. Within minutes, we were in the heart of a little village of clapboard homes and old colonial brick houses that were now covered with moss. David and Myles split up to photograph and video the area. Dust kicking up at my boot heels, I marched down the road, attracting a small gathering of children that blossomed into a throng of curious villagers. I felt like the Pied Piper.

"Hello, mistah! Hello, sir. Mistah, hey, mistah!" they shouted and pranced around, trying to grab my attention. I smiled at the children, but said nothing. I walked up to a house where a matronly woman sat in a rocking chair on the rotting wooden porch. A brood of children surrounded her. Behind her stood two men, a father and son. The father had a stubbly gray beard. The son wore jeans and had his hair cropped short to the scalp. I walked up, my entourage of gawking children following my every step.

"Hello. My name is Ian Stewart," I called out to the men

on the porch. "I'm a reporter for an American news service. I wonder if I can talk to you for a minute?"

The son moved to the railing of the porch and leaned down toward me.

"Are you from BBC?" he asked.

"No. I'm from the Associated Press. It's an American news service like the BBC," I said, knowing that in much of Africa the BBC World Service reigns supreme among foreign news organizations.

"OK. What do you want to know?" said the son. His father moved closer as the crowd of children pushed in around me to be able to hear.

"What do you think of the rebels now that they are coming back?" I asked, my attentive audience of children hissing and booing the word "rebels."

"I hate them," said the son.

"We all hate them," the woman in the chair interjected.

I scribbled in my notebook. "Can you tell me why?"

"You ask why?" the son said, his voice now hinting at anger and exasperation. "I came to Freetown after the rebels attacked my hometown," he continued.

"Where was that?" I asked.

"I come from Bo."

I wrote the town's name in my notebook and kept scribbling as he spoke.

"These rebels came into my home—" he began, his voice faltering. His father put a supportive arm around the young man.

"They grabbed my wife," the son continued. "She was with baby." He motioned a round belly with his hands.

The rebels asked him, "Is it a boy or a girl?" The son had shaken his head and said he didn't know.

"Wouldn't you like to know?" one of them asked. As he told the story, the son shook his head, no. His father pulled him closer with his arm.

The son continued: one of the two rebels aimed his AK-47 at his head while the other held the now screaming woman to the dirt floor of their home. He pulled out a hunting knife and plunged it into her pregnant, bulging belly.

"She screamed and cried for them to stop," the son told me in a halting, breathless voice.

But the rebel continued to cut her open until he pulled out a seven-month-old fetus, dead of the stab wounds.

"The rebel said. 'I'm sorry, you have a girl.'" Then he tossed the fetus aside and slit the woman's throat.

I stared at my feet for a moment that felt like an eternity. The son and father backed away from the railing and stood against the front door. The son folded his arms in front of his chest, his face contorted with anger and grief.

Now feeling like an unwelcome intruder, I tucked my notebook into my back pocket and backed away from the porch, thanking them as I left. The cluster of children and curious neighbors now joined me in the middle of the road. We stood for a moment as I interviewed several other people for their opinions about the rebels and why the world wasn't coming to the rescue of Sierra Leone.

An army jeep quickly turned a corner up ahead and sped toward us. A young Nigerian officer stepped out once it stopped. "You've got to clear out of here," he said to me and the crowd of villagers. An Alpha jet screeched overhead again.

"They spotted the crowd and don't know whether or not you are rebels," the officer explained, pointing toward the jet. "They are going to bomb this spot in ten minutes if the crowd doesn't disperse."

We hustled to our car, Myles and David catching up quickly when they saw me running toward Sharif's white SUV. When we got to the hotel, I wrote up my notes and filed a feature story entitled "City of War."

OVER THE NEXT TWO DAYS, David, Myles, and I convinced Sharif to take us further into the city, away from the relative safety of Aberdeen. We made it as far as the ECOMOG checkpoints on the other side of the Aberdeen peninsula bridge, but we were repeatedly turned back and ordered to return to the hotel. On Saturday, January 9, Myles was fed up with this restricted access to the war. He clamored for pictures of combat. We climbed out a side window to the roof of the Cape Sierra Hotel and watched as screaming Alpha jets passed overhead and circled over greater Freetown. I couldn't see the shells fall, but the impact of the 500-pound bombs shook the roof of the Cape Sierra more than five kilometers away. Black smoke billowed up and over the part of town that housed the central power station. Myles filmed as I took notes and David snapped photos. Our Reuters and AFP competitors were nowhere in sight. With little else to do, I lounged around the hotel, slowly writing a dispatch from the snippets of news I heard on the radio, including a statement by Foday Sankoh, broadcast on state radio, calling on the rebels to lay down their arms.

I called Sam Bockarie for his reaction.

"It's a trick," he said.

I skipped dinner and worked well into the evening, writing and updating my story. Myles brought me cold beers several times during the day, stopping in to visit, chat, and smoke my cigarettes. I filed my story by eight in the evening (three in the afternoon, New York time). I waited an hour before calling New York to check whether there were any editing questions.

"It hasn't been edited yet," I was told.

"Isn't it on the budget?" I asked. The "budget" was the AP's daily list of the top stories on the wire.

"Nope," I was told. "The General Desk feels it's just another story about a little war in Africa."

"Well, if that's how they feel, then what the fuck am I doing here risking my life?" I barked back. I calmed down as quickly as I had snapped. "I'm sorry. I know it's not your fault. I'm just frustrated and tired," I said.

I hung up the phone, drank the last of my beer, and took a final long drag from my cigarette before stubbing it out in the overflowing ashtray. I lay down to read a bit of the Graham Greene novel *The Heart of the Matter* (the tale of an illicit love affair in colonial Sierra Leone) that I had brought with me. I skimmed a few pages until I began to feel sleepy, but before turning out the light I circled a line that struck me as interesting: "Perhaps you'd like to know a bit about what I'm doing in 'the white man's grave.'"

I turned out the light. David was already asleep. I listened to him snore and counted artillery explosions through the night. The ocean breeze kept me cool, but I couldn't sleep.

# 9

# A SUNDAY DRIVE

WITH THE THUD of a wooden door slamming shut, an artillery shell crashed down near the Cape Sierra Hotel. My bleary eyes popped open with the blast's echoing boom. Slowly, I dragged myself out of bed and peered out the window into the brilliant sunlight dancing off the ocean surf. I gazed east down the coastline; smoke still curled up from the many fires gutting Freetown's commercial district.

Along with mortar and artillery explosions, gunfire popped and crackled in the distance. War suddenly seemed very real and uncomfortably near in the unblinking light of day. I began to feel a flutter of panic in my stomach. *Maybe Aberdeen has been overrun.*

"David! Hey, David! Wake up!" I snapped.

"What's going on?" David asked as he sat up.

"I dunno. Sounds like things are getting worse. I'm just going to check now." I untangled the headphone wire of my Walkman and began tuning to the ECOMOG-controlled radio station in Freetown. I turned the knob and listened to varying forms of static that sounded like rain, sizzling bacon, or whining flies zipping near and far from my ears. Finally, I hit FM 98.1. In a singsong blend of West African English and Sierra Leonean Krio, the news anchor announced that rebel forces had broken open the city's main prison and freed scores of their comrades.

"Everybody must stay at home today. *No go in dee streets,*" the announcer said. "*ECOMOG say dee rebel-man be in dee streets.*"

I sat down at my laptop and began tapping out a quick update for the wire—just enough to freshen the story with a "Sunday" in the lead paragraph. I figured I'd be back by mid-afternoon to file a more comprehensive report. I transmitted the story via my sat phone, and then David and I set out to find Myles and get some breakfast before heading out for the day.

I walked out of my air-conditioned room into a heavy curtain of humidity that smothered my face. I was still half asleep. In a pool of sweat, legs tangled in twisted, cotton sheets, I had lain awake most of the night, staring at the darkened ceiling and listening to the thudding artillery shells juxtaposed with the licking sway of the surf on the shore just below my window.

David and I headed down to the Cape Sierra's restaurant. Myles was sitting with Michèle Leridon of Agence France-Presse. Michèle was sipping coffee and picking at the hotel's runny eggs without enthusiasm while Myles scribbled in a notebook. I saw her peek over his shoulder to see what he was writing, and I took a look, too. It was a list of charter airlines and their phone numbers, including Air Ivoire, the

Abidjan company that had flown us to Sierra Leone four days earlier. Myles looked up from his notebook and flashed Michèle a wide grin. "Just in case," he said.

After a last cup of watery coffee, we gathered up our gear and headed for the parking lot. Fearing the city was about to be overrun by rebels, Sharif had refused to drive us; instead, the ever-resourceful Myles had hired Joseph Koroma to chauffeur us around Freetown. A cocoa and coffee farmer from a nearby village, Joseph hadn't been home since fighting broke out in the capital the previous week. Michèle asked if she could join us, but there was clearly no room for her in Joseph's white station wagon.

DAVID AND I CLIMBED into the backseat of Joseph's car, while Myles sat up front. Finally, I was off to find Freetown's war. For days I had listened to its destructive wrath; now I was about to see it with my own eyes. For a few hours we rolled and bumped along broken, empty streets. We traveled down Aberdeen Road, past Pirate Cove, and over the causeway that separated Aberdeen from Greater Freetown. We pushed forward past Cockle Bay, where a lone powerboat sat anchored in placid waters. Just after we had arrived, Myles had inquired into hiring that boat to get the three of us out of Aberdeen if the rebels should capture the peninsula.

Along the way, we passed huddles of gaunt, frightened-looking civilians fleeing their homes. Caught in the middle of this merciless conflict, civilians carrying what few ragged possessions they could had become human shields for the rebels—a precaution to forestall a full-out counteroffensive by the ECOMOG coalition.

By mid-morning, we were making our way down a deserted road toward a checkpoint manned by Nigerian foot soldiers armed with M-16 rifles and shoulder-held grenade launchers.

"Stop!" they yelled, one after the other. "Stop where you are! Identify yourselves!"

Joseph hesitated until Myles shouted at him to stop the car. We all lurched forward when the station wagon's brake pads gripped the wheels. From behind stacked-up sandbags, the troops peered down their rifle sights at us. Behind the barrier, six more Nigerian soldiers chatted lazily and smoked cigarettes. The troops at the bunker ordered us to approach on foot.

"Hands up!" they shouted from about fifty meters away.

We stepped cautiously toward the makeshift bunker. *What should I do with this notebook?* I thought, clutching the yellow pad in my sweaty left hand above my head. *What if they think it's a weapon of some kind?*

Slowly but deliberately, I continued to walk forward. My legs felt as heavy as cement columns.

"Pressmen!" David and Myles shouted.

"We're reporters!" I yelled, following their lead.

We approached the sandbags and presented our bags for inspection. Once satisfied that we posed no threat, the young troops began clowning around and posing for the cameras. I relaxed a little.

*These guys don't seem too tense, considering it's a war zone,* I thought.

Their antics came to an abrupt halt when a burst of
gunfire popped like a row of Chinese firecrackers beyond
our car. David, Myles, Joseph, and I darted for the cover of
a nearby drainage ditch. Raw sewage oozed around my left
boot. My heart raced like a jackhammer and I desperately
sucked in air to catch my breath. I crouched and peered
down the road in the direction of the gunfire. I tried to
steady my shaking hands long enough to light a cigarette. I
gave one to Joseph. He lit both. A deep, long drag sent a
nicotine-induced calm flowing through my body and
cleared my head. Crouched halfway up the ditch's steep
side, Myles began mocking David and me about how slow
we had been to take cover after the first shots were fired.

"You're gonna get your asses shot off like that," he teased.

Myles flicked his cigarette butt into the ditch and began
humming the tune to Bob Marley's "Buffalo Soldier." He
started to sing, using words he had made up the year before
when ECOMOG drove the RUF from Freetown: "ECOMOG
soldier. Come from Nigeria—"

After the shooting had subsided, we regrouped over by
the sandbags. Standing in the middle of the road, I
stepped back a foot or two to make room for an oncom-
ing army jeep. It was heading in the direction from which
we had come. A Nigerian colonel wearing a black army
beret and khaki uniform trimmed with gold braid and
epaulets leaned out the driver's side door. The name
"Tongo"—stenciled in faded black letters—stood out from
his chest. Colonel Tongo kicked one foot out of the open-
sided vehicle and clomped it down to the ground. He

perched half in and half out of the green jeep, waving and gesturing with his handgun like a conductor's baton as he spoke.

"Go back the way you came and get out of here!" he yelled, the barrel of his gun flipping between us and the road in the direction he wanted us to go.

"Fine with me," I muttered under my breath as we climbed back into our white station wagon and Joseph turned it around.

AS WE HEADED BACK toward the Cape Sierra, a convoy of military trucks sped past us. In the lead jeep, Julius Spencer, Sierra Leone's heavyset and bookish minister for communications, was at the wheel.

"Catch up with them," Myles urgently ordered Joseph, who quickly slammed on the brakes and once again wheeled the car around to speed after the convoy.

We chased Spencer's jeep. Flashing the headlights and blasting the horn, we managed to draw his attention and the convoy ground to a stop. We jumped out and walked over to the lead vehicle. From the gossip at the hotel, I knew that Spencer was the only government minister still in the capital. An imposing six-foot-plus character, he wore a camouflage uniform and a jungle guerrilla's floppy sun hat.

Spencer emerged from behind his steering wheel, an assault rifle slung over one shoulder. In his free hand, a walkie-talkie crackled and occasionally bleated a flurry of frantic orders, interspersed with the hollow echoes of gunfire in empty city blocks.

Smiling and relaxed, Spencer explained the government was so sure of victory that he had been dispatched to recruit volunteers to gather bodies from the streets. Left rotting for more than a week under a cooking tropical sun, the corpses would soon pose a health hazard, he said.

"This thing will be over in three, four days, tops." He gazed thoughtfully down the empty street as if proof of his claim lay just out of reach. "We are winning this war. The rebels have been defeated."

"We are now just mopping up," he added. I scribbled the words into my notebook.

Sure of the government's upper hand in the fighting, the communications minister invited us to travel along with his convoy of two jeeps, a truck of volunteer undertakers, and another truck of soldiers. Eager for pictures and details of the carnage that had engulfed the city, Myles and David readily accepted the offer. I hesitated, thinking I would rather return to my hotel room, since already I felt that I had all the material I needed for my afternoon story. As on previous occasions, however, I followed the lead set by David and Myles.

Spencer instructed Joseph to drive in the middle of the convoy, which he did until we reached a gas station where the convoy was planning to refuel. Spencer left us there and said he'd be back in twenty minutes. He sped off toward the Cape Sierra, where he intended to pick up Clothaire Achi, the Reuters photographer.

Mercilessly, the midday sun beat down on my head. My exposed forearms began to turn bright red: it somehow

seemed unmanly to wear sunscreen in a war zone. I squatted at the curb and reached into the breast pocket of my
pale gray T-shirt. Rings of sweat had stained and darkened
the armpits. I pulled out a soggy crushed pack of Marlboro
Lights. A single drop of sweat rolled down my forehead
and between my eyebrows. It hung momentarily on the tip
of my nose. I hung my head down between my bent knees,
the sweat dripping off my nose and splashing into a tiny
puddle on the gray pavement between my feet. I watched
it evaporate in the fierce heat.

For more than half an hour we waited for Spencer to
return. Eyeing the abandoned streets for signs of the rebels,
I followed the path of the Portuguese ambassador's car as it
rolled past. *Things can't be that dangerous,* I reasoned, *if
Portugal's embassy is still open.*

A mangy black stray, its tail tucked between its legs,
scampered across the street and out of another car's path.
David and I play-wrestled in the driveway of the gas station,
killing about ten minutes. Another fifteen minutes passed.
Just when Myles was beginning to worry out loud that we
had been left behind, Spencer's jeep pulled up, followed by
another jeep with Clothaire. Spencer spoke briefly into his
walkie-talkie and received a reply. Joseph positioned his jeep
back into the middle of the convoy and we set off into the
heart of Freetown.

OUR STATION WAGON had just pulled up on the crest of a
small hill. At the top of the gentle roll in the road, we
looked across into a lush green valley, in the center of which

lay Freetown's Siaka Stevens National Stadium. At first, I didn't know why we had stopped.

"Snipers!" one of the Nigerian soldiers shouted and pointed across the ravine toward the bowl-shaped stadium. A lone bullet zinged past. Then the echoing ricochets of several more flew by overhead, bouncing off the craggy escarpment on the opposite side of the road. Soon the air was filled with the dizzying sound of bursts of automatic fire. With every round, I ducked lower behind our station wagon. My heart raced with that same exhilaration I always felt whenever I came under fire.

Myles, his TV camera propped up on his shoulder, was several yards ahead of me. He squatted in the grass by the side of the road, doing what Myles Tierney did best— capturing on video the stark terror of combat. Looking away from his viewfinder, he peered back at me over his shoulder. His face beamed with the excitement of a young child who has discovered the simultaneous terror and thrill of getting caught breaking the rules. I breathed more easily when Myles grinned at me; his smile assured me, saying, *It's cool, man. Everything's going to be fine.*

Up the road, Spencer stomped around. "Who is that?" I heard him demand impatiently into his walkie-talkie. "Who's firing at us?"

"We're not sure," one of the commanders behind him answered. He raised a pair of binoculars to his eyes and scanned the stacked levels of the stadium's bleachers. "I don't see anything," he told Spencer. "It could be friendly fire."

Spencer wheeled around and glowered at the young commander. "Well, find out, will you!"

The troops from the convoy had spread out, up and down the road in the ditches and tucked up beside the rocky overhang of the escarpment. Awaiting confirmation on whether the incoming fire was rebel or ECOMOG, they did not return fire.

Slowly, I crawled closer to David and Myles on the roadside, my head ducking with every incoming bullet. I marveled to myself that we had made it this far. Fear gave way to pride and a bit of the bravado that makes a war correspondent feel invincible.

It took several long seconds before the scene in front of me registered. I looked up and spotted a metallic-blue sport four-wheel drive. It was a Pajero, the kind common in the suburbs of most big cities in North America. It was directly in front of me, maybe ten feet away.

Its windshield and side windows were shattered. Tiny cubes of glass were scattered everywhere. The hood was twisted and crumpled in toward the windshield. The vehicle's interior was charred black; the seat cushions had burned down to their metal springs. A long, sticky trail of dried blood and human excrement ran from the bottom of the driver's door down onto the pavement and into the ditch where I was squatting. The raw, rancid, almost sickly sweet smell of decaying flesh wafted toward me—that stink of death still lurks in my olfactory memory today, triggered by scenes of war on the evening news or by driving past a car accident beside the road.

The two troops crouching beside me in the ditch explained that two rebels had been killed in that blue Pajero four days earlier when a rocket-propelled grenade slammed into the windshield just as the vehicle topped the hill's crest. Distracted by the grim details of death and decay on a Freetown street, I began jotting down their words about the earlier battle. I was so preoccupied that I barely noticed that the shooting had stopped and our convoy was again preparing to press forward.

WE GOT BACK INTO THE STATION WAGON. David slipped into the backseat on the passenger side; Myles and I walked around to the driver's side. Myles would now be joining us in the back, because Spencer had assigned two bodyguards to ride up front to protect us. Suffering from mild claustrophobia, I hesitated at the door to see if Myles would get in first, leaving me the seat by the door. He stalled as well. Finally I realized that he needed the window seat to shoot video. I opened the door and slid in beside David. Myles's bulk crammed in next to me. Instead of getting in, Joseph stood uneasily beside the driver's door, and suggested we return to the hotel.

"It'll be fine," Myles said, with that reassuring smile he had used to charm so many people so many times before. "We won't let anything happen to you."

Joseph reluctantly agreed, after the Nigerian bodyguards gave him encouraging nods and motioned him to get behind the wheel.

We approached downtown, moving down a slope, past

shuttered buildings, and over a short exposed bridge only a few hundred yards from the soccer stadium. It felt as if we were creeping across the bridge.

*We're sitting ducks here,* I thought. *This is WAY too dangerous.*

"Holy shit," David said in a subdued but emphatic voice. "D'you see that?"

I craned my neck to see out the back window.

"See what?"

"Those vultures eating the bodies over there."

I looked again, and spotted the group of heavy black-winged birds. One of them tugged at a strand of flesh until it snapped like a rubber band. The vulture gobbled it down.

I felt sick. My chest was heavy, as if someone were standing on it. I struggled to fill my lungs with the damp, heavy air. My shirt, saturated with sweat, stuck to my sides. Myles sat on my right. David was on my left. The added temperature of their bodies made the cramped backseat suffocating. A twinge of terror gripped me at the idea of being trapped in the car.

*I want to get out of here!* I thought frantically. *I have to get out of here!*

My thoughts hovered near panic. I shoved my elbows into Myles and David and spread my knees to claim more space. I still hadn't said a word. "Take it easy, man!" Myles finally snapped in response to my squirming. "You're in the safest seat in the car.

"If anyone starts shooting," he added as an absent after-thought, "you've got my fat body to protect you."

WE CONTINUED ALONG the abandoned street for another ten minutes or so until the convoy stopped near four rebels in jeans and flip-flops. Three of the men nervously clutched AK-47 assault rifles in their hands. One of the gunmen wore a black Oakland Raiders stocking cap and dark, black sunglasses. A second man had a knitted, rainbow-colored Rastafarian cap on his head. All four wore khaki army shirts similar to the kind worn by the ECOMOG troops. Under his unbuttoned shirt, the third gunman wore an orange-brown tank top. A black bowler hat sat askew on his head.

The Nigerians in our car ordered Joseph to stop. The rest of the convoy drove ahead about a dozen meters. One of the Nigerian bodyguards rolled down his window and leaned out to the gunmen.

"Who are you?" the bodyguard asked, his dialect instantly identifying him as Nigerian. The man in the bowler smiled. The corners of his mouth turned up as he began to chuckle to himself manically.

I sat perfectly still and held my breath. Every muscle in my body tensed, my heart pounded in my ears, and my mouth ran dry, my tongue sticking to the back of my teeth.

Myles carefully lifted his camera to his shoulder. He peered through the viewfinder.

"Oh shit," he said.

Before anyone could move, the bowler-topped rebel spun around on his heels. His AK-47 jumped in his hands; flames belched out of the thin barrel. The window beside Myles exploded as a hail of bullets tore into the side of Joseph's white station wagon. A wave of heat flooded the car.

Myles slumped forward onto his camera, blood pouring from his head and chest.

My head jolted backward, slamming into the seat. For a split second my left side went rigid, and then I slid sideways onto David's shoulder. I groaned as he pushed me to the floor in case the shooter fired again.

Suddenly I was no longer a war correspondent; we had become the story.

# 10

# WILBERFORCE

A SINGLE BULLET HAD HIT ME square in the center of my forehead, just five centimeters above what would have been a fatal hit between the eyes. I would never be able to remember the moment of being shot or the days afterward, but David and other people told me about it much later.

David pushed me to the car's floor and out of the way of more bullets if the shooter fired again. Then he slipped out and took cover behind the car. From that relatively safe vantage point he watched the next events unfold.

In the blink of an eye, the street erupted with more gunfire as the Nigerians in the lead truck returned fire, killing the shooter and another man. Both fell where they stood as scores of bullets ripped into their bodies. The two other rebels darted down the sidewalk and jumped into the burned-out shell of a Nissan hatchback. A Nigerian with a rocket-propelled grenade launcher on his shoulder took aim and squeezed the trigger. The grenade exploded with a *foosh*. It whistled, flying in a spiral toward the wrecked car. The street shook as the grenade slammed into the hatchback. On impact, it lit up the car's gutted interior like a Halloween jack-o'-lantern, killing both rebels instantly.

The convoy sped on toward Wilberforce Barracks— named for the English abolitionist William Wilberforce— in downtown Freetown. Joseph stepped on the gas and raced to keep up with the military vehicles. Dazed and badly cut by flying glass, David stood dumbfounded by the side of the road, watching blood ooze from the bodies of the dead rebels on the sidewalk. Quickly, he snapped to and began to run after the convoy, but he was already too far behind. He waved down a jeep that had been farther back in the line, and it slowed to pick him up.

David sat quietly and watched the tense Nigerian troops in the jeep. They nervously fingered the triggers on their rifles and glared at the white man perched on the backseat of their jeep. They began arguing over whose fault it was that the rebels hadn't been killed before they fired. Once at the base, David jumped out of the jeep and raced through the gates.

In the reception area of Wilberforce's cramped medical clinic, David stopped short at the sight of Myles's body on the floor. Then he spotted me writhing on the floor in my boxer shorts.

The Nigerian bodyguards from Joseph's car had dragged me from the car by my arms and left me near an examining room, where the medical staff cut away my blood-soaked pants and shirt. Reacting to my head wound, I had become combative and had tried to punch one of the Nigerians. In response, they hog-tied me at the wrists and knees.

A Nigerian army medic walked up to David and explained to him that they wanted to X-ray my head. Incoherent and oblivious to the ambush, I continued to squirm and chatter. Together they walked over and stood beside me. David finally squatted down to try to calm me.

"What happened? Where are we? Why can't we leave? Where's Myles?" David struggled to keep up with my barrage of questions. Over and over, he explained the shooting and told me that the convoy had rushed me to Wilberforce, where I could get medical treatment.

"Some flying glass cut your head. You're in shock," he said, dabbing blood away from the cuts on his own face. Unable to see the depth of the bullet hole because of the blood, initially David believed my wound was superficial. "You just hang on, man. We're trying to get you out of here."

David walked back to the medic and asked when the helicopter would arrive. ECOMOG's Mi-8 was the only way back to the international airport at Lungi. The medic shrugged and stepped away. He summoned a second soldier, and together they hefted my limp frame into an adjacent room that housed an enormous U.S. Army surplus X-ray machine. David waited alone while the medical staff scanned my head.

After the X ray was complete, I was again hog-tied. The medic and the soldier returned me to my spot on the cement floor. I cursed at the top of my lungs and fought my restraints like an animal until my wrists and ankles turned raw and red with rope burns.

"David! Cut me free, man!" I shouted, my voice cracking with panic. "You've got to help me!"

"I'm trying to help you," David said. "but you've got to stay calm."

The Nigerian medic reappeared and motioned David to come into his office.

"What's the news, doc?—" David's words trailed off as he froze in midstride. The medic was holding a profile X ray of my skull up to the window's light. It clearly showed a bullet—shockingly white against the shadowy negative image—lodged in the back of my skull. Despite the heat of the tropical day, a sudden chill ran down David's back, making him shudder involuntarily.

He looked out the office door to the floor where I continued to fight the ropes. His heart sank as he walked back toward me. He sat briefly with me, again trying to quiet my endless flood of expletives; after a moment or two, he stood up and headed outside.

"Where the fuck are you going?" I bellowed at his back. "Where's Myles?"

In the courtyard of the Wilberforce Barracks medical clinic, the sun was blinding after the room's gloomy fluorescent lighting. David put on his rose-tinted Serengeti sunglasses and looked away so nobody would see the tears rolling down his cheeks. Then he shook his head and went back inside, resolved to get me out of Freetown alive.

It didn't take long for news of the ambush to spread to the other foreign journalists in Freetown that Sunday after-

noon. Back at the Cape Sierra Hotel, Michèle Leridon, the
AFP correspondent, was sitting in the lobby, still fuming to
herself that she had not insisted on coming along with
David, Myles, and me. Suddenly Clothaire Achi, the
Reuters photographer, sprinted in the front door. Out of
breath and panicked, he was barely able to speak.

"We've been shot at!" he blurted out in French. "Myles
and Ian have been hit!"

Panting to catch his breath, he continued, "I don't even
know if they are alive. I don't know what happened to
David."

Moments later, Muhammad—the police officer we had
met when we arrived in Freetown—walked into the hotel
lobby. Grumbling that the white journalists were in the
way, he walked up to Michèle.

"I'm sorry, but your friend is dead," he said gruffly, and
then instructed Michèle and Clothaire to gather our
belongings and meet him in the parking lot.

They quickly gathered Myles's things and only the most
important items from the room David and I were sharing.
Michèle hurriedly stuffed everything into our packs and ran
out to the parking lot with Clothaire, where a car and driver
were waiting for them. They sped off for Wilberforce and
pulled up to the gate minutes later. Michèle found David
and handed him our satellite phone. Squatting in the
parking lot, David set up the phone while Michèle took a
turn watching over me. The sun shone in his eyes as he
dialed the AP in London and New York. "Myles is dead," he

said into the phone's handset in a flat, lifeless voice. "Myles is dead. Myles is dead."

There was still no word on ECOMOG's helicopter as the day dragged on. The sky turned a deep royal blue as the sun slowly sank into the Atlantic Ocean. Ribbons of orange, pink, and yellow edged the horizon, and a few stars twinkled in the twilight evening sky. David knew that nightfall in Freetown probably meant death for another journalist— the tenth in Sierra Leone in January 1999, nine of which occurred on January 10. On the day the rebels had overrun Freetown, the government had imposed a dusk-to-dawn curfew for the city, including the Lungi airport. And now the airport was just minutes from shutting down.

*He's never going to make it,* David thought as he gave me a quick glance and spoke reassuringly to me. "We'll get you out of here even if we have to swim," he quipped bravely.

"What about Myles?" I asked, and once again began chattering.

Sierra Leone's information minister, Julius Spencer, arrived at Wilberforce just after sunset. "The helicopter is on its way," he said. But, he explained, rebel fighters had pushed closer to Wilberforce over the course of the day's fighting, so the helicopter would be arriving at Cockerill, another nearby army base. A small caravan of vehicles carrying all the foreign journalists from Wilberforce to Cockerill was led through Freetown's darkening streets by Spencer's jeep. There was still no sign of the helicopter.

Once at Cockerill, David took out his notepad and a ballpoint pen. He scribbled in bold capital letters: "Myles

Tierney" on one line, "Associated Press" on the next.

And finally, "United States." He tore the sheet from his notebook and taped the page to the blue canvas bag into which Myles's body had been placed.

The journalists waited at Cockerill for about ten minutes before they heard the thumping of helicopter blades over the ongoing crackle of rifle fire and thud of artillery rounds. The helicopter's welcome black silhouette appeared against the indigo sky.

David covered my face to protect me from debris kicked up by the whirling blades. He, Michèle, and the BBC's Mark Doyle—who had come to Freetown to help out after learning of the shooting—climbed aboard, while Clothaire and his Reuters colleague lifted the backboard onto which I had been placed and positioned me in the center of the helicopter. They then hefted Myles's body bag and stowed it at the back of the helicopter near my feet. They hopped off and waved goodbye as the Mi-8's blades churned up a red dust storm and climbed away from the ground.

"What about Myles?" I screamed frantically, but I was drowned out by the roar. A Nigerian nurse sat beside me and held my left hand. The left side of my body was motionless, but the right side quaked violently. My foot began to shake and kick wildly with spasms.

The helicopter was airborne only moments before it again touched down. By now, it was pitch black outside. Above the roar of the helicopter blades, there were screams of terror and weeping as a small group of Lebanese merchants and Sierra Leonean refugees stumbled over one another to pile into the aircraft. Again it took off and headed for the narrow gap of water separating Lungi from Freetown. In ten minutes, the helicopter landed at the Lungi airport.

The refugees poured out of the helicopter and headed straight for a chartered aircraft waiting near the terminal. Myles's body was transferred to the plane, and I, still on my backboard, was laid in the aisle. Michèle kissed David goodbye and gave him one last hug before he climbed aboard the plane. Slowly it began to taxi toward the runway.

Standing near the terminal building, Michèle watched as the aircraft lifted off the ground. She followed its climb until the illuminated tail with the name "Air Ivoire" was swallowed by the night sky. A tear rolled down her cheek as she thought back to breakfast earlier in the day.

"Just in case." Myles's words echoed in her head.

The flight from Freetown was an uneventful forty-five-minute jump to Conakry, Guinea's capital. While we were in the air, Tim Sullivan, my AP colleague back in Abidjan, was arranging for another evacuation plane to pick me up in Conakry and fly me back to Abidjan, which had the best medical facilities in sub-Saharan Africa.

On the ground in Conakry, the chief customs inspector, a burly man with a large potbelly, poked his head in through the passenger door of the plane. He looked up and down the aisle and eyed David with a frown. With him were representatives from the Canadian and American embassies, who had been dispatched to the airport by the U.S. State Department in Washington, and Ottawa's Department of External Affairs.

*"Ou est le passeport pour le cadavre?"* the inspector demanded. David quickly rifled through the bags, but eventually shrugged and said he couldn't find it.

"Then you must turn around and go back to Freetown," the inspector barked in French.

The diplomats intervened and struck a deal with the customs inspector. David and I could wait on the tarmac for our evacuation flight that was en route from Abidjan. But Myles's body would have to remain at the airport to be retrieved later. The customs inspector stamped a three-hour transit visa into my passport.

The airport staff loaded Myles's body onto a luggage cart and laid me beside him. Dressed only in my boxer shorts, I noticed a warm breeze as it blew fine dust across my face and into my eyes. I rubbed at it with my right arm and bumped my head dressing. The smell of aviation fuel wafted across the airport's exposed apron. David draped a blanket over me and said, "Hang on, we're almost there." For the first time, David began to think that I might survive. But in what shape?

When the evacuation flight arrived about an hour later, I was loaded on board and again placed in the aisle. David sat a few seats away from me. Canadian diplomats had arranged for a doctor from the United Nations to join us for the 1,200-kilometer flight in case I went into shock or stopped breathing.

We were met at Abidjan's airport by Tim Sullivan, his wife, Michele—a teacher—and David's girlfriend, Cassy. They stood somberly watching as a medical team boarded the plane and slowly brought me out and loaded my back-board into a waiting ambulance. David, shaky and exhausted, slowly descended the steps from the plane. He hugged Cassy and whispered a word or two of encouragement to her.

Some twelve hours had now passed since I had been shot. The siren from the Ivorian ambulance wailed as the vehicle sped off through the busy streets toward Pisam Hospital in the city's suburbs. Tim, Michele, David, and Cassy piled into taxis and followed the ambulance to the hospital. At Pisam, the best the surgeons could do was stabilize me with sedatives to minimize my movements, which threatened to exacerbate the swelling in my brain. A catheter was inserted to collect the urine that flowed while I was under heavy sedation.

The hospital's corridors were quiet and clean. A few wooden armchairs lined the walls. Everyone waited nervously for news on my condition. Finally a doctor came out and explained there was little he and his team could do unless I was admitted for full treatment in Abidjan. I was running a perilously high risk of severe brain damage from swelling. Furthermore, the longer the slug remained in my head, the greater the threat of infection. However, having consulted with the AP's senior management in New York, who in turn were in contact with my parents, Tim made the decision to wait for a Swiss air ambulance to take me to London. The nightmare crawled by until the first light of morning peeked through the hospital windows.

By mid-morning the Swiss medical team—a nurse and surgeon—arrived in their air ambulance, a medically outfitted Hawker 800 corporate jet. The surgeon climbed down the aircraft's steps onto the hot black tarmac that baked under the building sun of equatorial Africa. The Ivorian doctor stood by a waiting ambulance and quickly briefed his Swiss colleague. Without delay, they climbed into the vehicle and sped off for Pisam. Within an hour, I had been loaded aboard the air ambulance and readied for the long flight to London.

Inside, the jet was equipped with a fully functional operating theater. A defibrillator, ventilator, emergency resuscitation kit, and CPR unit lined the sides of the narrow aircraft. The nurse and surgeon stooped to enter as they climbed aboard behind me. To ensure an uninterrupted flow of oxygen-rich air to my lungs and brain, the doctor put me on a ventilator by inserting a narrow endotracheal tube through my mouth and into my trachea.

After eleven months, nine countries, four wars, and far too many close calls, I left Africa just after noon on Monday, January 11, 1999.

# PART 2

# 11

# A 20 PERCENT CHANCE

THE REFLECTION OF the air ambulance's landing lights gleamed off the rain-soaked runway at Heathrow International Airport late Monday night. The pilot had radioed ahead for permission to land on a seldom-used runway in a remote corner of the airport that was closest to the M4 highway. The doctor on board had cautioned him that the minutes saved by not having to taxi to the terminal could make the difference between my life and death. Months later, my family and colleagues explained to me in great detail the events that unfolded in London.

It was just after 9 P.M., and the klaxon of the English ambulance wailed through London's darkened streets. I was still heavily sedated (in a chemically induced coma) when the orderlies wheeled me through the front door of the National Hospital for Neurology and Neurosurgery at central London's Queen Square. They rushed me up the elevator to the fourth floor's Surgical Intensive Care Unit (SICU). As I was wheeled into the unit, the portable respirator on my gurney beeped like a vigilant guardian each time it filled my lungs with air. My head was still covered in the dirty, turban-like dressing that the Nigerian medic had wrapped around my wound back in Sierra Leone. I lay motionless as the gurney moved past my horror-struck parents standing in the corridor. Overlooking the raccoon-mask bruising around my eyes, my mother absently noticed only the golden brown tan on my face. *He looks too healthy to be in a hospital,* she thought.

My parents had rushed to London on the first available flight, leaving my sister, Karen, behind to tie up loose ends before coming over herself. Leaving Toronto's Pearson International Airport before nine in the morning, they had landed in London just eight minutes ahead of my own flight. Not sure what to expect, they had raced to the hospital and awaited my arrival.

ALMOST THIRTY-SIX HOURS had now passed since the shooting. My brain continued to swell, threatening further damage to the fragile neocortex, which controls the immensely complicated cognitive and motor functions of the human body. I was wheeled into the radiology department for X rays and a series of CT scans, to determine what parts of my brain had been damaged by the bullet's trajectory.

Late Monday night, my neurosurgeon, James Palmer, rushed into the hospital dressed in a charcoal gray mackintosh over a tweed blazer and a dark tie. His trousers, beige and baggy, were creased at the knees. His blond hair, tousled and short, gave him a schoolboy appearance, but there was nothing boyish about his grim face and serious tone when he stepped hurriedly into the waiting room to meet my parents. They chatted politely, skirting the issue of my condition until Mr. Palmer had had time to assess the brain scans, though he knew from experience my odds were not good. The AP's Bryan Brumley, then a deputy international editor based in London, had found Mr. Palmer after a quick but intensive search for brain surgeons in English-speaking Europe. Mr. Palmer was the best, Bryan had been told over and over.

A nurse poked her head through the door of the waiting room and announced that the CT scan results and X rays were ready for the surgeon's perusal. Mr. Palmer shook hands with my mother and father and disappeared out the door, his footsteps echoing on the linoleum tiles. Holding hands for mutual support, my parents sat quietly on the wood-framed sofa under the quiet hum of the waiting room's fluorescent lighting. Tom Kent, then the AP's international editor and my boss, sat across the room and tapped away at his laptop's keyboard while reviewing the day's e-mail correspondence from news bureaus around the globe. Like my parents, Tom had caught the first available flight to London from New York once it had been determined that I would be flown to Heathrow.

About fifteen minutes later, Mr. Palmer returned to the waiting room along with an anesthetist who would be assisting with the operation. Both wore pale-green surgery scrubs and caps. The young surgeon squatted in front of my parents.

"You do realize how serious this is, don't you?" he asked in a sympathetic tone.

My parents nodded.

"Does Ian have any brothers or sisters? A spouse? Children? Is there anyone who should be here, in case?"

The last two words hung in the air. My mother gasped. Tears filled her eyes. My father's lips were pursed, his face severe with anguish.

"His sister is on her way from Toronto," my mother finally replied, her voice wavering.

"What is his outlook?" my father asked reluctantly, afraid of the answer.

"It isn't too good. I would guess he has about a twenty percent chance of surviving the first operation," Mr. Palmer said. "And if he does, he may have suffered very serious brain damage."

Jet-lagged and bleary-eyed, my parents were cruelly confronted with the horrible moral dilemmas that accompany any life-threatening injury. Could death be the lesser of evils? *What if Ian survives but needs life support? What if he survives but is no longer Ian because of brain damage?*

UNDER THE BRIGHT GLARE of the operating theater lights, Mr. Palmer took one last look at the CT scans of my brain. The bullet's path was thin and relatively straight down the brain's midline between the left and right hemispheres. He anticipated that most of the damage would turn out to be the result of swelling after the bullet's concussive blow.

He began by slicing a deep incision that started just above my right temple, arched over the top of my head and stopped about four centimeters from the left temple. The nurse assisting him dabbed with a gauze pad at blood seeping from the fresh incision. With gloved hands, he gingerly peeled the skin away from my forehead, exposing my skull and the jagged bullet hole, about one and a half centimeters in diameter.

Like a blacksmith's bellows, the respirator heaved and the heart monitor chirped as Mr. Palmer moved into the second hour of my first craniotomy. Respecting the anesthetist's medical knowledge and skill, Mr. Palmer consulted him throughout the operation, particularly as he cleaned the area surrounding the bullet hole. He swabbed the skull around the hole and delicately inserted a micro-thin suction tube into the entry wound. Very cautiously, he used the tube to remove dead brain cells (by the tens of millions), along with clotted blood, bone fragments, and any other foreign debris that had found its way into the hole while I lay writhing on the floor at Wilberforce in Freetown the day before.

Mr. Palmer then took a surgical drill and made a second, much neater hole to the left of the entry wound, into which a surgical bolt would be placed to measure intracranial pressure as it built and abated with the swelling of my brain. The bolt would further serve as a drainage valve, allowing for the safe release of excess fluid accumulating in my cranial vault.

Three hours after the operation began, Mr. Palmer began stapling and stitching my forehead back in place. Finally, he stitched the skin at the entry wound together. Shortly after two in the morning on Tuesday, January 12, Mr. Palmer—

still dressed in his scrubs, a surgical mask hanging from his neck—returned to my parents in the waiting room. He cautiously declared the *first* craniotomy a success.

*First?* my father thought. *How many will there be?*

As if anticipating the question, the surgeon explained that he would have to perform a second operation on the back of my skull to remove the bullet still lodged in my brain.

After one full day to recover, I was wheeled back into the operating theater. Mr. Palmer used a high-tech computer program in conjunction with a series of small magnets to pinpoint the exact location of the bullet at the lower back part of the brain, not far from the brain stem. Then he drilled a hole through the back of my skull. The swelling inside provided enough pressure to push the little brownish-gray slug out through the hole by itself. My brain was finally bullet-free.

For the next several hours in the ICU's recovery ward, the nurses kept a close eye on my oxygen levels. After years of heavy smoking in war zones, my lung capacity had diminished and I was incapable of providing my brain with the oxygen it needed, even with the help of a ventilator. As I began to wake from my chemical coma, I struggled against the endotracheal tube in my mouth and throat. My subconscious was sucked into a dream, or vision:

*The room around me is white. White walls, white curtains, white bed linens over my legs. Standing around my bed are my parents, my sister, and several senior executives from the*

*Associated Press, including the company president, Lou Boccardi. I reach out to shake Lou's hand, but a gray telephone cord appears from beside the bed and wraps like a creeping vine around my arm. A second cord appears and spins itself around my waist, up and around my chest, and finally around my neck.*

*I struggle with my free arm to pull the cords away, but more appear, entangling my legs and the free arm. The more I struggle, the tighter the cords become. They are the phone cords the AP uses to wire its bureaus overseas. I pull and yank and flail around in the bed until one last gray cord with a blue plug on one end emerges from under the bed. It hovers above me, poised like a cobra; it strikes at my face. It does not bite, but instead worms its way into my mouth and down my throat.*

*I can't breathe! I panic, kicking my legs. I try to scream, but no sound comes out.*

*In a desperate attempt to get rid of the coiled cord in my throat, I decide to bite it. I chomp down so hard that my teeth feel as if they are going to shatter under the pressure.*

"Ian!" I was jolted into reality.

My eyes eased open. Squinting against the bright lights of the ICU, I saw the murky outlines of people standing by my bedside. (It was later that I recognized them as my sister, Karen, and my parents.) A long, clear tube was running from my mouth to the chrome railing at the edge of the bed. Only aware that the wire-reinforced tube was a nuisance, I had bitten down on it and ground my teeth into the thick rubber.

"Ian!" The voices sounded scared, exasperated. "Don't bite the tube, Ian."

*Huh? Who said that?* My thoughts were slow, as if bubbling up through thick molasses. My eyes fell shut.

TIME SLIPS BY. TEN MINUTES? A day? I have no idea. I could hear soft voices calling my name:

"Ian, can you hear me?"

Then more harshly: "Ian!"

Commanding my attention: "Ian! Open your eyes, Ian!"

My heavy eyelids slowly unglued. I looked around with my eyes, but my head wouldn't move—it was heavy. I blinked. I saw blurry, nondescript faces; then, as if the focusing ring on a camera lens had been turned, my parents and Karen became clear images. Tom Kent was with them, standing just behind my dad.

My mom was dressed in a dark sweater. She sat low in a chair next to the bed. I could see only her shoulders and head. Her eyes looked concerned, filled with uncertainty and empathy. She held my right hand and tenderly stroked the back of it with her thumb. A tear filled my eye. I didn't know why.

That my family and my boss were gathered at my bedside never struck me as odd. I wasn't even aware I was in bed. It seemed easier to close my eyes and shut out the confusion of the world around me.

"Ian." It was my mother's voice and I reluctantly opened my eyes again and focused on her soft face.

"The doctors want to do another operation that's called a tracheotomy."

My mother explained the basic details of the operation and asked, "Do you understand? If you understand, squeeze my hand."

I squeezed acknowledgement, but I was unable to speak. If I could have, I would have said, *I know what a tracheotomy is! She knows I know what a tracheotomy is. Why is she explaining that to me?*

Then I thought, *Why is everyone speaking in slow, deliberate sentences as if I'm incapable of understanding?*

Although I had no inkling of what had happened to me, I was able very early on to think and reason. Like many brain injury patients, however, I would have to relearn even the most basic social skills.

My mind fell silent. My heavy eyelids once again insisted on closing.

ON FRIDAY, I WAS WHEELED OFF to the operating theatre for the tracheotomy, my third operation in four days. I remember little from the first hours afterward. I have foggy memories of my parents, sister, and boss staring at me. Occasionally they spoke among themselves, whispering in the subdued tones that people use in a funeral parlor. I recall only a void of curiosity and thought on my part. No questions, no interest, no glimmer of coherence of any kind.

Months after I was released from the hospital I slowly came to understand many confusing aspects of brain injuries.

No two brain injuries are alike, nor are they curable; but thanks to medical advances, brain injuries often are not fatal. Their consequences can be as mysterious as the brain itself. Relatively simple tasks can become difficult, if not impossible, for some patients, while complex thought processes remain intact. The reasons for these variations remain unclear, though neurologists continue to search for answers.

When not fatal, a brain injury can leave its victim trapped in a muddled world of gray confusion, where up and down are interchangeable and the distinction between left and right is lost in the twisted wreck that once was a healthy, *normal* brain. Frightened, disoriented, and isolated, a brain-injured person's world slows to the crawl of an overloaded mainframe computer grinding and churning in search of order among whirling words and familiar forgotten faces. Meanwhile, emotions careen between the peaks of unrealistic optimism and the suffocating valleys of gloom and despair.

For days back in the ICU, life remained a jumble of dream and reality. I'm still not sure which was which. Fluorescent lights flickered in the gray haze of my partitioned space. Busy nurses fluttered in and out of my wavering consciousness. Beige floor-length drapes were drawn around my bed. Like a puppet show, visitors occasionally poked their heads in through an opening in the curtains at the foot of the bed. A combination of heavy sedation and severe head trauma initially sheltered me from the reality of my wound.

My left arm and leg were paralyzed. Only days earlier I had been near death on an operating table, my forehead cut open, brain swollen, exposed, and bleeding: this was all too much to process at this early stage of what would be a long fight to win back my life. Understanding the frightening reality of my condition could come later. Right now my life was still on the line.

While monitoring my vital signs about twelve hours after my tracheotomy, an ICU nurse discovered that I was running a low-grade fever. She quickly alerted Mr. Palmer, who feared the worst: that I had contracted an infection in the brain. He immediately ordered a series of tests, meanwhile prescribing a course of intravenous antibiotics for me. My parents, who had hoped I was out of danger, once again waited anxiously for the results. But no definitive answer emerged from the lab.

As the ICU staff frantically worked to find the cause of my fever, I lay restless in my bed. Every time I fell asleep, my mind led me on a psychedelic journey of surreal images as my mind attempted to rationalize my condition in terms with which my brain could cope.

*I'm in an open-windowed medical clinic deep in the marshy forests of the Niger delta region of southeastern Nigeria. Through metal bars on the window, I watch green palm trees swaying in the breeze. The sky is bright blue with only a few tufts of white cloud drifting by.*

*A black nurse in a white uniform and cornered hat walks into the room. As she rolls me onto my stomach she explains that I have contracted a fever and respiratory illness from the swampy mangrove waters of Sierra Leone.*

*I picture tiny paramecia and amoebae swimming through*

*the winding waterways near Freetown. The water turns red; it becomes my bloodstream.*

*The nurse says her name is Wamba di Wamba.*

*"Hello," I say. "It's very nice to meet you."*

*Wamba explains that I have developed a highly infectious form of chlorophyll poisoning in my lungs.*

*"Mosquitoes spread it," she tells me.*

*I'm on white sheets in this medical clinic when Wamba begins pounding my back with rubber-gloved hands. She hops up on my bed and continues whacking my back with the heel of her open hand. I cough and wheeze and cough again until I vomit, spitting up green and black chlorophyll. Mixed in the bile are tiny black and green cloverleaf-shaped bits. Millions of these Lucky Charms–like bits stream from my mouth. The foul vomit pools on my sheets. The stench is unbearable, making me retch more.*

In reality, because of the tracheotomy tube in my throat, I was being fed a high-protein liquid diet through a naso-gastric tube. I vomited after almost every feeding following the tracheotomy. As well, a respiratory therapist from the ICU stood by my bedside and gently whacked my back, trying to stimulate stronger breathing and ward off pneumonia.

OF THE ICU AFTER THE TRACHEOTOMY, I remember the sounds most: the wheezing gurgle of my ventilator; the incessant beep of heart, blood pressure, and respiration monitors; the scratching sound of the tube used to suck mucus from my throat. Day and night, I wavered on that uncertain boundary between sleep and consciousness. I was unable even to lift my head from the pillow. A clear bag and intravenous tube hanging from a chrome pole fed saline and antibiotics into my bloodstream. I lay unaware of my condition, but resigned to it nevertheless.

But as the days wore on, the mist that had enshrouded my brain began to lift. I started writing notes—just hard-to-read scribbles, really—to communicate. I held up my right hand, index finger pinched to thumb and mimicked to the duty nurse, Paul, the motion of writing. He handed me the blue felt marker and the pad of paper I used to write notes to my parents. In tiny script, awkwardly crammed near the left edge of the blank page I scribbled a message:

"Ian go home."

# 12

# LEFT OF CENTER

THE DAY I WROTE MY FIRST NOTE—Monday, January 18—marked a significant advance in my recovery. Although still battling the mysterious low-grade fever and still awake only a fraction of the time, I began writing more notes. Deciphering the scrawl, my sister, Karen, sat by my bedside as I scribbled a long string of disjointed thoughts. In erratic script, I wrote "Keevlar blankit" in an attempt to communicate that I was cold and needed a blanket to keep me warm. Karen struggled with this one, guessing that I was trying to indicate that either I had or had not been wearing a bulletproof Kevlar-lined jacket in Freetown at the time of the shooting. The effort of writing just two words left me drained. My eyes grew heavy, and slowly I drifted back to the realm of nightmares.

*I'm lying in bed in a white room in a small medical clinic in Abidjan. The room has no walls; the floor is covered with sand. Palm trees and elephant grass enclose the area around my bed. Above me the sky is a brilliant aquamarine blue. As I lie there, Malik, one of the security guards from the AP's bureau in Abidjan, emerges from the elephant grass and stands by my bed. He flashes me a wide, toothy smile and says, "Hello, son."*

*"Hi, Malik." I hold out my hand, and a paper hospital identification bracelet is dangling from my wrist.*

*"Can you go get me a case of Coke?" I ask. "I'm dying of thirst."*

*Malik smiles and nods sympathetically.*

*Two men in torn jeans and plastic flip-flops creep up behind Malik. He doesn't know they are there. I try to yell, but no sound leaves my lips. I watch as the men grab Malik from behind and drag him to the floor. After a moment or two, his brown, leathery hand reaches up to the mattress, leaving a sticky, red trail of blood on my leg. Apprehensively I peek over the edge of the bed. Malik is lying on the floor in a puddle of pooling blood. His throat is slit open; a machete lies by his body.*

My agitated body twitched through the duration of my dream. When my eyes opened again, my face was blank, my eyes sad and lost. I motioned for the pen and paper. "Malik?" I scrawled over and over in jagged lines.

The following day, three nurses hefted me out of my bed and propped me up in a wheelchair. My motionless left arm was safely balanced atop a pillow on my lap. Half asleep and expressionless, I sat in the wheelchair as Mr. Palmer discussed my fever with my mother.

"We ordered a CT scan," he began.

My mother simply nodded, apprehensive about what was to come.

"I saw the results this morning," he continued. "There is a blurry spot on one of the scans. We're not sure yet, but it may indicate Ian has developed an infection in his brain."

Stunned, my mother processed this latest bad news. "And then what?" she finally whispered.

"Well, we'll try increasing the antibiotics," the surgeon answered.

Despite the fever, Mr. Palmer approved my transfer to the recovery ward. Later that same day, a nurse trailed behind the orderly who wheeled me from the intensive care unit to the Nuffield Wing on the National's fourth floor. There I continued to surface from the haze of my coma. Unlike the way it is depicted on TV or in the movies, there was no definitive moment of waking up for me. It was like surfing a tide in and out of reality. Consciousness was a cagey predator, quietly closing in on me. It seems to me now that my subconscious brain was safeguarding my conscious mind until I was strong enough to handle the shocking news of what had happened.

Throughout my eight-day stay in the ICU, I had had no idea that I had been shot. Of course, I had been told time and again by my family and the nurses: "You were shot in the head. You have been paralyzed. It will be at least a year before you can return to work, maybe two." I heard the words, but they fell harmlessly around me like dead leaves dropping from a tree. I was too exhausted to bother thinking. Language was empty and meaningless; it had no relevance and no definition.

I later learned that brain injury patients also struggle for years with bouts of fatigue, affecting their ability to remember, perform simple tasks, or express themselves coherently. Until a brain injury patient is fully assessed, fatigue easily can be mistaken for memory damage or cognitive impairments.

Under my sheets, my left hand, arm, and leg lay motionless. My brain wasn't even aware they existed. The trauma to my head had so disconnected my brain from the left side of my body that I was scarcely aware of anything left of center. (It was more than a year later that eye examinations confirmed my neglect of my left side was worsened by a small blind spot in my left eye—confirmation that at least part of my neocortex had been damaged by the rebel's bullet.)

Hour after hour, my father stood by the left side of my bed. He told stories and jokes, and read me the day's headlines, following Mr. Palmer's instructions to help me recognize the world to my left. He waited for some sort of response, but I stared straight ahead with blank, lifeless eyes, wearing the frighteningly flat expression of a lobotomized patient.

The damage to my brain also left me disinhibited—a common result of an injury to the brain's frontal lobe. Unaware that I was doing anything wrong, I'd whip off my sheets and expose myself to anyone in the room. At first my family and the nurses were concerned, but with time, as my brain began healing, my disinhibition abated and I kept my sheets on.

Knowing the bullet had almost certainly damaged at least part of my frontal lobe, my family was frightened. Had my personality changed? Was I still the same son and brother they had last seen in December 1997? Those answers still lay months in the future. At this stage it would be enough if I turned to look at my father.

Over the first few weeks in the National, sleep provided little respite from my ordeal. Every time I fell asleep, I slid into a surreal dream that blurred reality with hallucinatory fantasy.

*I'm in my hospital bed, but now it's in the freezer aisle of a 7-Eleven convenience store in the downtown Wan Chai district of Hong Kong. Tossing my bedsheets aside, I hop to my feet and walk briskly to the bank of freezers containing cold soft drinks and Popsicles. The door mists over when the cold mingles with the dense tropical air. I pull out a small carton of Tropicana orange juice. Tilting my head back, I pour the cold juice into my mouth, soothing my parched, cracking throat.*

"Ian! Stop that!" The Irish nurse's voice was sharp.

My eyes popped open. Head tilted back in the dark room, I was holding the liquid receptacle from my ventilator's nebulizer to my lips. The receptacle gathered condensation from the ventilator. Although it was essentially my own vaporized spit, I viewed the liquid as a quenching drink, like the juice in my dream.

Bridie, the Irish nurse and night supervisor, scowled at me.

"You could kill yourself, love," she snapped. She quickly relented after noticing my temperature had spiked to more than 103 degrees, a reminder of the unexplained infection that still threatened my life.

She gently explained that I could not eat or drink until the tracheotomy tube was removed from my throat. I listened, but the words were meaningless as my unfocused mind wandered.

"You poor lad," Bridie said tenderly, her voice dancing with brogue. "You don't know what's happening, do you?"

It was dark outside my window. Late night? Early morning? Light from the corridor streamed into my room from the small window in my door.

"Ian? Do you know where you are?" Bridie asked. I stared at her with blank eyes.

"You are in London, England," she answered for me, and then turned to leave the room. As soon as the door shut behind her I slipped into another wrenching fever-fed dream.

*It's night. The sky is indigo. Black silhouettes of palm trees rustle in the warm breeze wafting in from the ocean. The rolling surf quietly washes up on the beach. I smile and feel relaxed in this idyllic setting.*

*Smoke drifts past my nose. The smell of cordite is strong. I realize I'm in a sandy foxhole on the beach near the Lungi Coco Beach Hotel in Sierra Leone.*

*Long narrow bands of red and yellow light—like the lasers from the* Star Wars *movies—streak the sky just above my head. The bright streaks of the tracer bullets illuminate the night. A bright red flare is fired high into the sky; drifting back to earth, it brightens the surrounding area. Now the idyllic trees cast sinister, flickering shadows on the beach. The palm frond shadows look like long twisted fingers reaching out to grab me.*

*David Guttenfelder is beside me in the foxhole. We are both wearing army khakis. An Irish nurse named Paddy crawls toward me out of a darkened corner of the bunker. Her over-sized helmet sits crooked on top of her red hair. Her baggy army jacket cloaks her femininity. Her sleeve is decorated with a row of sergeant's chevrons. Bullets whistle at us, thudding into the sandbagged bunker.*

*I duck and look over to Paddy, who continues to inch toward me from out of the darkness. Once close enough, she leans toward my ear and whispers gently.*

*"Ian, there's a hot tube behind your head."*

*I understand a "hot tube" to be a loaded mortar cannon. My body is suddenly cold; I shiver despite the steamy air of the African tropics. I duck my head instinctively, knowing the weapon is aimed just inches from the base of my skull. Bullets are flying in all directions.*

*Behind Paddy, a Nigerian commander is sitting atop a wall of sandbags. He is impervious to the bullets tearing into his back in rapid succession. Holding a whistle between his teeth, he lets out a single shrill blast. It's a warning to allied troops that heavy weapons like the mortar behind my head are about to be fired. The whistle drops from his teeth and dangles around his neck at the end of a yellow string.*

*Body tensed and teeth clenched, I wait for the mortar to fire, blowing off the back of my head. I wait—nothing happens. I wait some more. Still nothing. The Nigerian commander blows the whistle a second time. Again I await my certain death—nothing. My heart is racing, palpitating. I can't catch my breath as my chest tightens.*

"Ian, are you awake?" asked my dad as he stood, arms folded, beside Bridie. Both were at the foot of my bed. Venting air from the nebulizer was whistling. I looked around. Sunlight was streaming in through the gap in my drapes. My forehead was drenched with sweat, but the fever had finally broken.

My father looked at me with soft eyes. "Ian, where are you? Do you know?" he asked.

I stared at him, hoping maybe the answer would come to me in a vision. Nothing: my mind was blank.

"You're in London, England, son," my dad said.

Moments later, Mr. Palmer walked into the room quietly.

"Ian, this is Mr. Palmer," my father said, introducing me to my surgeon for the first time. "It's *Mister* Palmer," he added emphatically, anticipating the obvious question. (He later explained that surgeons in Britain are called Mister rather than Doctor. But the exchange left me bewildered.)

*Mr. Palmer?* I thought. *My surgeon is a pro golfer?*

The following afternoon, Mr. Palmer ran excitedly into my room, holding the results of the latest series of lab tests. Smiling and relaxed, he announced to my parents that the source of my fever was indeed an infection, though not in my brain as he had feared.

"It was the trach incision," he said, motioning to his throat with a finger.

My parents let out their breath, their first sigh of relief in days.

• • •

THERAPY BEGAN WITHIN the first few weeks in the recovery ward; I would have to learn to stand and walk all over again, and possibly how to speak with a damaged throat. Rebecca, my speech therapist, leaned toward me over the side of my bed and stared intently at the clear plastic tube jutting out of the notch at the base of my throat. The incision, bright red from infection, looked painful and swollen, prompting her to worry out loud that complications could jeopardize my ability to clearly enunciate words and swallow.

She gently fitted a small plastic disc into the end of the trachea tube. I winced as she manipulated the tube around the inflamed skin. The disc, covered with a thin membrane-like drum skin, would exaggerate the vibrations of my vocal cords. Speech discs, Rebecca explained, are often used to assess whether a tracheotomy patient can expect to encounter problems in learning how to speak again.

With the disc in place, Rebecca stepped back a pace or two from the bed. She stood beside my mom at the foot of the bed. "Ian, can you say something for us?" she asked.

I braced for a sharp jab of pain from my traumatized vocal cords before taking a deep breath. Finally I said the word "something."

I smiled weakly at my own bit of cheeky wit. My mother exchanged a look of sheer relief with Rebecca. *Not only is his voice going to be OK but his sense of humor appears to be intact,* she thought to herself.

For two days I used the speech disc to relearn how to sound out words and test the limits of my weakened throat. Often I went too far: speaking just slightly above a whisper sent me into coughing fits that propelled the disc across the room.

Toward the end of my third week in the recovery ward, my trachea tube was finally removed. A surgical nurse sutured the incision and covered it with surgical sealing tape. Those few stitches in my inflamed skin were as painful as anything I had experienced.

The following week I began eating solid food, often pilfering a second serving of dessert. While I grew physically stronger, though, my patience began to wane; the littlest things sent me into a blind rage. When I bit my cheek or tongue during meals—a daily occurrence—I flew into an uncontrollable outburst, slamming my fist into my meal table in time with my emphatic exclamations of "Fuck! Fuck! Fuck! Fuck! Fuck!"

While my speech strengthened quickly, my conversation skills fell short through much of my stay at the National. Early one evening, around dinnertime, I was lying in bed and staring at the ceiling when the phone rang. My mother answered while I turned my head in slow motion to gaze at her.

"He's sleeping a lot of the time," she said.

*She's talking about me,* I thought.

"I think so, but he hasn't asked," she said cryptically.

"Ian, Ian?"

I was slow to realize she was calling me.

"It's your father." (My father and Karen had returned to Toronto shortly after I was transferred out of the ICU.)

"Do you want to say hello?" she asked, holding the phone's white handset toward me.

"Hello?" I said. My eyebrows knitted with confusion as I pondered how a telephone conversation worked.

"Hi there, buddy," my dad said cheerfully. "How are you doing?"

"I'm OK," I said, my voice flat and weak. Then, unthinkingly, I placed the phone by my side in the folds of my blanket and looked quizzically at my mother as if to say *What now?* Having said my piece, I thought the conversation was over. It never occurred to me that my father might have something more to say. It took me a long time to relearn the intricacies of phone calls; it was harder to focus on the conversation, because the other person wasn't in front of me.

Along with speech therapy, I began physical therapy. In my room, Leslie, my therapist, worked on my left leg—paralyzed as a result of damaged nerve cells in my brain. She had stretched and tested its range of motion while I was still in the ICU, but once I was in the recovery ward, in-room therapy began with very simple tasks such as sitting up in bed or in a chair.

About seven days after moving to the recovery ward, I was taken by wheelchair to the hospital's rehabilitation ward for the first time. It was time to stand again. The therapy gymnasium was dank and chilly on that gray Monday, January 25. Squatting down to look me in the eye, Leslie spoke softly in her Scottish accent.

"Good morning, Ian," she said. "Do you know where you are today?"

"Ahhhh—" I tried to summon the answer from the recesses of my mind. "Nope," I finally responded.

"You are in England. London, England."

Leslie then patiently explained that I must shift my weight forward in order to gain enough momentum to stand up. I heaved my shoulders forward and bent my waist as well as I could. My rear end lifted a few inches off the cushion on my wheelchair. Too weak to go further, I plopped back into the seat. A second stronger attempt almost sent me tumbling to the floor.

"Don't forget to straighten up as you go forward," Leslie advised, her *R*s rolling sharply off her tongue.

I rocked forward again, lurching harder with my shoulders; my butt rose. I tried to straighten from my trunk, but my abdominal muscles had atrophied after several weeks of lying in bed. Leslie helped me the rest of the way.

I cautiously looked around. I was teetering like a tower of building blocks stacked a few too high. I corrected the sway and overcompensated in the other direction. It took several minutes before I stopped rocking. Ready to break a fall, Leslie's hands hovered just centimeters from my body. Though unsteady, I smiled.

*Upright*, I thought, feeling a surge of self-satisfaction. *I can do this.*

For the next ten days, I practiced standing up under Leslie's close supervision, but the idea of taking even a single step at this stage seemed unthinkable.

Although my fingers began to involuntarily curl into a loose fist, it was too soon to begin working on my lifeless left

arm, where damaged neural pathways overreacted to the
effort of standing. (Later this was explained to me as an
"associated reaction.") As I became more lucid, I slipped
naturally back into reporting mode—only now I was reporting on myself. I began asking many questions about my
injury and the prognosis for recovery. Nobody could say for
sure, but I did learn that the rule of thumb for recovery from
brain injury paralysis is leg first, then arm, and finally the
hand—and here we are talking years, if ever, to regain function at a pre-injury level of agility, strength, and dexterity.
Over time and by asking many questions, I learned (and am
still learning today) that paralysis from a brain injury, unlike
spinal cord injuries, may sometimes be reversed; however,
it's a very slow and painstaking process of therapy.

Because of the very nature of a brain injury, it was difficult for me to comprehend and accept what had happened
to me. I can't even say for sure when I began to realize the
gravity of my wound. As the weeks at the National dragged
on, the afternoons became unbearably boring. That long,
quiet stretch in the day between lunch and dinner offered
too much time to think. Again and again I asked about the
shooting. Yet I can't recall ever hearing the words "you were
shot." Every day I struggled anew to comprehend why I was
in a hospital.

"Tell me what happened?" I would ask my mom or the
nurses. And patiently they would tell me again about the
shooting.

"And what about David?" I asked repeatedly. "Is he OK?
Was he hurt?"

"He was hurt a little," I was told. "David was cut by flying glass. But he's all right now."

But I never moved to the next logical question. I never asked about Myles.

One day, my mother walked into my room carrying a plastic bag from Selfridge's department store. She pulled out the board game Scrabble (one of my favorites) and laid it out on a table beside my bed. I sat in my wheelchair staring blankly at the board. I felt hypnotized by the grid pattern and the seemingly randomly placed pink and blue squares. My mom began explaining the rules, but unable to stay focused, my mind wandered.

"Yeah, yeah, I know," I said, as I began picking lettered tiles one by one from the bag. After I picked a letter, I turned it over and stared momentarily at the point value written in the corner; if I wasn't happy with it, I put the tile back and picked another. Once again I was falling victim to disinhibition from my head injury. Somewhere in my head I knew what I was doing was wrong, but I was simply unable to control my actions.

"Hey, you cheater," my mom said, feigning indignation. "You can't do that!"

This was fun. I began laughing uncontrollably at myself.

When it was my turn, I stared at my tray of letters, but could see no words despite the fact that I had several *A*s, an *N,* and a *D.* I reached across the table and turned my mother's letter tray to face me.

"Hey! Stop that," she said, becoming both a little concerned and bemused by my antics. She looked at my letters.

"You've got the word 'and,'" she said helpfully.

"But I need an *L* to make 'land,'" I said, giggling at my childishness.

Time continued to crawl slowly by in the hospital. I was hounded by exhaustion; it was an ongoing struggle just to understand where I was.

One morning my mom asked me, "Where are you, Ian?"

After hearing it often enough, I finally responded appropriately, "London, England." This, however, concealed my true dilemma: *Where the hell was London, England?*

In my mind, London was now a suburb of Halifax, Nova Scotia, near my parents' summer home in Canada. That's where I had last seen my family all together and it just didn't make sense that we would all be in England together. In the confusion of trying to situate myself in a world upturned, I talked myself into believing that London in all its historic grandeur had been reconstructed in Canada, like a theme park similar to Disneyland. For days I asked my mother questions designed to trip her up in what I perceived was a conspiracy to fool me into believing I was in England.

# 13

# MYLES IS DEAD

ANOTHER BORING AFTERNOON. I had just returned from therapy and eaten my lunch and now there was little else to do but think about what had happened to me. During the preceding weeks, as the swelling in my brain abated, I had slowly begun to remember details of the trip to Sierra Leone—the helicopter, the convoy through Freetown, the bodies, and the vultures. It was jumbled and out of sequence—at first I thought I had been shot during the gun battle near the stadium in Freetown—but it was there. What was hard for people, including me, to understand was that my brain injury had primarily affected my motor functions and mental organizing skills. For example, I could no longer walk, and tasks such as speaking on the phone were confusing. However, my cognitive and reasoning skills had largely been left unscathed by the bullet and the swelling.

As the confusing images of Freetown swirled in my mind, I lay with my head on the pillow facing away from my mother, who stood beside my bed. The wall behind her was covered with get-well cards and letters. The room was

warm and lit by sedate sunlight, filtering through the
brown curtains.

"Am I going to die?" I asked suddenly. Weeks after the
shooting it was finally sinking in, marking the start of my
tortuous struggle to accept the consequences of my actions.

"No," she answered. "You are not going to die."

"Is David going to be all right?"

"Yes, David is OK now," she said, repeating her oft-
rehearsed line.

I paused a moment.

"What happened to Myles?" I asked bluntly and without
emotion.

My mother drew in a deep, steadying breath and exhaled
slowly. "Myles is dead, honey," she replied, her voice strong
and even.

My mind fell still, the way a room does when the power
cuts out.

*Dead.*

The word echoed in my head, insinuating its way
through the bullet's damage and the thick, lingering stupor
of sedation. I didn't say much, but I was struck by a whirlwind of emotion. I realized I was very lucky just to be alive,
though it would be months before I, or anyone else could
utter the word "lucky" without provoking a bitter response.
*Lucky? How dare you call me lucky?* I'd think or say. *I've had
a bullet through my brain—if I was lucky I wouldn't have
been shot at all.*

My mind desperately tried to piece together the final
moments before the shooting.

As more time in the hospital went by I began to feel I had killed Myles. I hated myself. I hated life. I hated Sierra Leone and Africa and war. Hate was easy and safe. Outwardly I smiled and remained courteous (always the polite Canadian). Inside I seethed with rage that ate away at my will to work at my recovery. I acted as if I no longer cared. The hospital assigned a psychologist to help me work through my feelings.

I felt so responsible for Myles's death that I insisted on meeting his mother, Hanne, who had come to London from New York to attend a memorial service for her son. I sat in my wheelchair as Hanne entered the room. She looked tired and sad, her eyes red from crying.

"I'm so sorry," I said. Squatting by my wheelchair, Hanne just smiled and put her hand on my lap.

"I feel like Myles's spirit has been with me here," I said.

Hanne smiled again and squeezed my arm as she turned to leave the room.

Days later I remembered the cat-and-mouse game Myles and I had played as we hesitated over who would sit in the middle seat of Joseph's station wagon. I became quiet and sullen as guilt tugged at my conscience. *Should I have insisted on sitting by the window? Was Myles dead because of me? Should I be dead too?*

Alone in my room I ruminated over the news of his death. Although weeks had passed, the shooting felt ever present. I was nervous and scared. Loud noises made me jump. Nights became haunting and unbearable.

*This is no game,* I thought. *Myles was sitting right beside me—how can he be dead now?*

One night I lay in my hospital bed in the dark. The light from the corridor shone in through the window in the door and cast a weird, elongated column of light on the wall. I found myself staring at three coat hooks on the wall that looked like a crucifix when the light hit them.

*Myles can't be dead,* I thought. I wept and sobbed until my throat gave out and I began coughing uncontrollably. I tore at my sheets and pounded my mattress with a fist.

Images began to flicker like a kaleidoscope: Myles bringing cold beer to my hotel room in Freetown; Myles and I clowning around in the wheelchairs he found at the airport. I thought about our trivial arguments over news coverage in Guinea-Bissau and Nigeria. Sadness soon gave way to self-pity, confusion, and anger. I no longer blamed myself for getting Myles killed. Just as irrationally, I now blamed Myles for getting himself killed.

AFTER ANOTHER LONG, LONELY NIGHT in the hospital, my door opened a crack, and Tim Sullivan and David Guttenfelder peeked in. Not knowing what to expect of their broken bureau chief, they were shy to enter the room and very uncertain of what to say.

Dressed in a pressed navy suit and tie, Tim looked like a Wall Street wheeler-dealer to me. At this early stage in my recovery, I had no idea how instrumental Tim had been in getting me out of Sierra Leone alive. Unaccustomed to formal attire, David, whom I had last seen in jeans and a T-shirt in Freetown, wore a dress shirt and a tie without a jacket. However, as always, he had a camera slung over his shoulder.

Tim sat quietly in one of the hard wooden guest chairs. David plopped down into my wheelchair and grinned, but the grin quickly faded as he realized the chair was no longer a novelty for me; it was a necessity in my new life. We sat in silence for several minutes. I wondered what they thought of me lying in bed so pathetically. As a bureau chief I had felt I was their leader—a tough but benevolent supervisor. Now I felt small and defeated.

"I don't really know what to say," Tim finally offered. "'How are you?' seems trivial."

"Well, I'm doing OK," I said.

But I was a frightening sight for my colleagues. After several weeks without solid food, I was gaunt: my cheeks were sunken and my arms and legs looked spindly. I was dressed in a blue polo shirt that hung off my body and the pair of baggy exercise shorts I wore to therapy. A black Nike baseball cap sat askew on my head, a vain attempt to hide the scar in the center of my forehead.

Throughout the hour-long visit I alternately lay in bed or, with the help of Tim and David, stood up and moved the short distance to my wheelchair. Finally, I tried to make conversation.

"So, what are you guys all dressed up for?" I asked cheerfully.

"We were just at the church service for Myles," Tim said.

"Oh." I fell silent, while working to understand the meaning of the words. *But Myles is dead,* I thought. *He can't go to church. Don't they know he's dead?*

I kept my thoughts private and instead said, "Can I come too?"

Tim and David exchanged glances and looked at me to see if I was joking. It was then that they realized just how seriously I had been wounded. My mind, no longer sharp and agile, was muddled and confused like a badly beaten boxer's.

David began snapping photos of me in my wheelchair and in bed. He even sat down beside me on my bed. Holding his camera out in front of him, he snapped a picture of the two of us.

"I'm really sorry, man," he finally said.

"It's OK, man," I said. "I'll be fine."

A few minutes later, Miguel Gil Moreno, the AP cameraman from Abidjan with whom I had worked on assignment in Sierra Leone and the Democratic Republic of Congo, walked into the room. He sat quietly in a chair beside Tim. Miguel said little, but he offered to push my wheelchair out to the vending machines so I could get out of the room for a brief while. He, too, looked smart in a brown tweed jacket and cloth tie.

"You look good," Miguel said, "considering what you've been through."

David, Tim, and Miguel sat with me in my room until visiting hours were over. It was an awkward visit, as we all sat there sizing up one another. Tim said he was leaving in the morning to return to Abidjan. Miguel was catching a midnight flight to the Balkans to help cover the growing crisis in Kosovo. David, however, said he planned to stay in London for a few days.

That night, I lay in bed. The room was quiet. A nurse sat in a chair pulled close to the side of my bed. She explained to me that David had left behind a videotaped copy of the memorial service they had attended in New York a few days earlier. I watched as several senior AP executives paid tribute to Myles. Miguel spoke, then David. All gushed about the nice and not-so-nice aspects of Myles, whose larger-than-life persona had obviously affected many at the Associated Press. When the video ended, the nurse left, turning off the lights as she walked out the door. I heard the latch of my door click shut.

Alone in my dark room, my mind raced in a desperate search for a reason that could justify Myles's death.

*What did we do wrong? How could this happen?*

In my mind's eye I pictured the headline: "American newsman slain in West Africa."

I wondered: *How many stories like this had I written? And now, how had our names slipped from the byline down into the first paragraph?*

Questions and emotions poured once again like the tears that streamed down my cheeks. I felt angry, then guilty, then sad, and then angry again.

*Were we too cavalier about the dangers? Should we have been there in the first place?*

The night passed, as most did, with little more than a few catnaps. By six in the morning, the day-shift nurses began arriving. They would get me up soon, offering relief from the endless night.

By mid-morning, David walked into my room carrying a plastic shopping bag. He pulled out a new video game system.

"Wow. Thanks, man," I said, as he began hooking it up to the bracket-mounted television on my wall. It never occurred to either of us that playing a video game one-handed would be next to impossible.

I had only recently resumed eating solid food, and my stomach sometimes ballooned with gas. While David was fiddling with the television wiring, an enormous fart shuddered my mattress. David slowly turned to face me and with an evil grin he quietly said, "Doorknob."

"Ah, shit," I said, in mock panic.

I playfully looked around the room for the nearest door-knob, but then realized that, unable to walk, I was trapped. David slowly approached the side of my bed as I jokingly cowered under the sheets, and he began gently punching my arm until I began laughing so hard that a second fart escaped. David kept on playfully punching my arm, until I slipped into a coughing fit. After I had calmed down, David went back to wiring the video game as I calmly drifted off to sleep.

AFTER LEARNING OF MYLES'S DEATH, I went many nights without a sound night's sleep. Mr. Palmer prescribed anti-anxiety medicine to ease my busy mind at bedtime. But even with the medication, I fell back into a pattern of night-mares. Every morning I awoke with sheets twisted around my ankles. My pillows, hurled in frustration, were usually strewn about the floor.

In the daytime, I felt trapped in my bed. Through days and nights I tossed and turned endlessly in my prison-bed. Squirming from side to side, I struggled with one arm and weakened stomach muscles to sit up. Once up, I immediately lay back down, only to want back up. The nurses were driven to distraction, helping me sit up, move to my wheelchair, and back to bed.

In the predawn hours of my last night at the National, my room was dark and quiet. I had left the television on standby, and its blank, lifeless screen stared back at me in the subdued light filtering in through the frosted glass window in the door. The idle television hummed. In my mind, I transformed the static buzz into the baseline for the John Lennon song "Beautiful Boy."

The gentle sound of an electric piano echoed through my head and was joined by the melodic strum of an acoustic guitar. Over and over, Lennon's lyrics had kept me going while I was in the National, and they comforted me again that night.

# 14

# MY OWN TWO FEET

MY LEGS AND CHEST STRAPPED DOWN, I lay on the gurney as the orderlies wheeled me out of my room at the National for the final time on February 6. From my horizontal vantage point, I surveyed my room once more and hoped that the worst of my nightmare was over.

As we passed the main reception desk, we rolled by an elderly couple staring at me. Shaking their heads with dismay, they murmured a few words in subdued voices. I couldn't hear what they said, but at once I felt I knew what it must be like to attend one's own funeral. *Hey!* I wanted to yell out. *I'm not dead, you know!*

As my ambulance sped off into London's congested streets, I turned my head to gaze out the window while block after block of Old World, brick row housing flashed by. Horns honked, brakes squealed, and cockney cabbies cursed. As the cacophony of the city filled my ears, I fought to calm my nerves and the self-pity that swelled in my chest and pricked at my eyes. *How many times before had I wandered these streets?* I thought as we sped along. I began to daydream.

One year earlier, I had stopped off in London to get my visa for the Ivory Coast. During that brief stopover I had walked five miles down Regent Street in search of a particular map shop. I had bought brightly colored Michelin maps of Nigeria, Sierra Leone, Mali, and one massive Rand McNally map of central Africa, from the Republic of Congo to Cameroon and Gabon. In February 1998, they had still been nothing more than seductive names on political maps of red, blue, and yellow blocs, although I would soon visit most of them.

Lying in the ambulance, I cursed my naïveté for ever thinking I could change the world by reporting on the evils of war in Africa.

MY FIRST FULL DAY at the Devonshire Hospital began with a knock at my door. Without waiting for a response, a nurse entered the room with a stack of freshly laundered towels and announced with a bright smile that it was shower time. Having finally overcome my disinhibitions, I shied away at the indignity of peeling off my shirt and underwear in front of a stranger who by averting her eyes tried to remain unobtrusive. When I was sitting small and naked with only a towel over my lap in a special waterproof wheelchair, the nurse pushed me into the en-suite washroom in my room, positioned me under the showerhead, and left me.

I sat shivering under the tepid stream of water, my leg quaking with spastic shudders. As the water temperature rose, I began to work my sponge into a soapy lather. Washing was simple, if acrobatic. Shifting and squirming on the plastic blue seat of my shower chair, I almost slid to the floor several times. Washing under my right armpit posed my first significant challenge. Like a contortionist, I reached under my right arm with my right hand and began scrubbing.

After about ten minutes, the nurse burst back into the washroom. Cloaked now in a clear, disposable raincoat, rubber gloves, and a pair of bright yellow galoshes, she squatted down beside my wheelchair. Without a word, she reached under my seat to the opening and began scrubbing my rear end vigorously. Stunned by her callousness, I sat silently and stared at the tiled wall in a futile attempt to retain some semblance of dignity.

Breakfast was served after the shower. A different nurse arrived in my room, carrying a tray with juice, tea, cereal, and toast. She set it in front of me and promptly left. I suppose she had never considered the challenge of spreading jam on toast with just one hand.

Following breakfast, the day's work began with forty-five-minute sessions of physical therapy, occupational therapy, speech pathology, and a session with my neuro-psychologist.

Jenny, my speech therapist, entered the room. A prim and proper Englishwoman with thin, pursed lips, she was neatly dressed in a black skirt and matching jacket, covered by a white lab coat. Her blonde hair was pulled into a tight bun at the back of her head. She explained to me that her job was to help me recover any language skills lost to the bullet's damage. But there were problems from the start; she failed to take into account the differences between

Canadian and British English. On that first day, she began with a multiple-choice exercise. She read from a large white index card: "A man walks up to a police officer at the side of a busy road and says, 'I'm having trouble with the zebra crossing.' How should the police officer respond?"

Before giving me the options, Jenny stopped to let me absorb her first sentence.

*Why is a zebra trying to cross the road?* I was asking myself.

"Tell the zebra to go to the corner and cross with the traffic lights like everyone else," I finally responded. Jenny immediately began scribbling in her notebook.

"Do you want to try again?" she asked coldly.

"Why?" I said, having no clue that a zebra crossing is British English for a crosswalk.

After two more sessions with Jenny, I complained to the hospital administration, who promptly assigned the deputy head of the speech department to my case.

After Jenny's visit that first Monday, a tall blond woman in a gray skirt and black sweater quietly knocked on my door. Poking her head in through the open door, she smiled and walked toward me with her hand extended.

"Good morning, Ian. My name is Sherrie. I'm a neuro-psychologist with the Devonshire's psychology department. I thought we could talk a little bit about how you feel emotionally."

"Sure," I said with a shrug that raised only my right shoulder.

Sherrie explained that she was from the United States

and had worked with a number of veterans from the
Vietnam War who had suffered from post-traumatic stress
disorder (PTSD). Having read my reports from the National,
Sherrie was concerned that I might also be suffering from
PTSD. I was showing all the classic signs: I was overly
emotional, non-communicative, and struggling with undi-
rected anger, confusion, and guilt.

She began by asking about my nightmares. We also
discussed why, since I had been hurt, I seemed to cry at just
about everything. It turned out I was not simply over-
wrought. Sherrie explained that swelling of the brain often
puts abnormal pressure on the ocular nerves, making tears
flow much more readily. It was also a form of disinhibition,
Sherrie told me. Brain injury patients often lose their
command of emotional controls or inhibitors, allowing
ill-timed outbursts of anger, joy, sorrow, fear, and other
emotions.

Sitting in a gray, vinyl-covered chair beside my bed,
Sherrie scribbled notes onto a yellow legal pad during our
first visit. She told me that over the course of the next few
weeks she would try to help me cope with the trauma I had
experienced. She also planned to give me a series of tests
geared to measure the level of impairment to my cognitive
or reasoning skills and memory.

After Sherrie, an Australian occupational therapist
named Dina strode confidently into my room. She handed
me a pair of socks and asked me to put them on. Up until
now, either my mother or one of the nurses had been
helping me dress. Dina explained that she needed to assess

how much help I still required for my Activities of Daily Living, or ADLs. Everything from eating to washing and dressing make up the average person's ADLs, but a brain injury and its resulting physical disability can rob a patient of the knowledge and dexterity to perform even the simplest task. Dina taught me to put on socks with one hand and drag a T-shirt up my left arm so that I could dress independently.

The phone rang that evening, and my mom, who usually sat with me through my dinner, picked it up.

"Oh, it's just great," she said. Now understanding the concept of a two-way telephone conversation, I listened intently.

"He seems to be doing fine. He's got great therapists." She paused.

"Just a minute, I'll see." My mom held the phone away from her mouth. "Ian, it's Tom Kent in New York. Do you want to talk to him?"

I took the phone receiver and chatted politely with him until my mind began to wander and I suddenly announced: "Tom, I'm going to write about the shooting from a patient's perspective, OK?"

Taken aback by this abrupt statement, Tom stammered for a reply.

"We'll see."

AT FIRST SIGHT, Alfie McVey's cropped, spiky hair lent her the appearance of a British rock star from the 1970s, not a Scottish physiotherapist. A young and energetic woman,

Alfie was also the one who helped me trade my wheelchair's four wheels for my own two feet. She bristled with enthusiasm and passion for her work and was determined to have me up again as soon as possible. She wore the same pale blue uniform that all of the Devonshire's rehabilitation staff wore. The minute she called me "kiddo," I knew we'd get along just fine.

On my first day of therapy at the Devonshire, Alfie helped me into my wheelchair and pushed me to the gymnasium in the basement. On the way, I sat expressionless, numbed by my awakening realization that I was now an infirm rehab patient unable to walk, barely able to feed, wash, or dress myself. I couldn't even steer my own wheelchair, thanks to my useless left arm. Alfie told me about the Devonshire's rehab department, but lost in introspection, I barely heard a word she said.

We turned a corner and entered the brightly lit gymnasium. Wearing only my black workout shorts and a T-shirt, I shivered in the cavernous gym's chilly air. Assorted pieces of medical equipment—backboards, first-aid kits, a defibrillator, and an emergency ventilator—were stacked along the wall on the left side. For an instant, I flashed back to the National and the gurgling rattle of my ventilator in intensive care.

At the far end of the room, three therapists and Sherrie were working with a young man. He was suspended in hoist restraints above a therapy plinth. After the therapists eased him down, he lay motionless in a fetal position. His eyes were squeezed tight shut as if he were wincing in pain, but no sound escaped his pinched lips. In unison, the therapists struggled to straighten his spastically curled legs. They placed triangular pillows under his knees to keep his legs partially straight.

I sat long-faced and sullen during my first session with Alfie. She pushed me forward to an empty therapy table near the far end of the room. A large mirror—the kind in a dance studio—covered the wall in front of the table. I slouched in my wheelchair staring at myself and shaking my head.

*Look at yourself. How could this happen to you? Why did this happen to you?*

Slumped over in a wheelchair behind me, a middle-aged man with a heavy five o'clock shadow stared vacantly at my reflection in the mirror. His unblinking eyes, meeting mine, were lifeless. When he saw me looking back at him, he gave a reluctant and, I assume, reflexive smile, tilting his head to one side. I looked away quickly—the human instinct to avert one's eyes when caught intruding on another's privacy, be it in triumph or tragedy. I peeked at him again, then shut my eyes tight to hold back my tears. Through the other patients, I could see my own catastrophe.

For the rest of my time at the Devonshire, I wondered and fretted about how the world would see me now. Would I have to prove myself all over again?

The first day in the gym was little more than an assessment of what I was capable of doing, what my deficits and impairments were, and what kind of rehab strategy would be required to help me learn how to walk again. In Alfie's reassuring words, it wasn't a question of *if* I would walk again. It was how to get me walking as I used to, without developing a limp and subsequent back problems. This was about the only good news I had heard since waking weeks earlier in the National, but I was so obsessed with my left arm that I scarcely cared that I would someday walk normally again.

ABOUT TWO WEEKS INTO MY STAY at the Devonshire, my father and sister made a second trip to London. During their visit, I began to venture out from the hospital more frequently. As a family, we'd go out to dinner at restaurants near the hospital.

On one bright, sunny Sunday in mid-February, we all headed out, walking toward Regent's Park. I was layered in gray fleece sweatpants to fend off the bite of the chilly London air. My sister and father took turns pushing my wheelchair. For about twenty minutes we bumped and rolled along London's busy streets. I felt small and vulnerable hunched down in my wheelchair.

In Regent's Park, we wandered through neatly manicured gardens where the occasional tulip was already in bloom. We strolled past wide tracts of open parkland, where teenagers and young adults played soccer. Mute, I watched in covetous wonder at the ease and grace with which the athletes moved. My mind wandered back to high school and university when I had played football and rugby. *God,*

*I hope I'll do that again,* I thought, still staring at the soccer players gamboling across the green pitch.

My bum began to ache after sitting on the hard wheelchair seat for more than an hour. I shifted back in my seat and repositioned my left foot, which periodically and spastically bounced off its footplate during the jarring ride on the cobblestone paths.

We finally arrived at the entrance of the Regent's Park Zoo and aimed for the primate house, where black spider monkeys endlessly entertained the spectators with carefree acrobatics. Out of the corner of my eye I saw two small children staring at my wheelchair and me. Ducking behind their mother's skirt, they looked away when I turned toward them.

*Hey, kids! It's bonus day at the zoo! Watch the cripple watching the monkeys.*

We were approaching the aviary, when from a distance I spotted several large, black birds at the top of the enclosure. One jumped a few feet along the tree limb it was standing on; its wings flapped once lazily. My heart pounded hard and I struggled to catch my breath. Suddenly the raw London air felt hot and humid; beads of perspiration formed on my forehead. In my mind I heard gunfire echo through the crowded zoo. I looked away from the large black birds and cast a frightened glance over my shoulder at my dad, who was pushing the wheelchair.

"Those are vultures. Let's not go over there, OK?" I said urgently, my chest tightening in a noose of anxiety.

For the rest of the day, my nose was filled with the smell

of cordite and rotting flesh on a Freetown street, and my mind replayed images of vultures tugging voraciously at human cadavers.

MY MOTHER AND I PILED into a taxi at the front door of the Devonshire and made the fifteen-minute journey back to the National at Queen Square in west-central London to visit my surgeon, Mr. Palmer. His assistant beckoned us in through a side door and up a wheelchair lift to the surgeon's office. I remembered Mr. Palmer vaguely from my early, foggy days in the National, but this was really the first time I would meet the man on my own terms.

We spoke briefly about the operation, and the surgeon cautioned me that I must never have an MRI since the metal fragments from the bullet might still be embedded in my brain and could shift with the pull of the magnets. Then he handed me a pad of paper and had me draw a series of diagrams designed to indicate neglect in hemispheric brain injury patients. The most typical of these is a clock face— people suffering from neglect tend to be unable to fit all twelve hours on the clock symmetrically. After that, he said, "I'm going to say three words. I want you to remember them and repeat them back to me when I ask. All right?"

I nodded yes.

"Ball, tree, flag," he said.

I stared out the window to find something I could use as visual triggers to help me remember. In the park outside his window there were many large trees. On the spire of a nearby church, a flag flittered in the breeze. For "ball," I would just have to remember the old-fashioned way.

He went on to ask about my work as a reporter, when I would be returning to Canada, and what it was like to live in Africa. The line of conversation was clearly designed to distract my memory. After about ten minutes, he stopped abruptly. I saw it coming and glanced out the window.

"What were the three words?" he asked.

"Ball, tree, and flag," I answered proudly, without hesitation. My memory was fine and I knew it and could prove it too.

Mr. Palmer noted something down in my file and leaned back in his chair. He looked at me earnestly and said, "I have something saved for you. If you want it?"

I immediately knew what he meant, and I nodded yes. He picked up the phone and instructed the person on the other end of the line to search through the top drawer of his clinic desk for an envelope marked "Ian Stewart." After a moment or two, a man in a suit entered the room and handed a half-green, half-cellophane envelope to Mr. Palmer. He held it for a moment, feeling the shape of its contents, and then he reached over his desk to hand the envelope to me.

My heart raced as I took the small packet into my hand. After a moment of collecting my emotions, I turned it over and looked through the cellophane at a narrow little slug of brownish-gray lead. It was already corroding. The tip of the bullet was flattened, but it was otherwise fully intact—something, he explained, that probably saved my life.

I stared at the slug and wondered if the dark spots on its sides were my blood. The thought sent an involuntary shudder down my back. I handed the envelope to my mother and shook hands with Mr. Palmer.

"I don't know what to say—," I offered, and hesitated.

Anticipating my next words, Mr. Palmer interrupted, "To see you here, getting stronger every day, is enough." He gave a modest smile.

RED NOSE DAY IS AN ANNUAL EVENT sponsored by prominent comedians from around the world who lend their names to causes. In 1999, their cause was African debt relief. As Red Nose Day approached in mid-February, media attention once again turned to Africa and its problems. The British Broadcasting Corporation and Sky News began airing nightly features on Africa. One in-depth report on the BBC by Fergal Keene highlighted the plight of Sierra Leone, and one evening as I sat alone in my room channel surfing, I came upon it.

A frantic woman was on her knees beside the corpse of a soldier in bloodied green fatigues. The street looked familiar; I struggled to place it. Keene's voice-over explained the carnage that had gripped Sierra Leone's capital in January. It dawned on me that it had been just over a month since I was hurt, although it seemed like a lifetime ago. More video footage showed mob revenge attacks and a street-side execution by Nigerian troops. Children cried and a breathless woman wailed in horror into the camera lens. Sierra Leone's nightmare was dragging on.

That night I turned out the light to go to sleep shortly after 11 P.M., but I could not purge my mind of the re-kindled images of war in Sierra Leone.

*I'm lying on a beach somewhere in West Africa. The sun is full and stiflingly hot. Instinctively I run my hand across my forehead to mop away the sheet of dripping sweat. When I glance back at my hand, it is covered with blood. A thick stream of blood begins pouring from a gash in my forehead, which spontaneously splits wide open. I grope in the sand for a towel, but the blood is so thick, it blinds me. The taste of it is on my lips. I try to scream, but my voice is silent. Before long, my entire face is dripping with blood that quickly grows sticky under the hot sun. I can't open my fingers; they feel fused shut by the thick, crusting liquid.*

I sat bolt upright in bed as I woke from my nightmare.

Glancing over to my bedside table, I could faintly make out the digital clock face showing 2:30 A.M. I lay back in bed in the dark, panting for a moment. Instinctively I stretched my arm and felt my fingers wiggle. Still reeling from my dream, I wiped my forehead to check that there was no blood. It was only then that I realized my hand was working, the fingers moving. My heart raced with a eupho-ria that replaced the terror of my nightmare. *It was all just a bad dream,* I thought to myself, drumming my fingers on my chest.

*Thank God. It's over.* I laughed out loud in my empty room and relaxed for the first time in weeks.

A nurse who had heard me laughing popped her head in the door. "Is everything all right, Ian?"

"Yeah, I'm fine," I answered. "Everything is fine now. See?"

I held my hand up to the beam of light from the corridor and wiggled my fingers in all directions.

"My hand is fine now," I announced. "I'm all better."

Baffled, the nurse looked at my face. She paused before responding.

"Ian, that's your right hand." She slipped her head back through the doorway. To me, the latch clicking into place sounded like a key turning in a prison cell door.

I was left in the dark room with a crushing sense of gloom pressing down on me. *Shit!* I thought. *It's real. It's not a nightmare. This is really happening.* Warm, salty tears streamed down my cheeks and soaked my pillowcase as I once again struggled to cope with the horror that had overtaken me, Myles, and David.

In the morning, I spoke with Sherrie about my blood-soaked nightmare. She suggested that my subconscious brain was trying its best to make sense of my injury and deal with it in the non-threatening context of a dream.

I went down to the therapy gym and settled in for my first daily forty-five-minute session with Alfie. I told her about my nightmare.

She asked, "Where do these nightmares come from?"

I told her how Fergal Keene's news report on Sierra Leone the night before had once again filled my brain with horrific scenes from Africa.

"I remember this one time when I was in Kinshasa," I began to explain. "I went out onto the streets just a few days after rebel fighters were supposed to have infiltrated the city."

Kneeling at my feet, Alfie listened quietly as she fastened the Velcro straps of my ankle brace. We stood and she guided me as I took one or two steps away from the therapy plinth. During the last few weeks, I had made dramatic progress in my walking and I was no longer terrified. Alfie encouraged me to continue with my story to keep me distracted from my walking, which should come naturally, not consciously.

"I was on June Thirtieth Boulevard—one of the largest avenues in the city—about two or three kilometers from the Memling Hotel, where all the journalists were staying when the 1998 civil war broke out against Laurent Kabila."

My knee began to buckle and Alfie quickly propped me up under my armpits. I regained my balance and stepped forward again. I continued to tell her about the rebels I had seen executed during the final weeks of the civil war in August 1998, but my mind remained focused on the act of walking. *Squeeze butt, bend knee, raise toe, step forward. Squeeze butt, bend knee, raise toe, step forward.* The words had become my mantra at the Devonshire.

It took about five minutes, but I slowly crossed the room by myself. A grin stretched across my face from one ear to the other. I thought back to the childhood Christmas specials I had enjoyed as a boy. A scene from *Rudolph the Red-Nosed Reindeer* pushed its way into my mind, as the Abominable Snowman learns to walk.

*Put one foot in front of the other,* I sang to myself.

ALFIE TOLD ME TO STAY in my room for therapy on Saturday morning, March 20, a brisk spring day in London. Stubbornly, I ignored her instructions. I carefully transferred to my battery-powered wheelchair and headed for the therapy gym.

"What are you doing here?" Alfie asked. "You're supposed to be going home today."

Nevertheless she smiled and helped me through a truncated set of exercises, including a brief walk down the center of the gymnasium, which was empty on weekends. After a twenty-minute session, Alfie followed my wheelchair as we headed back to Room 104.

Sherrie and several of the nurses had gathered to say goodbye. Sherrie stood and left the room when I arrived, but quickly returned with a large sponge cake frosted with vanilla icing and garnished with slices of pineapple and kiwi. My eyes widened and I smiled self-consciously.

"But what about my high cholesterol?" I asked Sherrie.

"Oh, it's all right this time—we ordered a special low-fat cake just for you."

Not realizing Sherrie was having fun with me, I sat quietly and nodded appreciatively. The nurses in the room chuckled. I gobbled down my slice of cake as my mother double-checked that all my belongings were packed.

"The car is here," she said. "Anytime you're ready, we should go so we have plenty of time before the flight."

I transferred into my normal wheelchair, and balanced my silver cane—recently supplied by Alfie—on my lap. My limp left arm was propped on a pillow in my lap. Alfie pushed the wheelchair to the elevator and led me out the doors of the Devonshire into the subdued light of an overcast sky. Sherrie and a small procession of nurses followed us.

Working my way down the line, I hugged each nurse (with one arm) and said a teary goodbye. Sherrie gave me a peck on the cheek and wished me well. Alfie stood a little apart from the others. She moved toward me as I slowly stood to get into the car. I formally held out my hand. A lump the size of an apple caught in my throat.

"Thank you, Alfie. What more can I say?"

Tears welled in Alfie's eyes as she wrapped her arms around me. "You take care, kiddo," she said in a shaky voice.

I watched my friends wave goodbye from the sidewalk until we rounded the corner from Devonshire Street to Marylebone High Street.

I fidgeted anxiously throughout the forty-minute drive to Heathrow. My mom and I chatted about how I would get through the terminal and on to the Air Canada flight home to Toronto. The AP's London bureau chief Myron Belkind had arranged everything ahead of time, but I was still nervous about the airport.

Heathrow's Terminal Three seemed enormous. In years past I had reveled at the idea of hanging out at the airport, watching the world go by. Heathrow was an important and emotional place for me; it marked my coming of age as a journalist and foreign correspondent. It also represented my complete independence. London had been my jumping-off point for trips to India, Pakistan, and Africa, or journeys home to Toronto. Now I sat small in my borrowed Air Canada wheelchair and thought about the destination this time, and how long it would take to get there.

# 15

# BEGINNING AGAIN

I SAT FORLORN IN MY WHEELCHAIR, swaddled in a bulky parka borrowed from my father—I had been away from Canadian winters so long that I had none of my own. The sun sparkling off the rippling water of Lake Ontario jabbed at my eyes, and my thoughts wandered back to the murky shores of the Congo River dividing Kinshasa and Brazzaville. For a moment, my nose filled with dank humidity and the stink of rotting vegetation. In my mind's eye I saw bloated bodies instead of ice floes drifting in the water.

The cold March wind, biting at my bones, snapped me back to the present, back to my wheelchair rattling along Toronto's waterfront boardwalk. To keep warm I wore a wool scarf wrapped around my hands—my left hand was too clenched to fit into a mitten or glove. Dark sunglasses hid the circles around my eyes, red from my still very frequent episodes of sobbing. A baseball cap concealed the dent in my forehead. Although it was already well hidden by my hair, which I left longer than usual, I had become ultra-sensitive about people seeing it and judging me as abnormal.

Of course, when I was in my wheelchair, few people ever made eye contact with me, anyway. Jennifer Beamer, one of my closest friends from my university days, parked my wheelchair beside the dented aluminum hotdog cart that spewed steam into the cold air. She ordered one bratwurst for each of us. Handing the sausages to her, the vendor looked over my head and past me.

"What does he want on it?" he asked her.

"He just wants mustard," I announced petulantly, interrupting Jenn as she leaned down to ask me.

We moved on, along the boardwalk in the Beaches neighborhood of Toronto. With every uneven bump on the boardwalk planks, my left leg quaked with violent spasms, the foot bouncing rapidly up and down on the wheelchair's footplate. A dime-sized globule of mustard dripped out the back of my hotdog bun and plopped onto the lap of my brown parka.

*God dammit,* I thought as I smeared the mustard, trying to wipe it away with a thin tissue napkin.

Through April and May I sat gray and grim-faced, hunched over in my wheelchair, watching with envious fascination as people strolled by me on Toronto's sidewalks. *I'll never be able to do that again,* I thought over and over. I saw myself back in high school, sprinting across a football field or stealing second in a baseball game. I envisioned an autumn stroll in a park, with red, orange, and yellow leaves crunching under my feet. I remembered trekking through the foothills of K2 and Mount Everest when I lived on the Indian subcontinent.

To convince myself that I was getting better, I often hastily pushed myself up out of my wheelchair, took my cane in my right hand, and shuffled across my parents' brown parquet living room floor. Reaching the couch out of breath, I would collapse in a heap, my left arm rigid with spasms from the effort. I was now relearning what most children master by the age of two. But shaky legs as a thirty-three-year-old were a lot more frightening than shaky legs as a toddler. The hard ground or floor looked a lot farther down from five feet nine inches.

THE OFFICE WAS A MESS; reports stacked high on the desk, splints and braces cluttered haphazardly in the corners. It was April 5, less than four months after the shooting, and I was meeting Anna Greenblatt, one of Toronto's leading occupational therapists and the co-founder of Inter-Action Rehabilitation, a private clinic specializing in physical and occupational therapy for patients with neurological needs, such as stroke and brain injury survivors.

During my first meeting, my mother waited in a chair by the door. Although sleepy, I sat up in my wheelchair and listened intently as Anna described how she would aim to help me regain better mobility and functional use of my arm. She made no mention, however, of my left hand, which I had irrationally made the central focus of my recovery.

"Don't worry," she said confidently. "We'll have you out there shooting hoops again."

*Hoops,* I sniffed disdainfully to myself. *How am I supposed to hold a basketball with one hand?*

What Anna failed to explain at the time, although I learned it through experience, was that I *could* play basketball with one hand, balancing the ball with a good hand against the side of the disabled hand.

"What about my hand?" I asked firmly. "Will I be able to type again?"

"I don't know, Ian."

That marked the start of a painful summer of misery and self-doubt, as I pondered life with my new physical disabilities. There were no answers, only questions upon questions. Fearing to falsely raise expectations, good therapists make no predictions regarding one's recovery of motor function after a brain injury. What I learned that summer was that recovery from a brain injury is possible, but it's an uphill struggle to reassemble a world left shattered on a car dashboard, on a curb, at a construction site, or, in my case, on the front line of a war. It was as if my life had become a fragile glass bottle hurled against the pavement—in an instant it shattered into a million shards of fading dreams, dashed hopes, and out-of-reach goals. I felt the best I could do was begin piecing that life back together one shard at a time until my bottle was once again ready to be filled with my future.

There were no guarantees, I learned, and neurology-based rehabilitation therapy is a nascent science that only in the past ten years has progressed far enough to *sometimes* allow a patient to regain gross motor function in a hand. Meanwhile, Anna and Chris Peppiatt, a physical therapist at Inter-Action, began devising a rehab program that over the next several years would restore my ability to walk.

About a month later, I first met Dr. Mark Bernstein at the Toronto Western Hospital, where he would perform reconstructive surgery—a cranioplasty—to repair the unseemly and gaping dent in my forehead. Where once my skull had protected my brain, there was now only skin. As the chief of neurosurgery at Toronto Western, Bernstein had been recommended as the best surgeon to take on my case for follow-up care.

Bernstein's internist entered the examining room and began a thorough evaluation of my injury and the resulting physical disabilities. She tested my sensory nerves, my reflexes, my brain's ability to sense my arm's position when not in view—known as proprioception—and of course the arm's range of motion. I did poorly on all counts. The internist left the room. I waited quietly with my mother for Dr. Bernstein. A short, bearded man with a friendly hello, the surgeon breezed into the room and glanced at the X rays and CT scans taken in London. He looked quickly at my arm and asked me to show what movement I had, which was still next to none. Then he had me walk a few paces. He scribbled a few notes into my file and said, "Well, you know you'll never be normal on the left side again."

His curt words caused me to sink into a gloomy funk for days.

DURING MY FIRST WEEKS and months back in Toronto I typically got out of bed around 11 A.M. I hated to wake up in the morning, because it meant discovering anew that I had a lame left arm, that I could no longer pop out of bed to zip to the washroom. The greatest cruelty of my injury was its ability to play possum through the night. Lying in bed I felt fine, but once I was back on my feet in the morning the depressing reality came flooding back.

Out of bed, I slowly shuffled off to the kitchen for breakfast. After gulping down a bowl of cereal or an English muffin I'd eventually work my way to the shower, where I sat on a plastic stool to guard against a fall. Through the first few weeks, my mother furtively stood by the ajar bathroom door, listening in case I fell. I scrubbed my body and washed my hair and carefully dried myself, with my one good arm clinging to a towel, the other end clenched in my teeth. Once back in my robe and exhausted from the effort, I plunked down in my wheelchair and summoned my mom to guide me back to my bedroom, where I struggled to get dressed. Once dressed, I curled back in bed and napped for an hour just to recuperate from the exertion of getting out of bed, washing, eating, and dressing for the day.

Every day for months I felt as if I were waking up after a raucous night of drinking, burdened with headaches while feeling foggy and slow-witted. My brain injury resembled a daily hangover that never dissipated.

*What the fuck have I done to myself?* I lamented, as another groundswell of emotion tugged at my chest before the tears once again flowed down my cheeks.

*I've ruined my life.*

BEING BACK IN CANADA did not free me from my nightmares. Sierra Leone and Africa lived on in my head through
vivid flashbacks brought on by emotional triggers. For
instance, Toronto's island airport was within earshot of my
parents' waterfront condo. On and off I would hear the
*thump, thump, thump* of helicopter blades beating against
the air. Each time, my heart would race and my body would
tense as if I were preparing to run the hundred-meter dash.
I would begin to sweat and my mouth would run dry.
Gazing down the boulevard from where my parents live I
would see green armored personnel carriers and heavy
Soviet T-90 tanks rumble down the lanes. Of course they
were only in my mind, but the sense of terror and vulnera-
bility they evoked was very real.

Everyday activities such as showering also triggered
flashbacks. As I sat on my white plastic stool, with hot
water beating across my shoulders, I slowly washed my
face, scrubbing my forehead with a queasy feeling every
time my fingers slipped into the jagged, bony edges of the
dent under my skin. The steam in the shower thickened
when I increased the heat, and the sound of water drumming on the shower tiles reminded me of the monsoon
downpour on palm leaves and elephant grass in Congo
and Sierra Leone. The glass door fogged over. The shower
stall's walls closed in on me; in my mind the tiles appeared
to sprout leaves as jungle foliage pushed in around me. I
could feel the humidity of the tropics, the heat of *that* day
in Freetown. The stink of decaying flesh filled my nostrils.
The sharp crack of gunfire echoed in my mind. I began

hyperventilating, sucking at the air furiously. I felt faint and dizzy, and sitting there I cursed myself over and over.

*You fucking jerk! You had everything going for you and you blew it all on some macho stunt in a war zone nobody gives a shit about.*

For weeks my mother had been urging me to see a psychologist to help me cope with my post-traumatic stress disorder. She began calling various hospitals and rehab clinics that treat brain injury patients with trauma-related problems. Finally she learned that the best psychologist in Toronto for my kind of injury was Brian Ridgley.

I began seeing Dr. Ridgley every week of that first summer. He was a soft-spoken and bespectacled man who helped me understand my trauma-related neurosis. But even though we worked through many of the disturbing events I had experienced and witnessed, I continued to suffer from wild mood swings and volcanic temper tantrums.

Then, at one of my sessions, as he sat behind his desk as usual with his yellow legal pad, Ridgley leaned forward in his chair, stroked his white beard, and pointed with his pen to the empty chair beside me.

"Pretend Myles is in the room right now," he said. "Let's say he's in that chair beside you—" The psychologist paused. "Is there anything you'd like to say to him right now?"

I was stunned and momentarily speechless. Then my shoulders began to heave; I sobbed so hard I could barely breathe. I fought to get the words out, my mouth screwed up with anguish: "How could you do this to me? How could you die and leave me here alone and crippled? I thought you were my friend!"

The realization that I had been harboring so much anger toward Myles brought peace and closure to at least part of my ordeal. I continued to see Dr. Ridgley for another eight months, during which time we worked through other symptoms of my trauma. He also taught me a series of relaxation techniques.

By the late spring, my journalistic instincts began to kick in once again. From a reporter's point of view, what had happened to me, Myles, and David was a very compelling story. I began trying to write something for the AP wires, but early on, the computer proved to be my greatest enemy.

Propped up awkwardly on a wooden stool at the kitchen counter, I leaned in hard toward the screen of my parents' aging desktop. After about an hour of fiddling with the keys to reacquaint myself with a computer, I managed to launch Microsoft Word. With the index, middle, and ring fingers of my right hand I began typing away. First, I knew I should write a headline. I typed one letter at a time: "Back from the brink, a war correspondent's long journey home."

I spaced down a few lines and typed out my byline in the AP style. Another line down and I typed a Toronto dateline. So far, so good. But when it came time to begin writing the body of the story, I froze. No words came. After about ten minutes, I pushed the keyboard away in a huff.

"Fuck this," I cursed loud enough for my mother in the next room to hear.

"What's wrong, honey?" she asked from the couch in the living room.

"I can't do it anymore."

"Sure you can," she said. "You just need to give it time."

*Time? It's been four months already,* I wanted to say.

The next day I tried again. I sat at the computer and began searching for the file of the few lines I had written the evening before. My mother discreetly reminded me of the name I had given to the file. When the "Back from the brink" headline reappeared on the screen to remind me of the story I had set out to write, I found fresh inspiration. Although it was melodramatic, the first line of my own story finally flowed from the fingertips of my right hand.

"By all rights I shouldn't be sitting here writing this," I typed. "By all rights, I ought to be dead."

I pushed ahead, working in ten-minute sessions, and managed to write thirty words that morning before shuffling back to bed for a nap. During my long days at home I continued to tinker away at the story. While overseas I had often hammered out five stories a day; now I was lucky to get five paragraphs.

In the meantime, I continued to plug away at my therapy, learning to walk all over again. My therapists in Toronto picked up where Alfie McVey had left off in London. Although I was able to walk greater distances and found my strength improving, it was not until June that I could finally return my rented wheelchair to the medical supply center. I was determined that, from now on, I would walk everywhere.

AS THE SUMMER WORE ON, the spasticity on my left side worsened. My hand began to clench involuntarily into a tight fist most of the time; the arm bent up at the elbow and shoulder with the slightest exertion. With fist clenched and arm raised, I felt I looked as if I were challenging all comers to a bare-fisted boxing match.

*Did people know my arm was positioned that way on its own? Or did they think I was just trying to be threatening in a slapstick kind of way?*

When my arm and hand were relaxed, however, there were glimmers of hope for them. After a long session with Anna, who struggled to release the tight flexor muscles in my fisted hand, my fingers eased up and relaxed.

"Try to open your fingers," she instructed.

I thought about how it felt to open my hand to catch a football and all five fingers flicked open for an instant.

"That means the neural pathways are still there," Anna told me. There was hope of working toward a hand I could at least open and close on command. Activities requiring fine motor skills in the fingers, like typing, would have to wait.

In mid-July, I traveled with my parents to our home in Hunts Point, Nova Scotia. Relishing a chance to relax and enjoy themselves after struggling through the trauma and burden of having their youngest child seriously injured, my parents went golfing most days. I took advantage of my slowly increasing stamina and the solitude of an empty house; I sat quietly at a computer and continued to tap out my story for the AP. My first draft had been rejected

by my editors in New York and they had sent it to Bruce
Desilva, a talented feature editor, who had agreed to take
on the project.

Each day, with cane in hand, I shuffled across the expansive lawn of my parents' oceanfront property. I sat in a
yellow Adirondack chair by the rocky shore and listened to
the waves crash against the rocks; I gazed out in the direction of where I figured Sierra Leone would be across the
Atlantic. The longer I stayed in Nova Scotia, the more I
could feel my anguish over Sierra Leone fade. Although I
continued to harbor deep anger for allowing myself to get
so badly wounded, I tried to think it through logically: *You
hang around bits of flying lead long enough and eventually one
piece will catch up with you.*

Although I had readily accepted the inherent risks of
working in war zones, I had always figured I might get shot
in the arm, or the leg (something heroic, but not *too*
painful). Never had I imagined that I could be shot in the
head! Shot in the head—and live.

By the end of August I sent a new draft of my story to
Bruce, but he kicked it back to me, requesting more: more
detail, more emotion, more of Ian Stewart. Bruce pushed
me to rediscover the journalist now buried within.

Word by word, I continued to tap out my story. Now able
to work for longer stints at a time, I managed to produce a
detailed 20,000-word account of the shooting, my evacuation from Africa, and my recovery to date. It was by far the
longest piece of writing I had ever produced.

BY LABOUR DAY I WAS BACK in the hospital in Toronto, finally undergoing the cranioplasty to repair my forehead.

"Ian! Ian, can you hear me? Open your eyes, Ian."

I heard the voices long before I could pry my eyes open. I blinked several times to help me focus on the faces hovering above. Two black nurses stood by my bed in my room at the Toronto Western Hospital. They smiled down at me with relief. As if reliving a bad dream, I sensed the turban-like bandage that enshrouded my head. It plunged low over my forehead. I could just see the fringe of a gauze bandage hanging over my eyes.

"Ian, you had a violent episode in your sleep," one of the nurses began to explain.

It was then that I realized my wrists and ankles were restrained with canvas straps. I fought them furiously, yanking and wrenching until my wrists grew red with friction burns. I flailed my legs, kicking and jolting in a bid to escape from my bondage.

"David! Fuck, man! Just cut me free!" I shouted.

The nurses looked at one another.

"Who's David?" one asked.

The other just shrugged.

"Ian, we're going to send you for some scans," the first nurse said.

Realizing I could not escape my bonds, I calmed down and listened to the nurse who spoke, repeating that I was going to be sent for brain scans.

"OK," I eventually agreed.

"But don't let them do an MRI. I can't have an MRI," I said, with desperation in my voice.

"Why not?" the first nurse asked.

I explained the shooting, my evacuation, and Mr. Palmer's concern that bullet fragments could still be lodged in my brain. The whole time I was speaking I kept thinking:

*Good God, they didn't even bother to read my Medic Alert bracelet.* (Shortly after returning to Toronto I had purchased one that described my medical history and the MRI warning.)

In the morning Dr. Bernstein walked into my room.

"Heard you got a little agitated last night," he said smiling. "How are you feeling now?"

*Like a million bucks,* I thought sarcastically, but mumbled, "I'm fine, but my jaw is really sore."

"Yeah, we had to cut into your temporal muscle," Dr. Bernstein said matter-of-factly. "It'll be sore for a few days. Eat lots of steak to work the muscles."

Describing it as a "psychotic" episode, Dr. Bernstein assured me the late-night fit I had encountered was unrelated to my brain injury. "The CT scans were normal. We don't believe you had a seizure."

By the end of September, I visited my family doctor to have the stitches and surgical staples removed from the incision that ran along the same line as Mr. Palmer's initial craniotomy operation. One by one the staples were gently pried from my head and dropped with a tinny plunk into a metal dish.

I went home that afternoon and shaved my head bald

to match the band of hair that had been shaved for the operation. I looked admiringly into the bathroom mirror at my neat, smooth forehead. No more unsightly dent. No more daily reminder of the shooting each time I looked in the mirror. The lingering effects of my cranioplasty—chronic fatigue, pain in my jaw muscles, and tender, itchy scars—had completely faded by the end of the year.

I regained strength through October and finished up my story for the AP. With Bruce's help I edited it down to a 3,000-word piece—extravagantly long for a wire service article—which was scheduled for use by newspapers on American Thanksgiving Sunday.

Response to my article—called "What Price, the News?"—was overwhelming. It appeared in hundreds of English-language newspapers around the world, including the front pages of the *Los Angeles Times,* the Cleveland *Plain Dealer,* the *Tampa Tribune,* and the Toronto *Globe and Mail*'s "Review" section. Letters from well-wishers—strangers, colleagues, and friends alike—began to pour in. I began producing occasional columns for the *Globe and Mail*'s "Comment" section and even tackled my first couple of magazine articles. Requests began flowing in, many of which I turned down because of my still limited energy. Meanwhile, my editors in New York had nominated my story for a range of awards, including the University of Michigan's Livingston Award for Young Journalists and Ball State University's Eugene S. Pulliam National Journalism Writing Award.

• • •

AS JANUARY 10 APPROACHED, my family quietly wondered whether to mark the one-year anniversary of my survival. Still wanting to sweep *that* dark day into my memory's dustbin, I told my parents, "Let's just treat it like any other day." Privately I marked the anniversary of Myles's death by calling his mother, Hanne, in New York.

I moved into my second year of rehabilitation therapy noticing more rapid changes and concrete progress. In the spring of 2000, I once again began doing the little things most people take for granted. I started walking up and down stairs, albeit slowly. I began riding Toronto's streetcars and the subway more frequently, thus reclaiming a little more independence.

By the end of April I was noticeably stronger; so much so that I traveled with Kim, a woman I had recently begun dating, to Arlington, Virginia, to attend a memorial service for journalists killed in 1999. Over the roar of a Delta Airlines Boeing 767 that passed low overhead, a gong chimed solemnly as a man in a black suit read dozens of names. The vast majority of the deaths had occurred in Sierra Leone, making it the deadliest place on earth for reporters in 1999. For each name the gong rang out once. It was a steamy May morning—my thirty-fourth birthday.

I fought to keep my emotions in check. Kim held my hand, squeezing it tight when Myles's name was read out. Hanne Tierney and Myles's father, "Big" Myles, sat two rows behind us along with Myles's adopted brother, his nephew, and a former girlfriend. Afterward, I wandered over to the memorial—a modern sculpture of blue-tinted glass and black steel girders. I stared vacantly at Myles's name. I ran my fingers across the indented lettering of his inscription:

"Myles Tierney, Associated Press. 1964–1999."

Later in May I drove a car for the first time and found I could walk on the beach at my parents' home in Nova Scotia with greater ease.

And then things got much worse.

On Tuesday, May 23, I was sitting in the foyer at the Inter-Action clinic waiting for Anna to begin her treatment session of my still dormant left arm. Flipping through the *Toronto Star* from the day before, I spotted a large headline on page A2 about several corpses discovered in Sierra Leone. It was suspected that they were the bodies of several missing UN peacekeepers. I noticed the byline under the headline:

"By Miguel Gil Moreno, Associated Press."

Leaning back in my chair, I smiled and beamed with pride. *Way to go, Miguel,* I thought.

I knew how rare it was for television journalists to get credit for their work in newspapers. I asked Anna Greenblatt if I could keep the paper. I thought I should send the clipping to Miguel along with a note of congratulations.

On Thursday morning I returned a call from Bryan Brumley at the AP in London.

"Hi, Ian," Bryan said softly, cautiously. "How are you?"

"Well, I'm doing fine, thanks. Why do you ask?" I responded.

"You haven't heard yet, have you?" Bryan said.

"Heard what?"

"I'm sorry to be the person to tell you," he said, pausing. "It's Miguel."

*Please, no,* I thought immediately. I braced for Bryan's next words.

"There was a shooting in Sierra Leone," Bryan continued. "Miguel was killed yesterday morning."

I felt as if I had just been punched in the stomach. I slumped into a chair next to the phone and closed my eyes.

*"Myles is dead, honey."* My mother's voice rang through my mind as if I had just woken up at the National Hospital in London. Anger, sorrow, grief, denial, and more anger flooded through my head.

*Fuck, it's happening all over again.*

For a time, I was completely derailed. I lost interest in therapy, becoming very moody and unpredictable. Renewed anger at Myles and now also Miguel began to fester inside me, spewing forth as petulant temper tantrums.

For months, Anna, my occupational therapist, had been suggesting I visit a clinic in Arizona that specialized in myofascial release therapy to loosen muscles and fascia tightened as a result of neurological traumas. Fascia—like a net—is the stringy tissue that surrounds our bodies under the skin; it covers the body from head to toe. If it becomes twisted or tight following an injury, it can inhibit normal movement. Myofascial release, or MFR, is a relatively new therapy that aims to loosen and "unwind" the body's fascia. Some therapists also believe that MFR can alleviate emotional distress after traumatic injuries. When it became clear that I was nearing a complete breakdown in the wake of Miguel's death, I finally agreed to give the clinic a try for a week.

The Sedona, Arizona, clinic, named Therapy on the Rocks—with airy mood music, burning incense, and a miniature waterfall trickling over a Japanese rock garden— was a sort of New Age Mecca for flower children still searching for the summer of love. But the clinic has also earned a global reputation as a first-rate center for patients suffering chronic pain and residual physical impairments resulting from neurological trauma. Its founder, John F. Barns, was a stocky physical therapist somewhere in his sixties. His protruding belly, round, cherub-like face, and thick, white beard gave him a striking resemblance to Ernest Hemingway—that is, if Hemingway had worn a shoulder-length ponytail, tie-dyed T-shirt, and mirrored sunglasses.

On my third day in Sedona, John led a group of patients and therapists training at his clinic on a hike through one of several Red Rock conservation areas. Sitting under a baking June sun we took turns telling our stories of the events that brought us to Sedona. I enjoyed listening to the wind whistle through the junipers and birds chirp in the distance as the others in the group related how they were injured and still struggling to overcome longstanding injuries. Still, I cynically rolled my eyes at the hippie-commune feel of the exercise. Then I noticed that the air around us was still and quiet, and the wind had stopped blowing just before I was to speak.

*This is bullshit,* I snapped in my mind.

Now that my turn had arrived, I choked up and was barely able to describe the shooting. I finally coughed up the details, blinking quickly as I did so, to keep tears from spilling from my eyes and running down my cheeks. Then it dawned on me that, as I spoke the words "I took a bullet right through my brain," a pack of coyotes in the distant hills began howling with haunting cries that echoed through the valley. A chill ran down my spine; the hair on my neck bristled. Nobody said a word when I had finished speaking.

With every session I was able to let go of more pent-up frustration, more hostility that had been eating away at my soul. Throughout the week in Sedona I vented and purged. I cried daily and went back for more. Returning to Toronto, I felt I had pulled back from the brink of utter collapse. My mind was sound once again. The incessant voices of fear and paranoia had ceased. I resolved to overcome any obstacle, any barrier, and any disability with a healthy mind at my command.

Shortly after my return, I got a call from Tom Kent in New York.

"Ian." He didn't wait for a reply. "Congratulations, you just won the APME award for feature writing." Each year managing editors from AP subscribers hand out a series of awards, called the Associated Press Managing Editors awards, for reporting, writing, and photography. Most journalists consider it very prestigious to win because it represents recognition from hundreds of their peers.

Stunned, I replied slowly, "Wow. I didn't even know I was nominated."

"If you're up to it, we'd like you to fly out to San Antonio to accept the award at the APME annual meeting."

I BARELY TOUCHED MY MEAL at the APME luncheon that afternoon. Waiting to be called to the podium, I fidgeted nervously with my cloth napkin. Peggy Kuhr, managing editor of the *Spokesman-Review* of Spokane, Washington, stood to introduce the award for feature writing.

She read a brief excerpt from the story and announced my award. The room erupted into applause and, one by one, the leading managing editors in the United States stood in my honor. I savored the moment and finally stood slowly and walked toward the rostrum. Jon Wolman, the AP's executive editor, gave me a pat on the shoulder as I passed him on the stage. I took the award from Peggy and faced the audience with a self-conscious smile.

I thanked everyone—parents, doctors, and therapists—who had helped me through my ordeal; then I thanked the editors who had stood by me during my very difficult eighteen-month absence. But I wasn't done. Fighting back tears, I looked at the faces in the audience and continued to speak:

"This award is not just a tribute to the work that all foreign correspondents do for the AP. It is a tribute to my friends Myles Tierney and Miguel Gil Moreno, who died in Sierra Leone. I'd like to accept this award on their behalf as well as my own. Thank you."

Flushed with adrenaline, I shakily made my way back

to my table, as once again my colleagues and peers stood to applaud.

ONCE BACK IN CANADA, I immediately headed east with my parents to Nova Scotia for several weeks of rest, sunshine, and solitude.

After about a week in Hunts Point, I pulled on my swimsuit and waded slowly into the pool behind my parents' house. The cold water made my arm tighten at the elbow, but I didn't care. As I adjusted to the bracing water, I looked at my dad, who was by the side of the pool skimming out fallen leaves and dead bugs. With boyish excitement I called to him, "Watch this!"

I took a deep breath and dunked my head under the surface. Kicking my feet off the side of the pool, I propelled myself forward; then the movement flowed easily, as if it were second nature; I reached forward with my right arm and plunged it into the water to pull myself through the water. Instinctively I turned my head to breathe on the left side as my left arm slowly, and laboriously at first, lifted up and out of the water, and reached up and forward. I plunged it in and pulled through the resistance of the water.

I swam six lengths of front crawl that afternoon. My father stood dumbfounded at the far end of the pool, his mouth agape, his eyes misting over. He dropped the skimmer and started to applaud.

I was breathless when I stopped, from both the exhilaration and the exertion. I stood in the shallow end for a moment or two. Water dripped off me and rolled across my shoulders. Sunlight glinted off the ripples in the pool.

*I can swim!* I thought euphorically.

THE BUSINESS-CLASS CABIN of the Canadian Airlines A340 shuddered as the massive aircraft lumbered down the runway at Pearson International Airport. *I finally did it,* I thought to myself. I was heading back to London. For months I had been talking about going back to *meet* and thank the nurses, doctors, and therapists who had saved my life and put me back on my feet.

I reclaimed my life during my two weeks in England. I visited museums and art galleries and strolled through the Tate Modern Gallery and the Imperial War Museum. I attended a performance of *Hamlet* at the Globe Theatre and went to see *The Lion King* at the Lyceum. Finally, I visited the AP bureau, where I had an emotional reunion with the many journalists who had been following my story. I sat with Myron Belkind, the bureau chief, in his office and discussed my recovery over tea. Myron offered me a job in his bureau "whenever I was ready." Through it all, I felt invigorated and alive as I wandered the streets of London, kilometer after kilometer, on my own two feet—even past "my" map shop on Regent Street.

On a quiet Thursday afternoon, I piled into a taxi near my hotel at Trafalgar Square and sped off for the London zoo at Regent's Park. I headed immediately to the primate section, where once again black spider monkeys and playful chimps entertained delighted audiences for hours on end.

I looked away for a moment and spotted through the fencing across the caged compound a father and his two sons, the youngest in a stroller. I smiled, remembering a chilly February day in 1999 when I sat in my wheelchair, while young children gawked at me as much as at the nimble monkeys.

*That was me in a stroller back then,* I thought. I looked down at my feet and grinned.

I strolled on until I neared the netted aviary that housed all manner of birds from around the world, including black hunchbacked vultures perched on bare tree branches. The birds didn't affect me at all as I walked past them and headed for the lion enclave.

During my second week in London I returned to the National Hospital for Neurology and Neurosurgery. Taking a deep, steadying breath, I went in through the sliding front door, where the old couple had muttered about my sorry state those many months earlier. I tried to visit the physical therapy department, but was told it had closed for lunch. I navigated the labyrinthian corridors and elevators to the Nuffield Wing, where only two nurses vaguely remembered me.

"Oh, you're that Canadian bloke who was shot," one said with uncertainty as she squinted at my face.

Back downstairs, I braced myself for a flood of disturbing memories as I walked into the Intensive Care Unit. Sister Sandra who ran the department and had overseen my care twenty-one months earlier greeted me with a smile.

"I'm not sure if you'll remember me," I began shyly.

"Don't be silly," she said as she gave me a hug. Like two old friends, we stood and chatted about the night I was admitted.

"I remember getting the call to ask if we had a bed for an emergency case flying in from Africa," she began, and then told me the full story—the first time I had heard all the medical details—of the operations my surgeon, Mr. Palmer, had performed. I asked about Mr. Palmer. Was he around? Could I see him? To my disappointment, I learned he had moved on to another hospital in Plymouth.

I thanked Sister Sandra and the whole ICU staff for their hospitality then and now. As I walked out the hospital doors into the bright afternoon sun I felt pleased and satisfied, but I knew there was one last thing I had to do.

LIKE MOST OLD WORLD CHURCHES, St. Bride's—the so-called journalists' church—is gloomy and subdued in its interior; it's a world of dark wood paneling and the soft glow of candles flickering from the altar. St. Bride's is an oasis of calm away from the bustle of Fleet Street.

I wandered down the aisle toward a small altar table set off to one side. The little flames from a row of candles cast curious light on the table, where half a dozen small white placards paid tribute to journalists from around the world who had been killed or wounded while reporting the news. Among the names on the altar were Dan Eldon, a Reuters News Agency photographer, and Hansi Krauss of the AP. Both were beaten to death in 1993 by a mob in the Somali capital, Mogadishu. Beside the card paying tribute to Dan and Hansi was another card, tightly tucked in between several others. It read:

"We pray for Myles Tierney, an Associated Press news producer killed in Sierra Leone, and for family, friends, and colleagues in distress."

Like a disciplined reporter, I scribbled the words into a notebook.

Choking back a sob, I continued to read the cards, and found my other friends.

"We pray for Kurt Schork of Reuters and Miguel Gil Moreno of Associated Press, killed in Sierra Leone; for their families and friends. Pray for all photojournalists in dangerous spots throughout the world and especially in Sierra Leone, Zimbabwe, and the Middle East." Once again, I jotted the words into my notebook.

An unusual card and the only one dedicated to a wounded journalist caught my eye:

"Please pray for Abner Machula, thirty-year-old photojournalist working for National TV of Chile; fighting for his life in an Italian hospital after being shot in the head on the border of Albania."

I vaguely remembered being told there once was a card with my name on that table. If there had been, it was no longer there.

I dug into my pockets. Pulling out a £2 coin, I dropped it into the donation box. Then I took two thin candles and lit each one from the flame of a larger candle on the altar. I set the candles near the white cards honoring Myles and Miguel.

After a few minutes, I turned to leave the church with a warm sense of peace. I felt I was finally able to let go. Just before I went outside, I impulsively opened the guest book by the door. I took out my pen. I wrote the date and a brief note:

*To Miguel and Myles. Goodbye, my friends. Ian.*

# EPILOGUE

MORE THAN THREE YEARS have passed since I was shot in Freetown. I have since made significant physical gains. My walking is less labored and I am now working on jogging. My left arm is growing stronger and has close to full range of motion. But the primary physical deficit from the shooting is an almost functionless left hand. I also struggle with spastic tone in my leg and arm, but that continues to improve with time.

In the weeks and months that passed after my shooting, Africa was also transformed, though only marginally for the better. For one brief glimpse, Africa's wars and crises captured the world's attention in the summer of 2000. In May of that year, Sierra Leone became a headline-grabbing story in the media as hundreds of UN peacekeepers deployed to halt yet another Revolutionary United Front assault on Freetown. I like to think the previous year's reporting by Myles, David, and myself set the stage for the UN's involvement. Following the peacekeepers' intervention, rebel leader Foday Sankoh was arrested and now awaits trial. The RUF reportedly disbanded as a fighting

299

force and now claims to be a legitimate political party (it even has a Web site). Peace—although tenuous—appears to be holding in Sierra Leone. Efforts are now being made to rehabilitate the thousands of children whose lives were ruined by the RUF, though it will be years before any results are seen.

The Democratic Republic of Congo, meanwhile, still awaits free elections as the war against Laurent Kabila, which I first covered in August 1998, continues to ravage the region and deplete scarce resources even though Kabila was assassinated—reportedly by his bodyguard—in January 2001. His son, Joseph, assumed power in the still embattled country. I am keenly watching to see if the younger Kabila ushers in a new era of kinder, less corrupt leadership.

Despite my injury (or perhaps because of it), my interest in and empathy for Africa deepened as the continent continued to face tragedy and global apathy. Even as I made steady progress during my recovery, I did not realize that I, like Africa, was not yet in the clear. Weeks after I had finished writing this book and had launched into the editing process, my world was rocked once more. On the morning of Super Bowl Sunday in January 2001—just days after Kabila's murder—I awoke at the foot of my desk, a trickle of dried blood on my chin and an enormous welt on my forehead. I was barely able to move my legs, and my left arm was rigid and locked at the elbow. My doctors quickly diagnosed that I had suffered from a Grand Mal seizure while working on the book the evening before. The very idea of my brain short-circuiting left me traumatized and once again horrified at the long-term consequences of my injury. Although I had been warned that I would be prone to seizures the rest of my life, I had gone so long without one that I thought I was in the clear. My doctor put me back on anti-convulsant medication.

Months later, I slowly and very cautiously resumed my life, including several more visits to my psychologist and a trip to California to interview for the John S. Knight fellowship at Stanford University. By the summer, I had finally made peace with the seizure, writing it off as an aberration, until in June, while vacationing with my mother in Nova Scotia, another massive Grand Mal seizure struck like lightning. This time I was rushed to a local hospital. My medication levels were increased, and I have been seizure-free ever since; with a bit of luck and healthy living, I hope to remain that way.

In September of 2001, I went to Stanford University to study how Africa's colonial and Cold War experience manifested into and nurtured a culture prone to conflict and violence across the continent. Ironically, the start of my fellowship was marked by the terrorist attacks on the World Trade Center and the Pentagon, triggering a new war—one that initially left more journalists than U.S. soldiers dead. At first, I was chomping at the bit to join the fray, but reality quickly hit home, and I accepted my new status on the sidelines. Afghanistan, where I got my first taste of danger, is once again being decimated by the bombs and bullets of foreigners, be they Arab, Pakistani, or American.

I've learned to live with my past, although it can still

come back to haunt me. Daniel Pearl's tragic death sent me into an emotional tailspin. He graduated in 1985 from Stanford, so the news of his death was particularly poignant at the university. Hundreds of students, faculty, and alumni came to Stanford's Memorial Church on a chilly spring day. They filled the quiet church at the heart of the campus's main quad to remember the understated but immensely talented young reporter. Sunlight streamed in through the stained glass windows, bathing the pews in a warm red and orange glow. Tucked in among his friends and admirers, I sat in the church listening to hymns, speeches, and tributes. In the solemnity of the moment, I couldn't help but think back through my own experience and reflect on the tremendous changes I have undergone—physical, psychological, and philosophical. Changes I have undergone even since I wrote the final words of this book. I am no longer the hard-drinking, chain-smoking, war reporter who needed so desperately to be in the thick of combat to find a purpose in life. I loved what I did, but I also now know that that is a part of my past.

Today, I am more balanced and happier than ever before. My recovery has been a journey of self-discovery. Now I savor life, and appreciate my friends and family. I no longer obsess over the next job promotion. The craving for adrenaline has abated. Sadly I had to almost lose everything to learn what I had. I suppose I had to stare into the heart of darkness to see through to the other side.

Ian Stewart, Stanford, March 2002

# BIBLIOGRAPHY

In addition to the numerous books, journals, and reports I used for research, I relied heavily on the AP's reporting from Africa, including my own. The dispatches, however, are far too numerous to list here. They span 1980 to the present. I have also depended on news reporting from Reuters, Agence France-Presse, the British Broadcasting Corporation (BBC), and other daily news organizations.

## BOOKS

Achuzia, Joe O. G. *Requiem Biafra*. Enugu, Nigeria: Fourth Dimension Publishers, 1986.

Boahen, A. Adu, ed. *General History of Africa: VII Africa under Colonial Domination, 1880–1935,* abridged ed. Paris: UNESCO, 1990.

Campbell, Mavis C. *Back to Africa: George Ross and the Maroons from Nova Scotia to Sierra Leone*. Trenton: Africa World Press, 1993.

Conrad, Joseph. *Heart of Darkness*. New York: Penguin Books, 1983.

George, Susan. *A Fate Worse than Debt*. London: Penguin Books, 1990.

Golding, William. *Lord of the Flies*. London: Faber and Faber, 1954.

Gourevitch, Philip. *We Wish to Inform You That Tomorrow We Will Be Killed with Our Families: Stories from Rwanda*. New York: Farrar Straus and Giroux, 1998.

Greene, Graham. *The Heart of the Matter*. London: William Heinemann, 1948.

Hancock, Graham. *Lords of Poverty: The Power, Prestige and Corruption of the International Aid Business*. London: Macmillan, 1989.

Hibbert, Christopher. *Africa Explored: Europeans in the Dark Continent, 1769–1889*. New York: W. W. Norton, 1982.

Hochschild, Adam. *King Leopold's Ghost: A Story of Greed, Terror and Heroism in Colonial Africa.* New York: Houghton Mifflin, 1998.

Lamb, David. *The Africans.* New York: Random House, 1982.

Ojukwu, Chukwumeka Odumegwu. *Biafra: Selected Speeches.* New York: Harper & Row, 1969.

Peterson, Scott. *Me against My Brother: At War in Somalia, Sudan and Rwanda.* New York: Routledge, 2000.

Reader, John. *Africa: A Biography of a Continent.* New York: Alfred A. Knopf, 1999.

Stallworthy, Jon, ed. *The War Poems of Wilfred Owen.* London: Chatto & Windus, 1984.

**PERIODICALS AND OFFICIAL REPORTS**

"Nigeria: Privatization? Forget it." *The Economist* (January 25, 1997): 39.

"Nigeria: The President Who Never Was." *Africa Confidential* 39:14 (July 10, 1998): 1.

"Congo-Kinshasa: Embattled Kabila." *Africa Confidential* 39:14 (July 10, 1998): 4.

"Sierra Leone: Disaster Waits." *The Economist* (January 31, 1998): 47.

"War and Peace in Congo." *The Economist* (April 29, 2000): 41.

"The Hopeless Continent." *The Economist* (May 13–19, 2000): 17, 22–24.

"Congo in Crisis." *The National Post* (August 21, 2000): D1–12.

Cahn, Dianna. "Hearts in Darkness." *Brill's Content* (June 2000): 76–83, 128.

Crosette, Barbara. "A Ghastly Campaign of Terror in Sierra Leone." *The International Herald-Tribune* (July 30, 1998): 1.

Fisher, Ian. "Kisangani Journal: Where War Is Forever, the Diamonds Are Cheap." *The New York Times* (December 25, 1998).

Fisher, Ian, et al. "Many Armies Ravage Rich Land in the 'First World War' of Africa." *The New York Times* (February 6, 2000): A1.

French, Howard W. "Congo Rebels, Moving Fast, Boldly Replay Last Uprising." *The International Herald-Tribune* (August 5, 1998): 1.

Hawthorne, Peter. "Diamonds in the Rough." *Time* (November 29, 1999): 34–35.

Hochschild, Adam. "How the Bicycle Led to Bloodshed." *The Globe and Mail* (March 23, 2000).

Kaplan, Robert D. "The Coming Anarchy." *The Atlantic Monthly* (February 1994).

Marby, Marcus, and Obi Nwakana. "Nigeria: President Dictator." *Newsweek* (April 20, 1998): 22–23.

Pratt, David (Canada's special envoy to Sierra Leone 1998– ). "Sierra Leone: The Forgotten Crisis." Report to the Canadian Minister of Foreign Affairs, Lloyd Axworthy, April 23, 1999.

Ross, Oakland. "Corners of Darkness and Places of Light." *The Toronto Star* (June 4, 2000): B3.

Saliou, Mohamed Yessoufou. "Congo: Un Passage politique recomposé." *Jeune Afrique Economique* (February 15, 1998): 110–16.

Simmons, Ann M. "Saving Sierra Leone's Ex–Child Soldiers." *The Los Angeles Times* (October 18, 1999): A1.

Smillie, Ian, Lansana Gberie, and Ralph Hazelton. *The Heart of the Matter: Sierra Leone Diamonds and Human Security.* A government-sponsored report prepared for Partnership Africa Canada (January 2000).

Stackhouse, John. "Is Africa's Future All That Dark?" *The Globe and Mail* (May 20, 2000): A9–10.

Stackhouse, John. "Diamond Battle Just the Tip in Congo." *The Globe and Mail* (July 15, 2000): A2.

Tshitenge, Lubabu. "Armées: Nationales ou ethniques?" *L'Autre Afrique* (November 11–17, 1998): 14–17.

UNHCR. *"Liberia and Sierra Leone Update."* Occasional report published by the United Nations High Commissioner for Refugees (April 22, 1999).

Wilkinson, Ray. "The Heart of Darkness." *Refugees* (winter 1997): 5–13.

# ACKNOWLEDGMENTS

If I were to name everyone who helped me put this book together, it would require another chapter. There are, however, a number of people who deserve special credit for their help and support. First and foremost I want to thank the people who saved my life, starting with David Guttenfelder and Tim Sullivan, who worked tirelessly to get me out of Freetown and onward to London, England, where Bryan Brumley had scrambled to secure the air ambulance that shuttled me out of Africa. Bryan also found and alerted neurosurgeon James Palmer. Mr. Palmer deserves my deepest gratitude for his swift and skilled treatment, without which I probably would have suffered from much more severe brain damage.

Thanks to the entire medical staff at the National Hospital for Neurology and Neurosurgery, but of particular note is Sister Susan of the intensive care unit. Thanks also to the nursing and rehab staff at the Devonshire Hospital. In Toronto, my family doctor, Bruce Rowat, deserves special credit for proofreading the medical aspects of this book. Thank you also, Dr. Mark Bernstein, for reconstructing my forehead, and Dr. Neville Bayer, for taming my seizures.

For visits to London that brought light back into my life, thank you, Eric Weiner and Sharon Moshavi, Jim Collins and Carrie Wright (and their beautiful daughter Daisy), Dick Schumacher, and Jeremy Grant. In Canada, Stephen Smith, Jennifer Beamer, Christine Ketchen, Kim Cole, Michelle Huang, and Nadia Burger all came to my rescue. Michèle Leridon in Paris, thank you for filling in so many gaps in the story for me. Phil Goodwin's uplifting e-mails from New Delhi and Lisa Twaronite's cheery phone calls from Tokyo made all the difference when I was down. There are so many other people I should thank: new friends like Amor and Alma Valdez, Gayle Vezina and the entire Knight Fellowship class of 2002 at Stanford. Old friends like Terrence White, Maya Vidon, and John Trotter.

To help me escape from Africa, Canada's Department of Foreign Affairs and International Trade came to my assistance. There are countless ministry employees to thank in Ottawa, England, and Africa, but special thanks are owed to the Right Honourable Lloyd Axworthy, then the Minister of State for External Affairs, and Suzanne Park. I'd like also to thank the staff of the U.S. Department of State in Washington.

And then there are my therapists in London and Toronto, who worked to bring my dreams back to within reach. In London, Alfie McVey started me on the long journey of recovery, while in Toronto, Anna Greenblatt and

Chris Peppiatt worked stubbornly to get me walking, biking, and using my left arm. Sherrie Baehr in London and Brian Ridgely in Toronto—my psychologists—eased the pain and taught me how to cope.

And throughout my recovery, the Associated Press stood by my side, encouraging me, and patiently awaiting my return. Of particular note at the AP, I would like to thank my editor Tom Kent for his concern and attentiveness, Myron Belkind and his wife Rachel, now in Tokyo; they offered kindness and unflagging support while my family and I were in London. Lou Boccardi, Kelly Smith Tunney, Jon Wolman, Sally Jacobsen, and countless others have been wonderful to my family and me; thank you all.

When it comes to this book, a debt of gratitude and thanks are owed to Janette Shipston, who helped launch this project, while Denise Bukowski gave me her full support and encouragement. At Penguin Canada, Cynthia Good gave me a chance, while Barbara Berson pored tirelessly through those messy first few drafts. Thank you both. Barbara Hehner, a skilled and patient wordsmith, you deserve huge credit and thanks for transforming my first wordy ramblings into a coherent manuscript. It wasn't easy writing such a personal book, but my editors understood and handled this project with kid gloves. At Algonquin Books in New York, thanks to my editor, Antonia Fusco, for bringing this book to the United States.

And finally, my family. I did not go through this ordeal alone; my sister, Karen, and my parents, David and Penny, were unwitting participants in a nightmare no family should ever have to endure. To them I offer an apology and my most heartfelt thanks for standing by me through many long months of toil and temper tantrums, ups and downs, triumphs and failures. On top of my injury, they have endured and cheered me on during the lonely, tear-filled hours I spent writing this book. Without them, I'd have thrown up my hands long ago. I couldn't have walked this road alone. Thank you all.